THESE ARE UNCORRECTED ADVANCE PROOFS
BOUND FOR YOUR REVIEWING CONVENIENCE

In quoting from this book for reviews or any other
purpose, it is essential that the final printed book be
referred to, since the author may make changes on these
proofs before the book goes to press.

SUBSTANCE OF THINGS HOPE $5.95

2201033286431 PROCTOR, SAMUEL DEWI   USED 07
Powell's 01   AFAM-GENERAL 104/11

P9-DMM-225

In this call of hope and celebration, the Pastor Emeritus of the Abyssinian Baptist Church in Harlem reflects on faith's role in his own life and in the African-American experience.

Honored by universities and institutions nationwide, Samuel DeWitt Proctor, has established a reputation as a preeminent theologian and educator in the United States. In this compelling memoir, Dr. Proctor invites us to share his lifetime of experiences and their lessons. He chronicles his family's journey—from his grandmother's slavery through the monumental victories of the NAACP, to his own involvement in the King Oasis and through subsequent presidential eras—to show the common thread in the lives of millions of African-Americans: pure, enduring faith. He tells us ". . . the faith that piloted the emancipated slaves remains the substance of things hoped for and the evidence of things not seen." And he reveals that the roots of that faith still flourish despite continued prejudice and deceptive racial stereotypes.

The Substance of Things Hoped For passionately illustrates the author's tenet that lessons from the past can help create a more promising future. Ultimately, Dr. Proctor affirms that faith—which was durable enough to overcome perennial waves of racist campaigns—is powerful enough to respond to the despair of alienated young blacks locked in a cycle of denial and defeat today. At this pivotal time in a long and grievous struggle, Proctor believes faith can drive a national quest for a new kind of community—the first "genuine community" in which all African-Americans will participate fully and equally. Both reassuring and inspiring, here is Proctor's prescription for today's society: pragmatic, controversial to some, and founded on a lifetime of faith and reflection.

Samuel DeWitt Proctor is Professor Emeritus at Rutgers University. He served as associate director of the Peace Corps and as president of two colleges, among his many appointments. He lives in New Jersey.

The Substance of Things Hoped For

Samuel DeWitt Proctor

THE

SUBSTANCE *of* THINGS

HOPED FOR

A Memoir of
African-American Faith

G. P. Putman's Sons   New York

G. P. Putman's Sons   New York
G. P. Putnam's Sons
Publishers Since 1838
200 Madison Avenue
New York, NY 10016

Copyright © 1996 by Samuel DeWitt Proctor
All rights reserved. This book, or parts thereof, may not be reproduced in
any form without permission. Published simultaneously in Canada

Library of Congress Cataloging-in-Publication Data TK

Printed in the United States of America
1 3 5 7 9 10 8 6 4 2
This book is printed on acid-free paper.

To my wife, and the mother of our four sons,
Bessie Louise

Acknowledgements

With deepest appreciation I acknowledge the encouragement and assistance of the following persons, who read my manuscript in its early stages and made invaluable suggestions: Stephanie Porter Freeman, Margaret Knispel, Dr. William Turner, Dr. Charles Booth, Dr. Jean Dorgan, and Reverend Sherry Austin. I owe an especially heavy debt to Charlayne Hunter Gault for patient, skilled, and sacrificial contributions to this effort.

The project was born in the minds of my literary agents, Barbara Lowenstein and Madeleine Morel, and nurtured by the faithful and talented assistance of Josleen Wilson, an accomplished writer in her own right. My editor, Laura Yorke, guided me from beginning to end, and she and the other Putnam professionals were zealous in their care for the finished product.

My wife, Bessie, and my sons, Herbert, Timothy, Samuel, and Steven, as always, were burdened with the tedium of laboring over every sentence at the initial stages. All this came to pass with the loyal and unstinting devotion of my secretary for twenty years, Lorraine Smoller.

However, while my thanks to those named above remains boundless, responsibility for the final outcome is mine alone, by the grace of God.

SAMUEL DEWITT PROCTOR

Somerset, New Jersey

1995

Contents

Foreword

I was honored to be asked to write this foreword. If you've never heard Samuel Proctor speak, you're in for a treat here. This remarkable, wise, and beautiful spirit has graced us with a thoughtful overview of the history of African Americans in our country since the 1600s, an inspiring portrait of his own call to the ministry and his struggles and successes, and a vision of how "the substance of things hoped for" can be achieved. I was moved by this book, as I always am by Sam Proctor. His writings and sermons ground me with his realism and awe me with his infinite optimism and faith. And he never fails to make me laugh.

Samuel Proctor has spent his life as a professor and college and university president, a public servant and adviser to presidential administrations and candidates (including Hubert Humphrey), a preacher and counselor, and a thinker and community leader in good political times and bad. He followed Adam Clayton Powell, Jr., as minister of the Abyssinian Baptist Church of Harlem and is equally at home in black and white churches, small and large, around the country and the world.

Sam tells us how he never absorbed the racist environment in which he grew up and has always chosen to believe unfailingly in God and the "moral order of the universe." He internalized his parents' and grandparents' definition of him, not the definition of him pronounced by many southern whites in the first half of this century. Like so many black children, Sam was blessed with loving and affirming family and neighbors and teachers, whose message was clear: You are important; let no man or woman look down on you and you must not look down on any other man or woman. He learned to share their vision of a world where committed persons do what their talents, interests, and opportunities lead them to do, forgetting about recognition and rewards, ignoring who is the "first," working hard and giving back.

In this wonderful book, Sam talks about the crises in our communities, leads us through the causes and consequences of what is happening to us as a people, and shows us paths we might take out of our wildernesses of drugs, poverty, and violence.

Those who are born to privilege, he states unequivocally, have the responsibility to help those who are not. He has devoted his life to this belief and encourages us all to follow where he has led. He has counseled, mentored, and inspired thousands of young people, always lovingly spurring them on. He has been a friend and adviser to many names which will ring through history, including Martin Luther King, Jr., Medgar Evers, and Jesse Jackson, and many more who will not be recorded in history but who are today doctors, lawyers, teachers, successful business people, and ministers instead of drug addicts and criminals.

Serving in the Kennedy, Johnson, and Carter administrations, he worked in the Peace Corps when it was changing the world and the Office of Economic Opportunity when it was changing our country. He saw and still sees government not as the enemy but as the recourse, the means to drive a wedge and then a stake into racial and economic inequities. Government, in the hands of honorable, wise, and compassionate men and women, has always addressed many of the evils of the world, and can again. It can also stoop to represent the basest, most selfish instincts of our darker side.

I share Sam's horror when, as we see countless children, families, and communities in crisis, we also see some members of the United States Congress propose radical, indiscriminate, unfair, and anti-child provisions which, if they become law, would leave millions more children destitute, hungry, and homeless.

As our society struggles to find solutions to the horrors of poverty and violence, Sam Proctor preaches the unity of mankind in which he has always put his faith. He is equally critical of white racism and black separatism. The African cultural advocates and black separatists who want to turn their backs on America ignore the struggles of four centuries of our forebears who have fought to make this their America as well. We have earned a place at the table. The answer to many of our problems is not to leave the table, but to put in all the leaves necessary to accommodate those who still stand outside looking in. And the leaves, Sam stresses again and again, are fitted in place by education and unity. Most scathing of all is Sam's indictment of blacks who blame blacks for the problems and pain we still face, who join right-wing, thinly veiled racists who say every child born in America today starts out with an equal chance. He has utter contempt for so-called conservative, well-known blacks who are "either stupidly ahistorical . . . or mendacious parasites," who use "obscure language to say virtually that blacks caused their own problems and deserve to suffer."

Sam also discusses a terrible myth among blacks that blacks who succeed are not black enough, that they are giving in to and joining in "white" society. Sam writes, "When young people put achievement out of reach for themselves and pretend to prefer ignorance, noise, drugs, and sex . . . it is a kind of suicide, or in the case of a generation of young people, genocide." He's seen angry reactions to his success from black adults and black young people. When he was a youth, he says, he expected prejudice from whites. But now it is heartbreaking to see it in blacks. And he is concerned about people who criticize his commitment to reach out to all people, to try "to make any new communication a positive one."

As Sam talks about our people and government, he naturally turns to ethics and religion. The impact of religion on human existence, and particularly on the black experience in this country, is beyond measure. And is it a coincidence that now, as violence and drugs and gangs seem to be replacing family and community and faith among our young people, we see a turning away from moral values and from God? In case after case, Sam Proctor shows us God-fearing and God-loving people who have overcome the most grinding poverty and degradation, staying together as a family and rising above their environment and bitterness. And he offers, too, the tragic stories of children born into "homes," if you could call them that, where parents have abandoned hope, and, I believe, not coincidentally, abandoned God.

My father was a minister and I was raised in a family that worshiped God in how they lived as well as how they prayed. I can't imagine what my life would have been like without that foundation of faith in God's presence.

Some people believe in God but seldom see the inside of a church or synagogue. I believe a religious congregation, a home church, plays an important role in children's lives. While it cannot replace the love and support children receive from their families, religious congregations can act as an extended family, helping children find the faith and hope they need to remain strong and find their way. In the face of the pervasive breakdown of family values and bonds today, religious congregations have to be a positive support system and the moral locomotive rather than the moral caboose for fair opportunity for every child.

We each need to find the way to peace in our heart and soul, and bedrock values on which to ground our life. The quality of one's life depends so much on one's interior climate, and that is where religion and a relationship with God make such a difference. While I won't say that you can't succeed without it, so many young people without faith are, as Sam writes, "giving up on any concentrated, sustained hard effort."

Sam characterizes two kinds of people: "Those propelled by their faith that we can make it here [are] making it come to pass." Without faith, "those for whom racist intransigence [is] too rigid and endemic, poverty too burdensome, political indifference too powerful and resources too shallow [are] wallowing in the muck and mire."

In this book Sam sounds the warning that "the crisis is upon us." Violence and hopelessness spiral together. Families disintegrate or never existed to begin with. Drugs and prisons are the future for so many of our children. Children who should be dreaming of careers and homes and families of their own are planning what to wear at their funerals.

Pride and self-respect, Sam declares, "derive from the spiritual core within," and there is a need within every man and woman "for a strong religious faith and a worldview that holds things together. If you believe that there is a purpose and a power available to each of us, you have an inexhaustible source of evergreen inspiration." Amen.

I believe, as Sam writes, that "we must reach back and find ways to help others" who are "mired in poverty, alcoholism, violence, and immorality . . . or the whole American nation may sink. This is the new tenet of our faith." We must reach out most of all to children and commit to mentoring and healing. And we must understand that the solutions lie in family, education, wise public policy, and a return to moral values that are lived and not just preached.

Here Sam offers ideas for a new kind of school, a National Youth Academy, and new ways in which our society can give a hand up to the last and the least. He calls upon us to address "questions of [our] purpose and destiny" and sort out our own individual "place in the scheme of things." He presents us with the vision of a "new human paradigm" of love and respect for each other in a world without poverty, hunger, and hatred, and offers an achievable dream of a community and a nation committed to realizing *The Substance of Things Hoped For.*

Thank you, Sam, as always, for your wisdom.

MARIAN WRIGHT EDELMAN

President, Children's Defense Fund

May 1995

Prologue

Most Americans know only those African Americans who appear on the 11 o'clock news—super-rich entertainers and car hijackers; phenomenal sports figures and rapists; a four-star general and a subway murderer; a poet laureate and a drug dealer.

But the main flow of life among African Americans occurs largely unnoticed: the millions who fill ghetto churches, whose children overrun the hundred and five historically black colleges and swell the ranks of minorities in the land grant universities, who maintain good credit, pay taxes on good incomes and investment returns, and maintain homes with order, love, and deep devotion.

Racial separation hides from public view the African Americans who have remained true to the resolve of those who marched out of slavery standing tall, who sought education immediately, who kept their hope alive and created the bedrock of the African-American middle class. They have refused refuge in otherworldly cults, ignored separatist movements, and rejected all pernicious theories about their genetic inferiority. They continue to fill the buses, subways, and superhighways, finding their way to banks, schools, factories, construction sites, hospitals, and stores, where they serve the public and pump up the economy.

A persistent faith propels them—faith in God, faith in their own worth and dignity, and faith in the idea that America's 250 million diverse peoples can cohere in a true community that gives space to ethnic preferences, but gives loyalty to the basic values of equality, compassion, freedom, and justice. Through the long, winding trail of political fortunes, with a disciplined transcendence over movements and individuals who would impede their progress, they have survived every challenge and still press forward toward helping America fulfill a unique and unprecedented role in the history of humankind.

Yet there never was a time when the future of black Americans has seemed so cloaked in contradictions and so wrapped in ambiguity as it does today. On the one hand, so many blacks have overcome the burden of discrimination, the drag of poverty and poor education, and seem to be finding a place for themselves in this society. On the other, highly visible, young black failures are seen on the news every night, handcuffed and stuffed into police cars. These powerful images project a frightful future where angry, alienated blacks seem to live in perpetual chaos. Many Americans buy into the notion that the spiral of racism and violence is swirling furiously downward and cannot be reversed.

This downdraught in race matters has culminated in a volcanic political eruption, and a chorus of politicians has won approval by chanting the refrain of black failure. They magnify data on crime, welfare, and dependence, and minimize such images as two black Rhodes scholars from New Jersey, ten black women in Congress, and a black governor elected in Virginia. It has become acceptable for civic and intellectual leaders to deprecate all blacks in cocktail party repartee, around oak boardroom tables, and more subtly in television talk-show interviews.

In the face of such lingering racism, black people pulse with pride, rushing to their churches, their asylum of hope and their fortress of faith. There, ushers are in place, choirs sway in rhythmic consent, and the pastor, healing priest at one moment and clarion prophet the next, is their incarnation of the spirit of transcendence. And there they are assured, week after week, in an unbroken refrain, that their dry bones of despair can live.

Like millions of other black Americans, I am heir to the faith that was born the day twenty frightened black captives were unloaded at Jamestown in 1619. Their slow, courageous journey from the Dutch slave boat to the present, in the face of unrelenting oppression, is the story of their faith; and therein I believe lies the clue to the answer to today's dilemma.

Faith put steel in their spines to endure physical bondage, and zeal in their souls to prevail against evil; it illumined their minds to keep the vision of a better day, and inspired their hearts to learn and embrace the great human conversation. Faith gave them a sense of eternity, a mystical transcendence that transposed their pain into song and their agony into a durable, resilient quest for complete humanity, the substance of things hoped for.

Despite the pall of suspicion and fear that hangs in the air today, I believe that enough idealism and faith remain among all of us to generate a soaring national quest for a new kind of a human paradigm in which all the diverse peoples of America can participate. I think of it as potentially the first of real community in the world. I believe in this vision because of my own family's experience up from slavery.

My father's mother and my mother's grandfather were born enslaved. As a child, I could not fathom how my grandmother, a dignified, intelligent woman of impeccable character, could ever have been someone's property. To me, she seemed the zenith of human completeness. She was still living when I became a college president and I can remember how she congratulated me with cautious restraint in her voice, and with challenge and high expectation shining in her eyes.

My parents raised their six children in the rigidly divided South during the Great Depression. For most of our lives my sister and brothers and I rode in separate cars on trains, ate in separate dining rooms and used separate bathrooms, all designed to diminish our sense of worth. At times I felt ready to give up, but in the long run nothing really penetrated my shield of faith.

This faith was like the air we breathed throughout my youth, and it has followed me throughout my days. It is a habit of the heart that constrained us to focus on the stars rather than the canopy of darkness. All of us went to college and three of us hold graduate degrees. My sister became a school teacher, and my four brothers became, respectively, an Air Force Bandmaster, a dentist, a postal clerk, and an ophthalmologist. My own professional life began at age ten with a shoe-shine box at the gate of the Norfolk Naval Base. I ended up a professor at Rutgers University, and pastor of the Abyssinian Baptist Church in Harlem.

My wife, Bessie, saw a similar passage in her own family. Her father graduated from the pharmacy school of Shaw University, a small, black Baptist school in North Carolina, and opened a pharmacy for black physicians and their black patients in Virginia. Her brother, Maurice Tate, graduated from the Philadelphia College of Pharmacy, and in the 1950s became the pharmacist who attended President Eisenhower at Walter Reed Hospital in Washington, D.C. Today, our son Timothy is vice president and associate general counsel of Glaxo, the world's largest pharmaceutical company.

The Substance of Things Hoped For chronicles my own family history against the larger history of the black struggle for equality in America—from slavery through the Reconstruction, from urban migration and the Great Depression through the monumental victories of the NAACP; from the tedious Eisenhower era to the King oasis and the Great Society, from Nixon neglect and Reagan-Bush hostility all the way to the Clinton debut. Looked at in perspective it is like a series of doors opening and closing. In between, however, real progress leaks through.

Make no mistake, none of these were easy journeys. Every generation of black Americans has been forced to overcome new hardships. Yet I believe the faith that brought our forebears out of the midnight of slavery into the daybreak of Emancipation is still powerful enough today to respond to the despair of alienated young blacks.

As a people we still have tremendous societal deficits to overcome, particularly among marginalized youth without hope, but I believe the glass is more than half full. As I write, millions of black people are leading productive, principled lives; forty blacks are in the Congress; a black woman is in the Senate, Riverside Church has a black pastor; five black Americans serve in the presidential cabinet; one has been chairman of the Joint Chiefs of Staff, another heads the Ford Foundation, the world's largest philanthropy; a black woman is America's poet laureate; one has directed the National Science Foundation; another directs the Centers for Disease Control; and another has headed the TIAA, the largest pension fund in the world.

Their achievements prove that we are more than composites of others' definitions of us, more than a reflection of dismal government reports and negative data in sociology textbooks, and more than the sum of our deprivations and deficits. We are created in the image of God, with the same human equipment as the Queen of England, the same intellectual potential of all others, evenly distributed on the same normal curve. Differences in outcomes derive from differences in opportunities.

We are at a pivotal moment in a long and grievous struggle. In 1865, freed slaves faced their emancipation secure in the belief that their cause was just. I believe that ultimately their experience may be a prophetic precursor to this new human paradigm in the world, one that underlines the absolute equality of all persons. This new paradigm is the fruit of high religion, and the concomitant of true democracy. It will foster the maximum cultivation of all human potential, and celebrate justice, fairness, and compassion. Evidence that such a model of responsible and decent humanity might come into being is shadowy, but the faith that piloted the emancipated slaves remains the substance of things hoped for, and the evidence of things not seen.

The Substance of Things Hoped For

CHAPTER ONE

The Crucible of Faith

IT'S SAID THAT ONCE FREDERICK DOUGLASS WAS GIVING A speech in upstate New York and Harriet Tubman, the inimitable captain of the Underground Railroad, was in the audience. During the speech, as Douglass's zeal appeared to be flagging, she stood up and shouted, "Frederick, Frederick, is God dead?"

Whenever I see our faith waning today, I think of that desperate, inspiring call to arms. And I also think of my grandmother and her own unflagging belief that God was not dead. When I was a boy, my father's mother lived with us, and I would find myself absentmindedly gazing at her, wondering how she had felt being a little slave girl. I had seen images of slaves in the movies and in a few books: they always wore shabby clothes and spoke in crude and halting words; they couldn't read or write, and cowered in a pitiful broken-down manner.

None of this jibed with the image my grandmother presented. She was highly refined and poised. Her speech was perfect, her spelling and penmanship flawless, and her expectations of her children and grandchildren demanding. Grandma had a frightening piety about her. She was never tentative or ambiguous about anything. Her own early suffering had generated strength, just as the wood from trees able to survive at the frigid timberline in the Alps made the sweetest-sounding violins.

Grandma's intrepid confidence rested on a single uncomplicated notion: God created all people; any inequalities among us were due to unequal opportunity. From her we learned that hatred and vindictiveness were always destructive. "No use fretting or crying," she would say. "If you do your part, God will do the rest."

If we listened patiently, Grandma told us stories about her childhood. She was born around 1855 on a small tobacco plantation situated on the James River, a region now completely enveloped by Richmond, Virginia. On the day she was born, without rights and with a general consensus that she was an inferior being, she was named Hattie Ann Virginia Fisher, after the family who owned her. This family was not very rich or influential, which may explain why, compared to most planters, they had a somewhat benevolent attitude toward their slaves. Hattie Ann was never whipped or separated from her family as other slaves were. However, she was worked hard. Slave children were usually treated like farmyard animals, doing whatever came to hand and eating cornmeal and scraps of fatback at a common table. Because the plantation was near the river, Hatti Ann's father may have been able to supplement his family's meager fare with fish and small game.

Like all slave children, Hattie Ann imitated the work done by grown folks and, even as a small child, learned to sew well. Her skill with a needle earned her a job in the "big" house. When she was around seven or eight years old, the Fishers entrusted their youngest children into her care. "When the Episcopal priest came around to teach the white children," she told us, "I was allowed to sit in the circle and learn right along with them." Hattie Ann was the only slave on the Fisher place who was permitted to learn to read. Although rare, her experience was not unique. Historical records show that from time to time some planters defied law and custom and taught a few slaves to read. Literacy meant that a slave could perform more sophisticated tasks.

However, the vast majority of slaves were denied any access to education as part of a well-documented conspiracy to forge a racial stereotype: namely, that blacks were less intelligent than whites and fundamentally unable to learn. Slaveholders' worst nightmare was the image of slaves carrying oil-soaked torches, waving bread knives and meat cleavers, and wildly rushing the big house where white women and children slept. To protect themselves, they denied blacks privacy, time, literacy, and teachers who might stir them to action.

Apart from forestalling rebellion, there was a more subtle reason to withhold education. Bible-reading Christians had a basic conflict between their religious beliefs and their brutal ownership of other human beings. To resolve their hypocrisy, they concluded that Africans were some sort of retarded offspring of *Homo sapiens* and, therefore, not quite human. To support this fiction, slave owners put out the lamps at night, snatched books from questioning hands, separated blacks from their tribal groups, and created around them a cultural vacuum. This extremely effective practice of first denying education then saying the victim cannot learn continues to compound all other problems facing us today.

Slave owners had reason to worry. Behind the docile masks pulsed nerves strung tight with the desire for freedom. These were the "hands" who were up at the crack of dawn, as the dew still glistened on the grass, mumbling to each other in hushed tones while they fed the chickens and the pigs, led the cows to pasture, filled the dog's water pail, started the fire in the oven, and put the skillets and flatirons on the stove top. All day long they acted out their charade, pretending stoic compliance while seething with indignation; humming songs of transcendence, while silently massaging their pain and waiting for twilight's sweet relief.

For nearly three hundred years, house slaves had been listening to their owners' prayers and Bible readings. They heard how Joseph survived his brothers' selling him into slavery. They heard how praying Daniel walked out of the lions' den alive, and how the Hebrew boys emerged from the fiery furnace unscorched. Bit by bit they memorized these stories. They would sneak among the unlighted slave quarters in the quiet hours of the night, risking their lives to pass these stories along to the other slaves and give hope to drooping spirits. They edified one another with prayers and made chants about freedom, reciting rhythmically the mighty acts of Moses, Joshua, Elijah, and Daniel.

From these epics of deliverance, they were able to interpret their own inexplicable situation and give themselves reasons to stay alive. From the Bible came a vision that one day, somehow, they too would be free. And by repeating the narratives over and over again, slaves began to fashion the faith hypothesis that would see them through every conceivable scheme of dehumanization. You might say that they found their source of faith in the very religion their owners had violated.

In Hattie Ann's youth this new faith was the single source of relief. Every Sunday morning she was saturated with the pure, undiluted, spirit-filled worship of the small makeshift plantation church, where God seemed to lean into the church-house windows.

Then early one morning word spread from the big house to the slave quarters and likely all the way down to the riverbank where ten-year-old Hattie Ann was picking berries with the little children: freedom had come. I can only imagine how she must have felt—excited, but also frightened. Where would she go now? How would her family survive?

Emancipation was like being born naked in a wintry world. Clothed in rags, their color a badge of shame and inferiority, freed slaves had no means of sustaining themselves. Most could not read or write, and possessed no worldly goods.

They were at the chaotic crossroads predicted by the distinguished French nobleman, Alexis de Tocqueville, during a visit to the United States in 1831. De Tocqueville knew that eventually the large slave population would become free, just as the slaves of South America and the Caribbean islands had already become free. When that happened, he said, the government would have to seize one of several options: ship slaves back to Africa or deposit them among the islands of the Caribbean; tempt them to violence and then kill them; deny them jobs, food, and shelter, and force them out of sight into the mountains and caves of the Appalachians; or compel fair-skinned slaves to meld with poor whites and Native Americans, and leave the rest to vanish slowly like flying fish or other unprotected mutants. De Tocqueville never realized that millions of slaves just like Hatti Ann had another option securely hidden in their minds and souls.

The spiritual resilience derived from their faith allowed most American slaves to come through their degrading experience whole, without losing their humanity. When the hour was upon them, they set out to create something entirely novel in the history of the world: In America, they dreamed of being free, side by side with their former masters. Their dream had been nurtured with prayer and watered with the briny tears shed by generations.

In their passion, they chose to redeem their race from centuries of dehumanization and make holy the ground on which their parents and ancestors suffered and died. With nothing but faith, they *imagined* the future. They fixed their trust in God and began the journey up the road to equality.

Itinerant black preachers tramped dusty backroads throughout the South, telling Bible stories, and stomping hope into the hearts of the people. The principal thrust came, however, with the founding of a chain of secondary schools and colleges across the South, beckoning the newly freed slaves to begin immediately to enter the life of learning. Booker T. Washington, born enslaved in the rough mining regions of West Virginia, walked from the Blue Ridge Mountains to the Chesapeake Bay, seeking admission to Hampton Institute, a school founded for Indians and freed blacks by Union Army General Samuel Armstrong. Throughout the South, other ex-slaves were also crowding into mission schools, ready and eager to learn. Within forty-five years after Emancipation, 259 of these black schools were established. In almost every instance, blacks themselves had started a school and appealed to missionary teachers for help, and those teachers responded by coming in droves from the Northeast. Virginia Union University, my own alma mater, was founded in 1865 in Mr. Lumpkin's jail for uncontrollable slaves, where dank cell blocks were converted into classrooms and bloodied whipping posts into lecterns.

After Emancipation, Hattie Ann and her family continued to work on the Fisher plantation. When she reached eighteen, the Fishers hired a coach and driver to carry her the eighty miles down the dirt road running alongside the James River all the way to "General Armstrong's school."

Hattie Ann had never been off the plantation and certainly didn't know what to expect at Hampton, but she didn't have much time to worry about it. Once there, she fell immediately under the scrupulous discipline of those puritanical New England school "marms" who followed behind their hard-working students as they scrubbed floors and washed windows, testing each immaculate surface with white-gloved fingertips. These teachers were determined to put new minds and hearts into the physical bodies that had outlasted slavery. Along with the domestic chores, Hattie Ann studied mathematics, chemistry, botany, art, music, anatomy, algebra, geometry, and the Bible. She became a superb seamstress. Hampton men followed a similar curriculum, and also learned carpentry, masonry, plumbing, and tailoring. Booker T. Washington, one of the oldest fellows in the school, stayed on to teach after he graduated, and his powerful presence emanated throughout the school.

Hattie Ann was not afraid of being brainwashed or made "white" by her teachers; she stood hopefully and willingly at the portals of her fuller emancipation, the freedom of the mind.

Most impressive of all was the lofty expectation of these white New England teachers and the black teachers they trained. As a young man, I was fortunate to have one myself—Dr. Joshua Baker Simpson, who taught Latin and Greek at Virginia Union in the early 1940s. He read and wrote those ancient languages with the ease of English and thought we should all do likewise.

Dr. Simpson had finished Colby College in Maine in 1895. He was old, but energetic, always standing at attention. Every move he made was precise. He wore a collar and tie every day of the week, all day long. In his class, you could not cross your legs or assume any relaxed posture. No excuse was sufficient for being absent or late. My soul, I never met such a demanding, unyielding creature in my life.

I recall that one day Lorenzo Shephard, the son of a prominent Philadelphia pastor, shook his fountain pen to cause the ink to flow, and a mere drop fell onto the floor. Dr. Simpson stood up, lit up his light green eyes, tightened his thin lips, reddened his mulatto cheeks, and barked: "Mr. Shephard, where do you think you are? Please, go to the janitor's closet, come back with hot water, soap, and a scrub brush, and clean that ink up from my classroom floor." As Shephard scrubbed, the lesson proceeded and not a soul giggled—we were all scared stiff!

Dr. Simpson was my first big academic challenge. Clearly, he was not preparing us for any lightweight assignment, nor for any subordinate tasks in life. Dr. Simpson was a child of that larger faith. He believed that black people were complete and equal. In every sinew of his body he believed that we could do whatever anyone could do, and that we should be held accountable to the highest standards. His photograph is on my desk at Rutgers now, fifty-two years later. He watches over my shoulder like my grandmother.

EVEN AS HATTIE ANN DEDICATED HERSELF TO THE FUTURE, powerful forces were getting ready to reject her claim to equality. In one of the strangest alliances in history, the Ku Klux Klan and the Supreme Court of the United States joined hands to thwart black progress. The Supreme Court had already emasculated the Fifteenth Amendment, which had granted blacks the right to vote. Then in 1876, in a squabble over electoral votes in the Hayes–Tilden election, Congress granted the presidency to Hayes if his supporters agreed to end Reconstruction.

The backlash was already in motion when Hattie Ann graduated from Hampton in 1882. She was no longer a rickety little slave girl. Gone was the child who had sat up nights painstakingly looking for words she recognized in the master's Bible, gone the ragged little body who spent endless hours hemming with delicate stitches a lady's fine handkerchief. In her place stood an educated and refined woman, her painful past and hopeful present joined. At this bright moment I doubt that she realized that the open door of Reconstruction had already clanged shut. And if she did, it wouldn't have mattered. Forward was the only way to go.

While she had been studying at Hampton, Hattie Ann's family had moved off the Fisher plantation and settled in Norfolk.

The new graduate joined them there and found a job teaching little children in a segregated schoolhouse. Recently, my sister discovered among her archives a picture of Hattie's father taken in Norfolk around this time. He is wearing a fancy black suit with a vest, a watch chain draped across the front, and a breakback collar with a bow tie. One hand holds a brand-new hat, and the other is shoved casually into his pocket. He looked like the future belonged to him.

The fragments we put together about the family's early life in Norfolk suggest that soon after her graduation Hattie Ann met a fair-skinned mulatto named George Proctor, who had been a slave in North Carolina. George was an itinerant musician and I think he came through town and caught sight of the cute little schoolteacher and that was it. Hattie Ann and George got married and started having babies—eight children, each born two years apart. George worked as a barber. It's clear from old photographs of the little wooden houses they lived in that he was not especially prosperous. Then young, handsome George suddenly died, probably from tuberculosis. And Hattie Ann was left to support and care for her eight young children alone.

The miracle of it all was that this skinny, itty-bitty woman kept them all in school. Hattie Ann supported her whole family on a black schoolteacher's pay, which was considerably less than white teachers were paid. Whatever her dreams, this was the job she would have for most of her life. All of Hattie Ann's children finished high school and all had some education beyond that. All of them knew music and played instruments well. My daddy played the piano, violin, and clarinet. One sister played the violin and a brother the trombone. All played in public concerts with various orchestras and bands.

Hattie Ann managed to defend her children and her home against all manner of intrusion. One famous family story concerns the night she set her house on fire when she threw an oil lamp at a burglar. The house burned down and the family lost everything. Grandma wasted no time looking back, she simply started over again.

We know a few more details about my mother's side of the family. Her grandfather, Zechariah Hughes, had been born enslaved in Gloucester County, Virginia, in 1849. *His* father purchased his family's freedom and changed their slave name, "Walker," to "Hughes," in recognition of the white man who had taught him to read. Zechariah grew up to become a preacher. As he preached, he also worked around the oyster beds of the York River. In 1878, he moved his entire congregation from Gloucester to Norfolk County and eventually built two churches that he served the rest of his life. He was an enterprising man who had eleven children by two successive wives. He made sure that all were educated, and all became achievers—ministers, businessmen, choir leaders, and teachers.

All of this happened at a time when blacks were being lynched for every and any trumped-up reason. In 1896, the disastrous *Plessy v. Ferguson* decision gave states the right to legalize racial segregation, and racial separation laws were immediately nailed up everywhere—in courthouses, trolley cars, universities, libraries, theaters, businesses, hospitals, factories, and even public beaches.

When I think about my grandparents making the giant step from slavery to freedom, I realize that none of my own achievements can ever live up to their legacy. Even though everything in the law and the society claimed they were inferior, through all the long days and long years of being beaten back, they held their heads high and made their mark. The lesson that I learned early from observing and listening, and trying to construct my own philosophy and pattern of life, was very simple. It was a way of seeing the stars, rather than the canopy of darkness.

WHEN MY WIFE AND I WERE VERY YOUNG AND ONLY RECENTLY

married, we used to spend our vacations at her mother's home in the old colonial town of Fredericksburg, Virginia. Nothing very exciting happened there, but next door lived an old woman who had a large fragrant flower called a night-blooming cereus growing in her front yard. When other flowers were dormant, after the last rays of sunlight dimmed and the rhythms of photosynthesis ceased, the cereus spread open its petals and effused its perfume. It seemed indifferent to the void. Unnoticed and unapplauded, it performed for its own sake and gave up its beauty without admiration. Around midnight on summer nights, when we were sitting out on our porch trying to catch a late night breeze, the old woman would call us quietly to come over and see her lovely flower blooming in the dark.

When the lights went out in the 1890s, when the political currents swirled against black progress and the nation draped itself in antiblack sentiment, hope still bloomed within the black community. We had learned that the key to the future was education. Somehow we believed that we, too, could bloom, darkness notwithstanding.

CHAPTER TWO

Come Sunday!

MY MAMA, VELMA GLADYS, WAS BORN IN 1893, THE daughter of Annie Gary and William Hughes, who was a choirmaster and a deacon in his father's church. When Velma was about twenty years old, she married Herbert Proctor, one of Hattie Ann's boys. They were students together at Norfolk Mission College, just as Velma's own parents had been when they met and married. On the eve of the First World War, Herbert canceled his plans for a dental career and got a job at the Norfolk Navy Yard. Soon he and Velma had two little babies, Herbert, Jr., and Annie.

In the winter of 1916, both babies were struck by whooping cough and died within days of each other. My parents never got over their deaths. For all of their lives they spoke of our little brother and sister who had died in infancy, and we all spent hours wondering what they would have looked like and been like.

It always impressed me that in addition to shouldering that grief, my father left the house every morning to work in a world of insults and humiliation, and my mother sang and prayed her way through long days of incessant labor at home, at the stove, the sewing machine, the wash tub and the ironing board.

Daddy and Mamma were children-oriented. They lived for us. Daddy left early every morning for the Navy Yard, where he seemed to take pride in earning a decent livelihood for his family. He was always upbeat and forward-looking. Our home, a nine-room frame structure in a long row of identical houses in Huntersville, the black center of Norfolk, was taken over by my parents from my mother's father when he became terminally ill.

There were six of us—first my sister Harriet, who was born in 1917, and then my older brother Vernon in 1919. I arrived in 1921. Four more boys came after me and all of us grew up in our grandfather's house at 918 Fremont Street. My mother's brothers and sisters lived nearby and were always in and out of our house. Their children were like our brothers and sisters, and we all had our eyes on the stars.

We lived behind a high wall of racial limits. I remember riding the ferry with my father between Norfolk and Portsmouth. No signs were posted to tell us which side was the "colored" side, but Daddy told me that our side was *always* the one reached by crossing through a heavy stream of traffic entering the ferry, clogging the area in the middle. Still fresh in my memory is the sight of a huge basket of freshly laundered linen, skillfully balanced on the head of a smiling, round-faced black woman ducking and dodging her way between teams of frightened, braying horses and loud, chain-driven trucks, as she struggled to cross the center of the ferry to reach the "colored" side.

Every day we lived with reminders of what our place was—what not to say, where it was safe to be, and how to make life a little smoother. To get a little raise in pay, or a slight promotion, we pretended to be "inferior." Any gesture that bespoke our desire for equality was saved for the black church. Speaking out elsewhere brought severe and final retribution. Some did, of course, and were willing to pay the price.

Church and family were like a seamless garment cloaked about us. Hymn-singing, praying, and Bible reading and quoting were as close as breathing and nearer than hands and feet. We never sat down to eat anything—a bowl of oatmeal, a piece of buttered spoonbread, a chicken leg—without bowing our heads and mumbling a fast prayer. When I wonder about the substance of things hoped for, I look within and remember the source of our hope for the future. The answer always was, in Duke Ellington's words, "Come Sunday!" Shoes were shined, music practiced, and the Golden Text memorized; the fish were frying in deep grease, the dog was fed and watered, the old Buick was wiped down and cleaned out, the rolls were in the oven, and every radio was tuned to the "Wings Over Jordan" choir led by Glenn T. Settles in Cleveland, singing, *Shine on me, shine on me. Let the light from the lighthouse shine on me.* "It was church time, and faith would be rekindled.

Our whole family was active in church life. My aunts and uncles sang in choirs and played the organ in several churches. Four of my uncles were pastors and two of the largest churches in Norfolk were those founded by my great-grandfather Zachariah Hughes.

Our father never sent us to Sunday school. He took us with him—all six of us—shoes gleaming, trousers ironed, hair trimmed (by him!), and the Sunday lesson learned by heart. Most families in our neighborhood welcomed Sunday in the same way.

Everyone was identified by the church he or she attended.

"Did you know that Mr. Crocker died?"

"Which Mr. Crocker?"

"The one who goes to St. John's Church."

If you attended no church at all, it was like having no identity at all. Church was a social hour, a time to compare clothes, exchange news, share a sad note, celebrate a new job, look for a partner in romance, exchange recipes, learn about bargains, or pick up the name of a better doctor, tailor, or automobile mechanic.

In the Sunday school orchestra, my daddy played the violin, Vernon played the tuba, and I played the clarinet. Our church sang with a rhythm and bounce. People often made up their own songs, adding verses as the Spirit led them, and the new verses became a permanent part of the song. Like their songs, their prayers were also memorized and repeated.

Church was also preaching time. I was generally bored by the worship service, although I was intrigued by the pastor. When I was a child, preachers wore long frock coats, high collars, and striped trousers. Week after week, they told the same familiar stories, giving content to our faith and rhythm to our emotions. People, anticipating every word, signaled the best points with verbal and, sometimes, bodily responses. Nowhere else could a group of people move from moaning and groaning to clapping and shouting for joy in so short a time. It was the same wherever black migrants gathered together and built churches up North and out West. These large urban churches, surrounded by mortuaries, cafés, blacksmiths, dry cleaners, barbershops, small stores, and professional offices, became the citadels of black American culture.

THE PEOPLE WHO MATTERED MOST TO US IN OUR YOUTH believed in the simplest virtues of honesty, sobriety, thrift, kindness, charity, and mutual respect. They abhorred dishonesty, boasting, unkindness, disloyalty, and sloth. Although such virtues bear no ethnic label, we learned them as patented human behavior from steady, predictable, devoted black Christians.

We learned Bible lessons from Grandma, who also taught us poems and hymns in her religiously correct English. She constantly policed our speech and grammar, correcting every split infinitive, every pronoun out of agreement with its antecedent, and every mispronounced word. I was perplexed that a woman as smart as my grandma could ever have been a slave.

When I was still too young for school, Grandma took me along to her classroom at the Cumberland Street School where I sat in awe watching her teach. Believe me, no one acted up in Mrs. Proctor's classroom. All of her friends and colleagues seemed to share the same secret: they had a mission and a destiny to meet. They spoke to us children in the subjunctive mood—not what is, but what *may be*, when our faith flowered into reality.

When I was old enough for school, my days brimmed with activities—rehearsals, contests, games, and programs of all kinds. For the most part, my classmates and I were insulated from harsh, daily racial insults. And we had an answer for the ugly incidents we did have to endure: they would not last. Our teachers kept our eyes pinned on the future, and our faith stayed alive, pulsing within us.

I remember sitting in an English literature class in a segregated school, using tattered textbooks with the names, addresses, and telephone numbers of the white students who had worn them out and scribbled all over the pages. We were in an old building, scantily built for the "colored," with outdoor toilets, no lunchroom, no gymnasium, and no music or art or physical education teacher.

I recall our tall, thin Miss Edith Green, teaching us a poem by Alfred Tennyson which described a tiny flower that managed to grow through a granite wall and bloom on the other side. That poem has lived with me through these long decades, a more powerful memory than the images of that "colored" elementary school.

It was not always easy being one of the Proctor boys. The old folks pointed me out as Reverend Hughes' great-grandson, which meant that my behavior had to be irreproachable. Even worse, many of my teachers had been students of Grandma's. So I also had to live up to Hattie Ann Proctor's formidable reputation. It was incredible how we learned to handle the paradox of being compelled to hold our heads high with expectation and hope, while the social landscape was etched with denial and rejection.

AS CHILDREN WE WERE UNAWARE OF THE FULL IMPACT OF the Great Depression. We never felt severely impoverished, and our parents imposed a strong sense of security around us, just as their parents had done for them. There was never enough of what we wanted, but always enough of what we needed. We learned early to discriminate between approved ways of getting by and disapproved ones.

My brother Vernon and I were lucky enough to have a morning paper route which we had inherited from an older friend who had gone off to college. On Sundays, the papers were so thick and heavy that we had to stack them at the corner of Lexington and Church streets, then break them down into smaller bundles and deliver them a few at a time. No one bothered the main pile because a popular bootlegger called "Bear" operated his joint near that corner. Early one Sunday morning, as we were separating our bundles, we heard loud sirens wailing and two police motorcycles screeched to a stop on our corner, followed by a big LaSalle limousine. Two white men got out of the car and unloaded about ten gallon-jugs of corn whisky. Then another limousine pulled up. Bear came out of his joint and handed the well-dressed passenger a large roll of money.

Then *another* car—this one a big Ford convertible carrying four plainclothes police—slowly cruised up, and escorted the second limousine as it drove away. Bear sure looked like a hero to us—a black man defying law and custom, handling big money, and collaborating with crooked white police.

We could not get home fast enough to tell Daddy what we had seen. He told us that Bear was a boyhood friend of his, but he had not been reared in a Christian home. Bear had dropped out of school and chose to hustle and scheme for a living. No matter how poor Christians were, Daddy said, they would never steal or sell whisky for a living.

My daddy made it perfectly clear that there were two kinds of people: those who tried to live with moral accountability and those who did not. Over and over in my childhood my parents talked about and *demonstrated* the distinction between the behavior of church people—those who reflected a self-affirming approach to life—and the behavior of the unchurched.

Some people, of course, were borderline. One very warm-hearted, generous woman in our neighborhood was the local numbers writer. Two or three times a year she was arrested and fined, then continued her business afterward. Although she lived in the midst of ardent church people, her whole lifestyle was something apart from the church. She smoked cigarettes in public, drank beer on her porch, and shouted profanity at her five children. Church people cringed at all of that. It saddened us boys because one of her sons was a friend of ours. He was embarrassed by his mother's behavior, but he was always getting into fights to defend her against one insult or another.

—

VERNON AND I USED TO LIE IN BED AT NIGHT TALKING ABOUT what we wanted to be when we grew up. Vernon said he wanted to lead a Broadway theater orchestra, although he had never seen one except in the movies. I wanted to be a lawyer, although

I had never actually seen a black lawyer anywhere at all. But Vernon and I already knew how to live on the substance of things hoped for. Our dreams took wing and soared beyond that little segregated dusty bottom in Virginia. Nothing—no ugly names, backdoor entrances, or raggedy, used schoolbooks—could stifle our faith.

Blacks living in other segregated communities around the country also made the best of their situation. They turned to each other and their neighbors and began to embroider the simple functions of life with a style and tempo that suited their taste and nourished their hope. In effect, they were creating a new black American culture that allowed them to survive with sanity in a hostile environment.

As we were growing up, that culture reverberated everywhere. Freedom's muse was joyous, profound, and often hilarious. We would dance a parody of our poverty, and sing a travesty of our pain. In our town, Saturday nights at Ashburn's barbershop, at the corner of Chapel and Anderson streets, was show time. Street messiahs, comedians, harmonica players, and poets performed routines for an audience of thirty or forty clients waiting on the five barbers.

ALTHOUGH BARRED FROM THE "LEGITIMATE" STAGE, WE also found creative ways to contribute to the larger white community. My father sang in the all-black Norfolk Philharmonic Glee Club, which comprised Pullman porters, bellhops, barbers, postmen, teachers, and even physicians, lawyers, and dentists. The Glee Club practiced every Wednesday night, and once a year they gave a concert in the city hall auditorium for a white audience. For that one night only, black families were permitted to attend and to sit in the rear of the auditorium. My mother always brought all six of us. Even though the whole society was rigidly segregated and lynchings were reported in the paper every week, the Glee Club closed each concert singing:

Dawn is breaking and a new day is born...

The world is singing the song of the dawn.

In reality, there was no new day. There was only the perennial belief that a new day would be born. Toward that end, church continued to provide the spiritual ballast needed for life's journey.

Before the Emancipation, slaveholders tried to convince blacks that God *wanted* them to be enslaved. In *Deep Like Rivers*, Thomas Webber recaptured the sinister words originally spoken to slaves by the Right Reverend William Meade, Episcopal bishop of Virginia:

> Take care that you do not fret or murmur or grumble at your condition, for this will not only make your life uneasy, but it will greatly offend Almighty God. Consider that it is not yourselves; it is not the people that you belong to; it is not the men that have brought you to it; but it is the will of God, who hath by his wise providence made you servants, because, no doubt, he knew that condition would be best for you in the world and help you better towards heaven. . . .

When blacks heard such things, they sucked their teeth, glanced at their fingernails, gazed into the deep distance, and slowly strolled away. It was not even worth a laugh. They knew their Bible.

We never accepted the self-negating religion offered by the slave masters. Our legacy flowed from preachers like Bishop Lucius Holsey, one of the founders of the Colored (now Christian) Methodist Episcopal Church, who was himself the son of a female slave and a slave owner; Bishop Holsey's wife had been the slave of a Methodist bishop. Holsey made a direct assault on Meade's words:

> Every man is made by the same hand. . . . Neither can racial distinctions, color, climate or geographical situation of birth and growth make any difference in the characteristics of his real manhood. . . . What, therefore, is possible for one man is possible for all men under the same conditions and circumstances.

Everyone we met at our church was looking up. They were educated, neat, polite, prompt, and serious. Incidentally, my Sunday school teachers were also my public school teachers. All week long they shouted at us in the name of algebra and Shakespeare, and on Sundays, with a little more perfume, more makeup, nicer clothes and higher heels for the women, and a blue suit for Mr. Newsome, they shouted at us in the name of Moses and Jesus.

Most of our churches blended religious instruction with education in citizenship and cultural history. Unfortunately, however, some preachers leeched on the poor and promised extravagant blessings in return for all their meager earnings.

One of our neighbors, whom we called Miss Lillian, appeared to be a balanced, competent person, the mother of several lovely, bright children who went to school with us. She ran a small grocery store that was a hang-out for us kids. Miss Lillian hardly made any profit, but the store provided a kind of stage for her.

Every afternoon, the excitement started when she began to talk about Jesus. She would get up from her chair and go into a foot-clogging, holy dance, and then tilt her head back, with her steel-gray eyes fixed on blank space, and begin speaking "in tongues" until she foamed at the mouth and passed out, often gashing her head on any object in her path as she fell. Within seconds, she was back in her chair, waving her hands placidly, saying softly, "Thank you, Jesus, thank you, Jesus."

Miss Lillian belonged to a church headed by a Cape Verdean charismatic preacher from New Bedford, Massachusetts. He came to town monthly, working with a local pastor and worshiping in a large tent. He baptized believers by the hundreds, keeping his congregants shouting and dancing for hours on end. We always rushed to Church Street, our main drag, to see his welcoming parade march in to the tunes of a mediocre brass band. Crowds gathered to watch the tall, dark-skinned honor guards, wearing brass-buttoned jackets and high leather boots, sporting badges, whistles, and whisking batons to keep back the crowds. Then along came the visiting chief minister, seated in the back seat of a white, four-door Packard convertible with the top down. He wore a pink satin suit, with manicured fingernails an inch long, and his curly hair down to his shoulders. Diamond rings flashed on eight of his fingers and two very rotund sisters sat on either side of him, fanning the Tidewater humidity away from his chubby face. The "divine one" smiled graciously, waving his open hands in a kind of blessing, as his admirers trotted alongside the slowly gliding Packard.

At night he sat on a gold-papered throne as crowds of devotees marched past the rostrum and kneeled before him, dropping five-, ten-, and twenty-dollar bills in bushel baskets held by the uniformed guards. He preached brief, teasing sermons without ever using a whole sentence. They were simply empty words about God's blessings and the joy of heaven that fell like dew on the hearer's ears. Then the brass band marched in and the preacher encouraged the faithful to fill up those bushel baskets with "quiet money," as he called paper bills. The baskets ran over. You couldn't ask for more exciting entertainment.

The preacher regularly visited eight to ten cities, with more than one church in some towns. He wasn't the only one. Many smooth charismatic preachers used the same patented procedure to break free from organized denominations. They were supervised only by the "Holy Spirit." And uneducated, innocent, frustrated black people who couldn't imagine participating in the American system were their prey. There were many white "bishops" who fleeced their uneducated believers in the same way.

Interestingly, white and black Christians followed the same Jesus who taught love and inclusiveness, but they never worshiped together. Black people hardly gave a thought to this peculiar contradiction. The black church met such a critical need, and was so independent of white control, that no one considered a merger of black and white churches.

In fact, the chasm between the white and black church was unbridgeable: any gesture that signified equality was unacceptable to whites; and any gesture that implied black inferiority was unacceptable to blacks. Rather than transcend the taboos of the secular society, the churches, both black and white, simply reflected things as they were.

Although customs varied from one congregation to another, black people had carved out a distinctive style of biblical interpretation and worship. White people spent most of their time preparing for heaven; although blacks did not reject a vision of heaven, they emphasized that a better day would come, here on earth. Whites emphasized God's holiness and judgement; blacks saw God as the liberator of the oppressed. Whites asked, "What if you should die unsaved?" Blacks believed that God would help them to bear their daily burdens. Whites said that they wanted to be ready when Jesus came again; blacks that God would make a way out of no way.

IN OUR TOWN, AS IN BLACK COMMUNITIES ACROSS THE country, preachers were thumping on pulpits proclaiming that deliverance would eventually come to the faithful. In every black lodge hall in America, the brothers and sisters were drilled in voting and home ownership, and in every segregated schoolhouse, black teachers held up photographs of C. C. Spauling, founder of the prosperous black life insurance company in Durham, N.C.; Mary McLeod Bethune, who build Bethune-Cookman College from an abandoned freight car; W. E. B. DuBois, the black Harvard Ph.D. who founded the NAACP; Booker T. Washington, who built Tuskegee Institute; and George Washington Carver, the black Iowa-trained Tuskegee scientist.

The NAACP was bringing cases before the Supreme Court, and John L. Lewis and the United Mine Workers were fighting to get blacks, who had been shut out of the AFL, included in the new CIO labor camps.

But even then not all of us were running on the same track. The patience of some black intellectuals ran out. Some gave up and turned toward the American Communist Party, which made a big pitch for the black vote. Eighty-six percent of all blacks were still living in the South, most in rural areas where they barely survived on sharecropping. The party assumed that the blacks' stagnant poverty and cultural isolation made them ripe for revolution. The swelling ranks of segregated trade unions in the United States added more impact to their argument.

In the midst of this, Marcus Garvey appeared, a Jamaican with a passion for black liberation and a dramatic plan to repatriate blacks to Africa. He had a poorly financed steamship line, an untrained "African Legion," composed of American blacks, which he said would run a new African state.

Garvey's whole movement had a lot of flair that was especially appealing to urban people who didn't have much education. He emphasized the beauty and promise of blackness, but most blacks knew that blackness without intellect, blackness without money, blackness without character or discipline, was just blackness without content.

The Communist Party's vision of class war and Garvey's vision of a new beginning in Africa failed to enchant large numbers of blacks. When Garvey urged American blacks to resettle in Africa in 1933, he discovered that our faith was like a rock, impenetrable; like a tree, deeply rooted. Despite the toughness of the times, no one was interested in abandoning the struggle here. Most blacks wanted solid, irreversible success here in a *changed* America, not a new start somewhere else.

Looking back now, it is clear to me that two strata of blacks in America had become solidly entrenched. Those who had been shut out still lived on subsistence wages, in cheap tenements or rural shacks along unpaved backroads, far removed from any talk of black destiny. By contrast, those who had made it through the open door of Reconstruction felt that their faith was being validated; they were leading lodges and churches, some had professional careers, and they were in the forefront of organizations dedicated to black education and black liberation.

When Franklin D. Roosevelt began to remake America's future, these heirs of the mission schools were ready, and theirs was the dominant black voice. They saw the worm turning.

CHAPTER THREE

The Turning of the Worm

1935–1945

ONE DAY IN THE FALL OF 1935, I WENT TO SCHOOL AND learned that our vivacious and self-assured biology teacher had been fired. She, along with four other black schoolteachers, had sued the city of Norfolk for equal pay with white teachers. We were suddenly thrust into the churning vortex of history.

The salaries of black teachers were 30 percent less than that of white teachers with the same training and experience. In many instances, black teachers were actually better educated than whites. While they were universally denied admission to graduate schools in the South, many black teachers had received state-funded grants to attend graduate schools in the North. (Southern states would pay any amount of money to keep them out of their universities—an example of how irrational racism had become.)

Thus, during the summer terms, the campuses of New York, Columbia, Indiana, Temple, Boston, Michigan State, and Penn State universities were dotted with well-dressed, serious black teachers from the thirteen southern states. Our biology teacher had been among them. Her graduate teaching degree gave her the credentials to become a plaintiff for the NAACP legal suit.

Even as children, we knew that there was a huge wall "out there" that no black person could go over or around, regardless of qualifications. It's difficult to describe our feelings about the "respectable" white Christians who sang in church choirs, served as deacons, trustees, and elders in downtown churches, who joined the Boy Scouts, and sat on city councils, court benches, and in the Congress, yet felt no shame in endorsing this wholesale racial discrimination. It's equally hard to describe our own absolute, unwavering loyalty to, and belief in, the principles of American democracy.

Our teacher's suit was filed by NAACP attorneys. It eventually ended up before the United States Supreme Court and our teacher won. The case dragged on for about three years, and in the meantime, all of the plaintiffs were employed elsewhere. At our Booker T. Washington High School, even though we had only a faint notion of the sweeping implications of that victory, we were jubilant. We were so proud of our teacher. She was a beautiful, lively woman with a sense of humor. She lived on the next street from ours, and anytime she caught us teenage boys staring at her as she walked down the street or the hallway at school she gave us a slow, sly wink and a sassy smile. We thrived on such ego inflation.

Now, she had leaped out of her role as our favorite teacher and become a celebrity. Her name, Alene Black, was in all of the black weekly papers and she was talked about in every black church, conference, or assembly. We were all aware that because of her, and other black teachers mounting similar lawsuits, blatant injustice was being beaten back for once.

Our leaders had always recognized the leverage of the Supreme Court. They knew that Supreme Court decisions in 1875, 1883, and 1896 had canceled the gains made during Reconstruction. When President Hoover appointed the avowed racist John J. Parker to the Supreme Court in 1930, we children, and adults, too, prayed hard for help to defeat those senators who voted for him. After the presidential election of 1932, we prayed that President Roosevelt's newly revised Supreme Court would be our deliverer. The Court was only waiting for the right lawyers to bring the right cases.

Thurgood Marshall and the other civil rights lawyers became our heroes. We read about them trying cases across the South where they were denied drinking water and access to restrooms and lunch counters. From where we stood, it took real courage to file a complaint in a federal court against a whole city, county, or state. These were the days when a black person couldn't expect any police protection, even if his life depended on it.

Dr. Benjamin E. Mays, the distinguished president of Morehouse College, was riding on a train from Atlanta to New York. In order to eat dinner he had to sit behind a curtain which had been installed to hide black diners from the white diners. Dr. Mays protested and filed suit. The curtain, the last vestige of legal separation, came down even while much prejudice remained, unprotested.

In our dining room at home we had a huge arcola stove, with registers cut into the ceiling to conduct some of the heat to upstairs bedrooms. Every night we would gather in that dining room for warmth and enjoy listening to our radio, tuning into Fibber McGee and Molly, Jack Benny and Rochester (Eddie Anderson), Edgar Bergen and Charlie McCarthy, Amos and Andy and the Mystic Knights of the Sea. Almost always, blacks were parodied, made to appear (even though ironically that was a program in which white comedians imitated and stereotyped Black life) ignorant, superstitious, easily frightened and deceived, and childish. They were never taken seriously. But even then certain sweet victories swelled our hearts with pride.

Every time heavyweight champion Joe Louis fought, our community was quiet as a morgue—until Joe floored another opponent, and a sudden burst of shouts and screams shattered our end of town. His victories were reason enough to wear a wide grin to work the next morning. And when Jesse Owens startled Hitler by winning four gold medals at the 1936 Olympic games in Berlin, black communities rocked with rapture.

When the Daughters of the American Revolution, descendants of the nation's earliest defenders, barred Marian Anderson from singing in their auditorium in 1939, decent people everywhere felt disgraced. Mrs. Eleanor Roosevelt, an aristocrat by anybody's standards, along with other concerned persons, arranged for Miss Anderson to sing outdoors in front of the Lincoln Memorial. Harold I. Ickes, Secretary of the Interior, set the date. More than fifty thousand people turned up for that concert on Easter Sunday, many thousands more than would ever have attended a concert in an auditorium. Blacks everywhere breathed in the fresh air of vindication.

As I approached high school graduation in 1937, other tiny apertures began to appear in the thick wall of segregation. Just before daybreak one Sunday morning my father hustled us out of bed and rushed us to our church, which was located at the far edge of our section of town. Flames were cracking and leaping across the church roof, enveloping its distinctive colonial spire. Everyone in the neighborhood gathered around, helplessly staring as the fire engulfed the whole building. Among them was Dr. Sparks White Melton, the venerable pastor of the nearby all-white Freemason Street Baptist Church. I can still see his striped pajama sleeves sticking out of his overcoat as he stood there in the predawn darkness, tears streaming down his face. Our church was in ashes and we were bereft. But Dr. Melton spoke up and invited our pastor to bring his congregation to worship in Freemason Street's auditorium, where Sunday school was held for the white children. We were welcome to stay, he said, until our church was rebuilt. His offer seems a small thing by today's standards, but at that time and place, when the two races did literally *nothing* together voluntarily, it was radical.

Today, I look back through the corridor of these long ago events and see the doors trying to creak open on their rusty hinges. Dr. Melton's congregation comprised businessmen, government supervisers, and city administrators. These white people employed blacks in menial jobs, but they never acknowledged their total personhood. I remember my father writing letters and filling out tax forms for his white supervisers and co-workers who didn't know how to write such items, sometimes even writing an obituary for a deceased white worker.

Nothing required Dr. Melton to get out of his warm bed to stand with us as we wept over our church fire. He violated the mores of his own society when he invited us into his church. His action was indelibly recorded in my mind—I knew that God was moving.

Alexis de Tocqueville said that white people would never accept blacks as equals, unless black people radically changed in their education and culture. He assumed that blacks wouldn't and couldn't change. He never even speculated that white people might change. But my own faith package always included that prospect, too. In my limited life's experience I had already seen that not all white people were programmed for bigotry. Even in the South, where racism was a way of life, they were capable of change.

I remember Mrs. Annie Griswold, proprietor of the big drugstore near the beach in Ocean View, a suburb of Norfolk. I worked for her the summer after I graduated from high school, delivering prescriptions and cases of Rheingold beer to the vacationers renting the waterfront cottages. That was the nearest

I was allowed to get to the beach where white youths lounged and played on miles of soft sand. As they watched me walking down the boardwalk in my white apron delivering beer to a party of drunken naval officers holed up in a tacky beach motel with six teenage prostitutes, they never dreamed I was working for my college tuition.

My main job was to keep ice and syrup on the soda fountain, clean up the floor when a drunk dropped his beer or vomited, and make sandwiches when the waitresses were too busy. I made nine dollars a week while the white soda jerk, who was a high school drop-out, made fourteen dollars. I had plenty of cause to see the world as unfair.

On my last day of work that summer, Mrs. Griswold told me to go in the back and find a cardboard beer box with my name on it. The box was packed to the brim with Lifebuoy soap, Gillette blades, Colgate toothpaste, Mum deodorant, Lucky Strike cigarettes (though I didn't smoke), writing paper, a pen and bottles of ink, Bayer aspirins, cough syrup, Mennen talcum powder, and, of all things, a dozen Trojan contraceptives. That last item was embarrassing because my conservative church rearing didn't even allow talk about such things. I'm certain that Mrs. Griswold didn't think I was promiscuous at age fifteen, but if I did stray she didn't want my schooling to be halted by having to stop and become a teenage father.

In her own way, Annie Griswold was breaking through that thick wall of racial separation that kept me off Ocean View beach, and showing me that she was happy that I was headed for college. Her gesture fueled my hope that the future was worth a gamble.

In my freshman summer of 1938, I worked as an elevator operator at Ames and Brownley, a fashionable department store in downtown Norfolk. When traffic was slow, I would close down my elevator, get a duster, and help the black maids clean off the counters and mop the floors. Here, affluent women came early, had lunch, and toyed with the merchandise all day. As they walked in the marble corridors of that glittering store, they seemed separated from the larger society. They talked to the clerks, and some of the more motherly ones paused at the elevators and talked with us. Many of them knew I was in college and they gave me little gifts and words of encouragement. On the surface, at least, they gave no sign of hatred or contempt.

On my last day there before going back to school, Mr. Proescher, the vice president, darted into the back room where the "colored" help ate lunch and received their daily assignments. He addressed Harry, thecontemptouwhite shipping clerk who was boss of all the "colored."

"Leave Proctor's card on the clock after he leaves for school."

Harry said, "For what?"

Mr. Proescher planted himself in the middle of that junky room, cluttered with broken merchandise and empty cardboard boxes. Twelve curious, tired black faces stared at him as he looked Harry in the eye. "So he can come in here and make some time whenever he comes home from college," he said, "even if it's only a half hour or a Saturday afternoon."

"Doing what?" scoffed Harry.

"Doing any damn thing he wants to. He's smart enough to find something we need to have done."

The chorus of colored porters ducked their heads and enjoyed a sniggle of triumph. This white man had broken through the barrier of racial etiquette and dressed down another white man in our presence; just like Annie Griswold, he was applauding the ambitions of a young black man trying to make something of himself.

True, some famous white voices were also sounding a clarion call for change at this time—Ralph McGill, Mrs. Eleanor Roosevelt, Walter Reuther, Eugene Carson Blake, John L. Lewis, and Branch Rickey to name a few—but to me, these small, personal episodes, like intermittent Morse code tappings, really signaied that change was coming. Each one helped keep my faith alive.

MY FIRST TWO YEARS OF COLLEGE AT VIRGINIA STATE IN Petersburg were turbulent. Money was a big problem. Three of us siblings needed college money at the same time; I had skipped three grades and finished high school with my brother Vernon, and our sister Harriet was still in college. I had to find ways to help pay my tuition.

In addition to my savings, I had earned a music scholarship with my clarinet audition of Schubert's "Serenade." I was also lucky to get a National Youth Administration job assisting the band director. I learned to play the alto sax and got a job with our college dance orchestra, called the Virginia State Trojans. We had more money in our pockets than most faculty members.

I tried hard to behave like my idea of a jazz musician; collecting cute girls, dancing, and fraternity capers crowded my agenda. I had no energy left for serious matters. College was a kind of smorgasbord—no one guided you through the menu, you just took whatever you wanted. The trouble was, I didn't know what I wanted. I was bored with books and lost in daydreaming, spinning through my days at school, but going nowhere.

It's curious how black folk have a life within and among themselves which has no reference to white people. On campus, we lived in a kind of social cocoon, since all the students and teachers were black. We imagined a world that suited our whims, a world without the presence or control of whites, where we chose our own heroes, reeled in a fantasy future. Like my brother Vernon, I even dreamed of directing my own pit orchestra on Broadway, which was a long way from reality.

Then, we were compelled to attend our black colleges in the South. Now, integration in education at every level is irreversible as a social goal. But what was intended to be a disadvantage, we converted into a solid benefit.

My college professors had managed to escape the limitations imposed by segregated schools with poor facilities and makeshift resources, and to succeed in obtaining graduate degrees in practically every field from highly reputed institutions. One can only imagine the personal sacrifices those black scholars and their families must have made to achieve such academic laurels at that time.

My professors believed in the future. They were committed to service and never stopped to question whether they would be personally rewarded. I can see my history professor, Dr. Luther P. Jackson, wearing his one blue suit, his arms filled with papers, hurriedly walking toward his beat-up old Plymouth, getting ready to set off for some small town in rural Virginia to organize a voter registration drive. When he wasn't registering voters, he was bringing young black men together to form glee clubs. He worked constantly and never looked back.

My own uncle, Dr. Tommy Carter, was a French professor at Virginia State. When he was a student at the University of Michigan, he paid for his room and board by living in the attic of a fraternity house and serving meals to the white undergraduates. He used to send me beautiful shirts, shoes, and jackets that the white fraternity boys had discarded. When the members of his campus French Club went out to dinner to practice their conversational French, Tommy wasn't allowed to go because the restaurants in Ann Arbor barred blacks. None of this stopped him.

Tommy Carter headed the French department at Virginia State for twenty-five years, then served as a Peace Corps administrator in French West Africa (Senegal) and Morocco; and *then* became an official in the U.S. Information Administration and a higher education program officer in the United States Office of Education!

I had always been troubled by the chasm between our home, where learning was emphasized, and other homes where it was neglected; and the conspicuous contrast between those who were literate and had good jobs, and those who were not and worked as hands. That divide seemed permanent and untraversable.

It was dawning on me that black people in America were actually living in a three-tiered society. At the very bottom, some could hardly read; they had children out of wedlock, never attended church, moved constantly, and a few even bought stolen goods, drank, and fought in the streets. These were people who had a weak beginning, and believed their future held only poverty and marginality.

Above them was a wide, deep layer of black people who believed they had a place in society and that sooner or later they would enter fully into the American system. My parents and their friends were among these hard-working, self-reliant, and compassionate black people. They headed the lodges; led the Sunday schools; presided over the social clubs; owned homes; educated their children, lived with modesty and sobriety, and could be counted on to support every good cause. They represented the large center of black society—government workers, Pullman porters, postmen, artisans, building contractors, shopkeepers, ice and vegetable merchants, nurses and longshoremen, hotel waiters and barbers, insurance and real estate salespeople, teachers and entrepreneurs.

And then, as I entered college, I learned that there was yet another stratum—those who had been trained in the professions and at the Ph.D. level, as well as a handful of artists, like Marian Anderson, who had soared above most humans of whatever origin. They set a fast pace for the rest of us.

Some of my professors were part of this last group. From childhood these men and women, often descended from free blacks, had been nurtured by caring, intelligent parents. They were overwhelmingly mulatto, and by virtue of their partial white ancestry, or the powerful mythology of light-skin supremacy, their own communities placed favors on them and held high expectations for them. As children they had enjoyed early initiation into academics; later, they had been able to enter the best colleges because of their privileges and their advanced academic performance. If white universities had been allowed to hire them, no black college could have competed for their services.

All of my professors, whatever their background, were visibly impatient with the low academic aspirations of many black students, and indignant that some of us thought ourselves inferior. They didn't want to turn us into white people, but they wanted to pour new content into the color black, to destroy stereotypes and to kill rumors about our indelible inferiority.

WHEN I WAS YOUNG, BLACKS DIDN'T HAVE MANY CAREER options. Large law firms, big industrial giants, state and federal governments and universities excluded blacks, regardless of qualifications. Certainly, blacks never had jobs that supervised whites.

Within the black community the career that was always open with unlimited access was the ministry. Role models like Howard Thurman, Mordecai Johnson, Benjamin Mays, and Adam Clayton Powell, Sr., were widely known.

The role of the minister as social advocate had always gripped my imagination. Yet whenever the idea of being a minister crossed my mind, I felt a strange revulsion. For one thing, many black ministers at that time went at it without proper training; they simply declared that they were "called." Many ministers were given to gaudy dress, unbridled egotism, and self-aggrandizement; they exploited women willing to do anything to be close to the "pastor." Of course, similar behavior occurred among judges, lawyers, teachers, and even presidents of the

United States, but it turned me off when I saw preachers behaving in such contrast to the One whose life displayed simplicity and humility.

I also thought that the institutional church, with its dogma and display of riches, was often unfaithful to the person of Christ in the gospels. I didn't know about the various kinds of literature in the Bible or about the many different ways writers expressed religious ideas.

Despite my confusion, I was haunted by the notion of becoming a minister. I read the life of Jesus over and over in the gospels. When my great-uncle, Reverend Everard Hughes, came home on vacations, I talked with him for hours on end. He had graduated from the Oberlin Graduate School of Theology and worked with very enlightened churches. Our conversations helped open my view of the ministry.

Meanwhile, months passed at college without my gaining any clear direction in school. Then I faced my own Gethsemane. This is what happened:

I had been sixteen years old when I entered Virginia State. Like everyone else, I joined a fraternity. I loved my fraternity and felt close to my brothers. But all fraternities tolerated a few thugs who loved to engage in excessively brutal behavior at initiation. They would drink themselves into oblivion and proceed to beat on the pledges with long, oak paddles that had the leverage of baseball bats. I mean, they floored them with fifty to sixty strong strokes to the buttocks.

After surviving my own initiation, I complained to my fraternity brothers about their behavior, but they ignored me. I threatened to report them, and they threatened to kill me. Even my uncle, Dr. Tommy Carter, told me to keep my mouth shut. He thought I had become too obsessive about it.

I sought advice from Dr. Harry Roberts, a professor of sociology who was also a Methodist minister. He listened patiently to my troubles and said I was on the right track.

I tried to launch a campaign among new members of all the fraternities to report these activities to the dean of students. Many agreed to speak up, but when the agreed-on day came to present the case to the dean, no one showed up.

Somewhere during that time I broke the peer rules against religious practice and slipped off campus to visit a local church. There, a short preacher with a sharp West Indian accent seemed to know that I was coming. His text that morning was from Joshua 1:9 (King James Version):

> Be strong and of a good courage; be not afraid, neither be thou dismayed; for the Lord thy God is with thee withersoever thou goest.

His words were aimed straight at me. After the sermon, I went forward and talked to him. Baptists practice believer's baptism, meaning that you're supposed to accept Christ on your own. As a boy I had accepted Jesus Christ several times as my Lord, but every time baptism day came, to my parents' dismay and consternation, I discovered at the last minute that I just wasn't ready. Now, I felt something unseen working in me. Within a week or so, I was baptized with about twenty small children between the ages of nine and twelve.

Then, I reported the fraternities to the dean. When the Greek letter organizations found out what I had done, I was ostracized by everyone on campus. For the last six weeks of the school year I lived alone, like a leper. I went to classes during the day, and at night I prayed by myself. I looked within for help and found those old faith propositions that I remembered from church:

> I can do all things through Christ who strengtheneth me.

> The Lord is my strength and my salvation; whom shall

I fear?

I will lift up mine eyes unto the hills whence cometh
my help.

When I went home for summer vacation that year, I fumbled
around trying to sort out my future. War preparations had
begun, and for the first time President Roosevelt had opened the
door for young blacks to enter government-sponsored training
programs. Instead of returning to college, I decided to take the
examination for the Naval Apprentice School in Norfolk, and in
September of 1939, I went to work for the navy as a shipfitter's
apprentice.

I rode to the Norfolk Navy Yard every day with my daddy and
five of his buddies, who were all a part of the civilian workforce,
laughing to some of the funniest stories I had ever heard and
soaking up globs of homespun philosophy and folklore. Being
one of the "men" helped me see the bigger picture. It was strange
how these educated black men could talk about race with a cool
objectivity that seemed to save their energy for the immediate
tasks of life.

Since this was an official government program, I expected to
be accepted by the other shipfitters and apprentices in our shop.
One day I took a break from my workbench and walked over to
the water fountain; it had two faucets, one for a right-handed person, and the other for a left-handed person. I leaned my shoulder against the wall and turned on the fountain with my right
hand. Before my lips touched the water, I heard a voice shout
from halfway across the building: "Hey, boy! That ain't your
faucet. You drink out of the one on the left."

I called back, "But I'm right-handed."

"You're colored, ain't you? Coloreds use the left faucet." Hot-
faced, I lifted my head without drinking, and walked away from
the fountain. What small, sinister mind thought up the idea of

having two faucets, so that every black person who came for a drink would be reminded that he was unworthy to share anything, even basic water, with whites? However, I too had been trained to conserve my energy and temper for significant battles. Like other black youths of my generation, I had learned never to absorb, to accept, to internalize unworthiness; I rejected the rejection that was aimed at us constantly.

The ministry seemed to be following me. I became friendly with the Rev. D. C. Rice, the new young pastor of Bank Street Baptist Church, whose engaging sermons spoke realistically about Christian living while preserving the awesome mystery and majesty of God. Reverend Rice shared several hours with me each week helping me to get a better view of the ministry. I wanted to be just like him. The broader issue of black destiny in America began to loom large before me, and building parts for battleships no longer seemed challenging.

I was absolutely convinced that I had to become an agent of that persistent faith that kept our people inching forward, living on the substance of things hoped for. I wanted to find an answer to the dilemma of black progress in America, an answer to world hunger and poverty, an answer to colonialism and imperialism.

One day I was at my workbench making a small steel cabinet with a combination lock for the captain's private papers aboard ship. My job was to punch dots on the steel sheet. It was a tedious, mindless job. I was partway through the process when I had one of those flashes of insight, like Moses at the burning bush or Isaiah in the Temple. The truth did not come in segments; rather, like falling in love, it descended in one luminous, existential moment. Suddenly I knew that I would make any sacrifice, pay any price, endure any inconvenience to go back to school and prepare for the ministry. I had to find a place to serve that would nurture the faith of my people, challenge the pervasive injustice, and complete the task of those who died, laboring in the quarries where the rocks were hard indeed.

I put down my hammer and puncher and took off my apron. Then I headed for the Labor Board to resign. Out in the yard, a man named Booker, a friend of my father, drove by in one of those huge, indestructible navy trucks. He stopped abruptly and cut off the deafening sound of the huge diesel motor.

"Proctor, where are you going?"

"To the Labor Board to resign," I answered.

"Are you crazy? We fought hard to open up that school to colored boys. You can't quit."

"Mr. Booker, I believe I'm called to preach, and I want to get ready for school."

"You don't need to go to school to be a preacher. We have a fellow cooking in the commissary right now who's a preacher, and another one working in the coal yard. They never went to any school."

"But I want to do it differently," I said. "I want to go to college and to the seminary. I want to give it my best and be ready for any opportunity that comes."

He shook his head in disbelief and moved on, the truck's noisy chain drive erasing our conversation.

That fall, as soon as all my friends left town and returned to college, I announced to the church and my family that I was giving my life to the ministry and asked for their prayers. I knew I couldn't go back to my old crowd at Virginia State who were already laughing at the idea of me studying for the ministry. So, in the fall of 1940, I enrolled at Virginia Union, a black Baptist school known for training ministers.

In my new college I immediately organized a school band, which technically made me a college "bandmaster." One day I received a smudgy, ink-smeared letter addressed to "All Colored College Bandmasters," inviting me to join a pool of musicians to be trained as a "Colored Army Bandmaster" in Fort Bragg, North Carolina.

Well, my brother Vernon, who played piano, tuba, and the

bass violin, was fresh out of Alabama State College with a music major and about to be drafted. I sent the grimy letter on to him and told him to hurry and go to Fort Bragg. Thirty years later he retired as an Air Force Bandmaster after a most fruitful career. Today he lies in eternal rest in Arlington National Cemetery.

VIRGINIA UNION WAS THE CENTER OF BLACK LIFE OF Richmond. Although the school had little money and modest facilities, the campus throbbed with intellectual excitement. The big questions in philosophy, theology, political science, sociology, and economics were grist for our mill. Chapel was compulsory, and every Monday, Wednesday, and Friday we heard outstanding black speakers from every section of the country, as well as a number of liberal-minded white intellectuals.

In the summers, I was back working as an elevator operator at Ames and Brownley. As part of the store's decoration, we wore maroon uniforms with eight brass buttons down the front, a round hat with gold braid, and black leather gloves. I would stand next to my gleaming elevator car chanting, "Going up?" One day, as I made my announcement, a jovial black porter passed by saying, "Go the hell on up, Reverend; don't nobody want to go up with you!" Standing in front of my car about to board was Dr. Sparks White Melton, the same white pastor who had cried with us the night our church burned down. "Are you a reverend?" Dr. Melton asked, looking at me with surprise.

I told him that I was still in college at Virginia Union. He asked me to let him know when I was ready for the seminary.

A year or so later, I saw him again. This time I rode him up to the sixth floor Tea Room, a racially exclusive dining room used for the Business Men's Bible class. While Dr. Melton conducted the Bible class, he could see me parked at my elevator, listening attentively. When he heard later that I was graduating from college, he arranged a full tuition scholarship for me at Crozer

Theological Seminary on whose trustee board he sat. He also sent me a box of books that I have used for over fifty years.

While fully a party to the racial policy that excluded me from that Tea Room, Dr. Melton eroded the whole system by helping me to go to Crozer. I'm sure he never dreamed that one day I would be invited to preach to his white congregation in Norfolk after he was silent in death, or that I would become a teacher and a trustee of that same Crozer, and even invited to be considered for its presidency.

I ENTERED THE SEMINARY IN CHESTER, PENNSYLVANIA, IN September of 1942. On my first day I learned that I was the only black student there. In fact, I was the only black anything there! There was not a black janitor, cook, yardman, or even a black cat or dog. I was it! That afternoon, I sneaked off campus and rode a bus into a black neighborhood. I walked around awhile and ended up getting a haircut from a black barber.

When I returned to campus, the entire student body was assembled in front of the dining hall. I walked a long fifty yards up from the road, with every eye aimed at me. Then a huge redhead from Fuquay-Varina, North Carolina, stepped out and laid a big freckled hand on my shoulder.

"Hi ya doing, fella," he said. "I see you have a fresh haircut."

I admitted I had found a barbershop downtown, leaving out the "colored."

He squinted his green eyes, poked his finger in my chest and barked: "Listen, I'm the barber here. I cut all the hair on this campus. And I'm gonna cut your hair, too! If I catch you going downtown again, I'm gonna whip your ass. Heah me?" I mumbled in agreement, but it took several days for me to absorb fully that a North Carolina white boy was going to be my barber.

I took in a lot of new information in the space of twenty-four hours. During the orientation session that evening, we learned about class schedules, bills, mail, meals, and jobs. Because of the war, students carried out all campus services themselves. The faculty chairman of the student employment committee finally made all the assignments but mine. I raised my hand and reminded him that I needed an assignment.

"I'm sorry, Mr. Proctor, I forgot. Mrs. Moitz wants to see you in the kitchen."

Sitting in the front row, I instantly aged ten years. I could not believe that the *only* black student was selected for the *only* kitchen job. When I went down to Mrs. Moitz, a refugee from Hitler's invasion of Hungary, she was embarrassed. "You're the only colored boy and they sent you to me?" she said, shaking her head in disbelief. No ethical, theological, or sociological studies could match old-fashioned prejudice.

My first thought was to give up on these white theologians and go home. But another part of my mind told me to stay right where I was and be the best kitchen help they ever had—and finish my academic work with honors.

All day long I did well in classes and enjoyed the fellowship of my classmates. At about 9 P.M. every night, I descended to the kitchen to my assigned job where I spent the quiet hours of the night by myself, singing, praying, conjugating Greek verbs, and memorizing names, dates, and places while I washed dishes, scrubbed pots, and mopped the floor. I felt burdened at times, and sometimes tears flowed freely. White people seemed to think I was without feeling, like a robot. And they were scholars of Jesus, who was so filled with compassion. It hurt—not the job itself, but how it had come to me. Throughout those days of doubt and confusion, of wandering and searching, I found safe harbor at the home of a local Baptist pastor named J. Pius Barbour. Dr. Barbour and his family always had a space for me at their table, and he always had time to sit with me for hours and debate the issues confronting me. Dr. Barbour was a scholarly person with a penchant for such dialogue, and he understood my problem, having been a Crozer alumnus himself. (I would not be the only Crozer student he helped. Some years later Martin Luther King, Jr., and many more after him, also sought and received his counsel.)

During my studies at Crozer, another learning experience came to me from outside of the classroom. I worked in the summer of 1944 as a driver for a wealthy, blind real estate man. Every morning I drove him into town from his Delaware County summer estate, parking his big Oldsmobile in the empty lot behind his office building, then walking on to school. At the end of the day, I returned and drove him back to the country. During that summer I lived at the estate with him and his wife, and every night we ate dinner together. We all behaved courteously and, while not warm friends, we got along peaceably enough, veiling our distinctly divergent social views.

The following spring I helped him again off and on; one afternoon I was waiting with the car in front of his building when he came charging down the steps alone, waving his white cane wildly over his head. He shouted to me at the top of his lungs, "Thank God, that son of a bitch is dead!"

To me and my people, Franklin Roosevelt was like a messiah, and all of our hope was pinned on him. Alone in my room that night I had a long soliloquy with myself. My blind employer thought that Social Security, helping the poor, and other Roosevelt initiatives were a formula for disaster. To me, on the contrary, they looked like the partial fulfillment of our major faith proposition. I had no idea that our country was so deeply divided between those who favored government intervention in behalf of the poor and those who did not.

Incidentally, my dormitory at Croze had been a Union Army hospital for wounded Confederate soldiers during the Civil War. I could still see the hole in the door to my room through which food had been passed to a wounded Confederate soldier. Often, while reflecting on a racial issue, I would recall that a soldier fighting to keep my people enslaved had used that very room. Now, it was my room, and I was using it to learn how to harvest enough spiritual energy to achieve our full freedom.

I wasn't sure how it would happen, but I believed that God had a special claim on us. Black people, just like me, had always had a special ability to look beyond the hate and see something bright shining.

THE SEMINARY WAS SO RADICAL IN ITS APPROACH TO THE Bible that it actually ruined the religious beliefs of some of my classmates. We were shocked to discover that Bible study included learning the history and geography of the Near East and the land of the Tigris and Euphrates rivers; we also studied the various religions of Egypt, Assyria, Babylonia, and Persia, and examined their influences on Judaism.

We were learning that God was much greater than the oversimplified view of creation coming from the mind of a fourth century B.C. scribe. But many of my classmates still held on to a literal view of creation from Genesis. They had trouble accepting that God had not sat behind a cloud somewhere and dictated the Bible word for word, in English! Some gasped as one professor after another challenged them to revise their belief systems and to embrace a bigger God idea that allowed truth from the sciences to inform religion. For me, however, listening to religious scholars who respected scientific data was a relief. Hearing them was like walking through a verdant forest with a mild breeze, birds chirping from every direction, and a crystal stream of clear water singing and dancing on solid, ancient rocks. I loved it.

My seminary took the plastic off the Bible, and made it a living book with a message infinitely stronger than I had ever dreamed possible. My professors taught that certain books of the Bible reflected different types of literature; some were written

47

like poems or long parables to make a serious point. The teachers showed us how Bible stories had been revised by various writers at different times, and taught us how to look at biblical events in a larger context. Indeed, by giving a deeper interpretation of the Bible, the Crozer theologians showed us how religion could have social and ethical application in the modern world.

My seminary training helped me to see how orthodox, fundamentalist Christianity, with its credulous literalism about the Bible, ended up as a religion unrelated to the travails of humans living in the real world. It was a religion that found reasons in the Bible to accept slavery and the subjugation of women; a religion that ignored Jesus, its Lord, and became comfortable with the rich; a religion that subjugated and exploited all of the darker skinned people of the world for the comfort of the whites; a religion that quietly endorsed militarism and bloodshed everywhere. In the hands of the fundamentalists, Christianity had become an embarrassment to Jesus.

It had always bothered me that Christianity had become an antiquated religion, rather than a living one. While religion in the black churches always addressed issues of freedom and justice, in terms of the basic theological agenda it was stifling and narrow-minded. It too was filled with anti-science sentiments that were never discussed openly. Strongly wed to a literal understanding of the Bible, it was also fundamentalist, but benignly so.

I am so thankful that my seminary delivered me from such views while leaving my faith in God and the centrality of Jesus firmly in place. Intellectually and spiritually I had a bath, a new awakening. What I learned about philosophy and ethics freed me to step out of history, to examine all of my assumptions, and to reenter society with greater clarity and understanding. I came out of the seminary with a God more powerful, more worthy of praise than I had when I entered. I came out with a Bible far more relevant to our spiritual quests.

BY THE TIME I ENTERED MY SENIOR YEAR IN SEMINARY, I had become a committed "inquirer." I wanted clear, honest answers to the ponderous questions hurled at me by history, nature, and society. But it should not surprise anyone to know that a theological education raises more new questions than it offers answers to old ones. During my last year I was hungry for answers.

When we heard that Dr. Edwin E. Aubrey, a professor of theology at the University of Chicago, was coming to our campus as the new president, I felt the campus ignite with excitement. Needless to say, our seminary was branded "liberal," a term which then stood for an unstinted search for truth and for a generous response to need and suffering. It's strange that "liberal" should become a bad word for Christians today. In any event, when Dr. Aubrey came, we were pushed even farther away from center in theological circles. As a naturalistic-theist he was a theologian who emphasized the order and majesty of God's creation, and saw scientific marvels, rather than supernatural miracles, as evidence of God's power. Of course, he was held suspect by orthodox Christians. Both from the point of view of putting my personal faith together, and also from the point of view of pursuing social justice, I was standing on tiptoe, eager to learn more about Dr. Aubrey's ideas.

Meanwhile, my special friendship with a young lady named Bessie Louise Tate, whom I had met at Virginia Union University, had ripened. With a world in flux and a future in great doubt, Bessie and I took a leap and decided to get married. We planned to rent a student apartment and scuffle for food money and expenses for that senior year, and trust God for the future.

In 1944, young women were only beginning to assert their notions of absolute equality with men. It was acceptable for an occasional woman to have a career in law, medicine, or politics, but it was the exception. In our circles the optimal condition for a young lady was to marry shortly after college, begin having children, and manage a well-ordered home. The success of her children and her husband were her intrinsic rewards. Divorce was never contemplated and there was no premarital sex. No couples in our circle thought of "shacking" together before marriage. Customarily, therefore, we married young, and stayed married.

Traditionally, in a very self-regarding way, everyone looked for the best mate available, and a lot of bargaining, negotiating, and compromising went on. On a small campus of a thousand or less, in a few weeks after school began, the matching was over. It is unbelievable how parochial we were; all from the same basic backgrounds, similar parents, values, religious affiliations, socioeconomic status, and aesthetic preferences. Practically, we could almost have chosen our lifetime mates in a lottery, but it was far more fun to pick and choose. And there was nothing like the electricity that was sparked when glances met and a bold stare was sustained, and a smile confirmed approval. That happened to us, fifty years ago.

About that time President Aubrey and his wife, who was active in national volunteer organizations, were looking for a married student couple to live with them to help with domestic chores and to monitor their two young children when they were away from home. The Aubreys both traveled extensively for meetings, conferences, and on speaking engagements. In exchange the couple would receive room, board, and a modest salary. We hesitated, since neither of us had much appetite for being domestic help.

Since I had been at Crozer, I had already held jobs working nights in the post office, Saturdays at Sears in the warehouse, washing Bond Bread trucks, and cleaning up the seminary kitchen every night. Work was my companion and I liked being independent. To me, this new job was just another hustle to make ends meet.

Bessie, on the other hand, came from a small, financially well-off family. Her father, a prosperous pharmacist who owned his

THE SUBSTANCE OF THINGS HOPED FOR

own drugstore, did not encourage Bessie to work outside the home. Black women always had to fight for respect and, if they could, black families tried to protect their daughters from the profanity, sex jokes, and disrespectful male attention common in workplaces. She had two summer jobs for pocket change and novelties, but never was she compelled to support herself. But Bessie agreed to take the Aubrey job with me so we could be together and save some money for the next leg of my education.

Living with the Aubreys was a completely new experience for both of us. Dr. Aubrey and his wife were from upper middle class families. They loved books, opera, the symphonies and art galleries; they never listened to the radio, never knew which football team was out front, who won the World Series, or which basketball teams made the final four. They could not dance. In nine months of living in the same house with them (we had a private apartment on the third floor), I never saw her without heels, stockings, and makeup; and I never saw him without a collar and tie. Bessie and I studied them as though they were in a museum. I enjoyed talking theology with Dr. Aubrey, and Mrs. Aubrey wanted to teach my wife more about cooking than she would ever need to know.

The Aubreys had only long-distance friends—in England, Wales, Chicago, Boston, and Canada. Nobody local ever visited except for occasional faculty teas or lunches. They seemed to enjoy life, and were always warm and generous, but to us they looked like stage actors.

The real value of that experience was a sustained, close-up peep into a social class and a cultural stratum that neither of us had known before. We found out how different life was for people who did not have to be concerned with their survival, their identity, or their space and basic rights and freedom.

Looking back, our experience with the Aubreys also showed us how easily people from completely different backgrounds could find common ground simply by respecting each other's privacy and preferences, and trying to understand the interior of their lives and goals. Even though the gaps between us were formidable, we *communicated*. I learned that experiences that drag us, kicking and screaming, out of our small worlds and compel us to stand tall in another world, can stretch our minds, forge our character, and fuel our imaginations. I believe the Aubreys had the same experience. We all learned from each other.

Although Dr. Aubrey died at an early age, Bessie and I continued to correspond with his wife. I visited her in a rest home in California when she was nearly ninety years old. She wept with joy when she saw me, receiving me like a son who had shown up after a long separation. She showed me a scrapbook of news clippings of my activities she had kept for over forty years! And she cried as she leafed through it. My soul! I had no idea. Again, I saw how artificial and dehumanizing racial barriers can be. Unless we had come into her home, she would never have known a black person at close range.

BY THE TIME I GRADUATED FROM CROZER IN 1945, THE war had ended and the country was retooling for a postwar economy and the GIs were settling in. The poor had tasted relief with jobs in defense factories. They had listened to the oratory of Roosevelt and Truman, and had seen the revulsion of the world in the face of Hitler's vile atrocities against the Jews. Black soldiers were returning from the Pacific, Germany, England, and North Africa. They had risked their lives to make a new world safe for democracy. They had seen persons of all religions and cultures, and were fed up with the racial arrangements in their own country.

The worm was turning. The intellectual and spiritual transformation that I had experienced in the seminary was an omen of the change and openness that the world would see in the next thirty years.

CHAPTER FOUR

The New Emancipation

∎∎

1945–1960

I LEFT CROZER WITH A $2,500 JOHN P. CROZER FELLOWSHIP to study social ethics at Yale University, and $1,700 saved. At the same time, I was called to serve the Pond Street Baptist Church in Providence, Rhode Island. So, Monday through Wednesday I was at Yale in New Haven, and Thursday through Sunday I was at home with my congregation and my wife in Providence.

The town was extremely generous in extending hospitality and openness. While the black community was small, it had strong and loyal allies among white churches and educated liberals. Our parishioners were hard-working people, but there wasn't much money around. Bessie and I were so young that the church leadership treated us like we were their children, with exceptional warmth and care. We constantly felt the love and protection of the whole congregation.

We moved into a small apartment on the top floor of a three-story frame house. On the first and second floors of the house lived Mr. and Mrs. Blount, a senior family in the church. Each evening they treated us to dessert and coffee and told long stories about old times and interesting people in the black community. These talks were always laced with advice on what to do and say, and which people to trust. The Blounts' children and grandchildren were all grown up, and Bessie and I were like surrogate family for them.

I was only twenty-four years old, and among the first generation of black pastors to have access, on a large scale, to graduate study at seminaries which were lodged in large universities. As we earned doctorates in religion, social activism became as important to us as saving souls.

One night, soon after I had begun in Providence, all the black ministers and their followers met at a big rally in the black community center. "We're going to organize a movement here for fair employment practices in this state," one pastor announced, "and Reverend Proctor will lead it."

I had studied social change, but had never actually *practiced* social ethics. I was a student with no leadership experience in civil rights, but this public announcement meant that I had to take the plunge. Within a few days, I found myself raising money, bringing carloads of people with picket signs to march in front of the statehouse, and going on the radio to bring our cause to the public. As a result, the Fair Employment Practices Act was successfully passed by the Rhode Island legislature.

Social activism was only part of my job. I saw my task as an agent for change in the lives of individuals as well as an agent of social change. In an effort to revitalize what I saw as a conservative, dormant black presence, I hosted a Saturday radio show with our youth choir and wrote a weekly column in the black community paper. I solicited funds from merchants to equip a social hall in the church for neighborhood youth and recruited young people from the local community center. We started a basketball team and participated in the local church basketball league. One of our best players, a young man named Howard Blunt, grew up to become an admiral in the Navy and is today part owner of the Baltimore Orioles. Many other young people who joined the church at that time are the leading black citizens in Providence today.

As I went about my work as a young pastor, I thought that the more privileged blacks should have extended themselves to help improve the chances for those least well prepared. The poorer blacks insulated themselves from the scorn of whites, as well as from the scrutiny of the blacks who were better off. Most had abdicated all accountability for their own lives. And, at the time, I thought the best way to help them was through jobs, schools, church programs, athletic leagues, and black associations. Eagerly, I threw myself into the fray.

One day Bessie and I were returning home from church, driving through a poor section of the city, when suddenly a huge fellow dressed in jeans and leather boots came bursting from the screened door of a porch front, leaped into the street, and landed right in front of our car. Behind him came another big man, brandishing an open barber's razor in the air. Rage was written all over his face, with his lips drawn tightly over his teeth, his eyes bulging and veins protruding in his neck. With one quick slash he opened a deep gash in the jaw and neck of the first man, who fell with blood squirting in volumes from his neck. We hustled him into the car and I raced to the hospital, holding a car seat pillow over his wound. He lay silent as death. At the hospital the emergency team revived him, stitched up his wound, and bandaged him like a mummy. He remained in the hospital for several days and I earnestly visited him and prayed with him.

57

I learned that his assailant was his brother-in-law, and their argument had begun over nothing—a telephone bill, use of a bathroom, or repayment of a five-dollar loan. One insulted the other, and within seconds they had come to the point of murder. A fraction of an inch deeper, and that brief argument would have been followed by tearful regrets, calling on Jesus, kinfolk driving up from South Carolina, singing sad songs and walking slowly to a cold grave in a strange and distant cemetery. I probably would have been called in to do the eulogy.

None of it made sense on a rational level, but they were behaving extrarationally, responding to subcultural taboos, which included: don't talk about my sister unless you say something nice; pay me my money when you say you will; don't "dis" me in front of my friends; don't act like you think you are better than I; don't use my telephone for long-distance calls without my permission; don't raise your voice at me, and more of the same. Violation is punishable by death.

This is the way people behave when their raw need for respect and status is frustrated. These two men eventually reconciled and continued to live together in the same apartment. But I knew it was only a matter of time before another trivial disagreement would explode into violence. I believed then, as I do now, that an educated mind behaves differently, is able to canvass options, and solve misunderstandings without violence.

I was bitterly disappointed to find that so many young blacks in the North had no educational aspirations. Without any nearby black colleges, and few black college graduates in sight, many northern blacks were satisfied with menial jobs. One of our biggest efforts in Providence, therefore, was to send young blacks South to school. It's no small irony that blacks who had escaped the rigid discrimination of the South had to return there to receive a college education. There was no shortage of excellent schools in the Northeast. Brown University, the elitist Ivy League school, was first choice for most of the country's brightest students. But there was no point expecting Brown to accept average black students, and watch them struggle—and collapse—trying to keep pace.

The black youth of Rhode Island needed a more "user friendly" campus. They needed to see and hear black Ph.D.s, black deans, black choral directors, black treasurers and presidents, black cheerleaders, and black assembly speakers. They needed a higher vision of our destiny, an ocean tide of celebrative black oratory to lift them out of the muck and mire of inferiority. And they found it in black colleges. Those same black colleges that sprang forth across the South following the Emancipation and raised the veil of ignorance from the faces of ex-slaves were just as indispensable in the 1940s and beyond to save black youth from the stultifying atmosphere of failure endemic in the large urban centers of the North.

We generated a flow of young black students going to colleges in the South. One played basketball for Virginia Union, did very well academically, and then returned to Providence College to finish his degree and to teach in East Providence. Later he became a college basketball referee, then a certified NCAA "television" referee for national tournaments, and finally the head of Rhode Island's parole board. He is Dr. Kenneth Walker, and his father was the ashes man who collected furnace ashes from well-to-do Providence neighborhoods.

Another student, Melvin Clanton, played football, did well academically, then returned to his Providence high school as a teacher. He recently retired as a citywide school personnel administrator. And Dr. Wesley Mayo is a dentist in Bridgeport, Connecticut.

However, most of the students we sent South never returned. Robert Ventner is now vice president of a black-owned bank in Richmond. Janice Scott is counselor to students at Howard University in Washington, D.C.

With our efforts we were beginning to see small signs of

change. We also saw the resistance. In 1947, the Baptists opened their Wisconsin assembly grounds at Green Lake with a conference on "Christian Social Concerns." The Rhode Island Baptists selected me and two white Providence pastors, John Zuber and Art Goodwin, to attend.

With very little money to spare, we drove all the way from Rhode Island to Wisconsin, planning to stop one night in Detroit, where we had reservations at the downtown Detroit YMCA. When we arrived at about 1 A.M., we were greeted by a night janitor who had one stiff leg and hobbled with a cane. He poked the cane into my chest and shouted, "Get out of here, boy. We don't take no colored in here. Now, go!" My companions turned red as carnations. This was the YMCA in Detroit, not Birmingham, Alabama! They staged a thirty-minute dialogue in complete futility. That man was a hater, and the hate was deep.

With the rise of blacks, poor whites like him saw themselves being jeopardized economically. They also saw themselves losing the only badge of preference that they had, the advantage of simply being white. With my presence, this crippled janitor's fragile status was slipping away from him.

We got the telephone number of the black YMCA on "John R" Street and were able to get a clean, quiet night's sleep. Believe me, when we arrived at the conference on Christian Social Concerns, we had a real live story to tell.

ALONG ABOUT THIS TIME, BESSIE AND I FOUND OUT WE were going to become parents. I was hurrying to complete my postgraduate studies at Yale so I could get better situated after the baby came. Added to the acute awareness of the responsibility of parenthood and the anxiety about the Ph.D. program, I worried about keeping my performance high, representing my people well, and confounding those who thought I shouldn't be there at all.

Four other African-American males and one female were also enrolled in the Yale program. We found rich and warm fellowship among ourselves, but hardly did any of us have a single close, steady white friend. In the sedate, colonial student lounge of the Yale Divinity School in 1945–46, no matter where I sat no white student sat near me. I believe they were afraid that if they fell into conversation with me they might say the wrong thing. Here they were, the cream of the academic crop, yet they felt uncomfortable talking to someone with a background different from their own. Despite their training in theology and philosophy, they seemed not to recognize how much all humans shared the same uncertainties, the same primitive needs and fears, the same estrangement, and the same sense of awe and wonder about God and the potential transcendency of life. Our alikeness far outweighed our few differences. It was pitiful, but I was immune to insults.

I did spend many hours assessing their behavior, trying to envision the churches of the nation being served by a cadre of clergy so well educated in the history and philosophy of religion—as an academic subject—but so guarded and fearful of letting go their cultural inhibitions and embracing the habits of Jesus. The special efforts of two white professors made a striking contrast to the attitude of the students. Professors Richard Neibuhr and Liston Pope took the initiative to make sure that I was fully engaged and included in every aspect of the program.

One day Dr. Luther Weigle, dean of the Divinity School, sent for me. It scared me to death. What on earth had I done? "Mr. Proctor," he began, dragging his chair close to mine, "why is it that so many of you colored fellows do so well here, when your Graduate Record Examination scores are so skewed? You are all far above average on the verbal tests and the social science tests, but your mathematics, sciences, and fine arts scores are far below other college graduates in the same majors, both regionally and nationally."

I was relieved, because I knew the answer. I looked in his eyes and spoke slowly. "Dean Weigle, we do better on verbal tests because we do a lot of debating and discussing. We are a talking people. We survive by images and analysis, analogues and metaphors, so we get to know words. We take flight in language as a buffer for our wounded psyches. The social sciences are all dealing with our past and our future; so we live with the social sciences, too.

"On the other hand, we are hardly ever considered for jobs in the natural sciences and technology. Our schools have no well-equipped laboratories and our teachers were educated without any hope of being employed in the sciences, either. Therefore, our knowledge in those areas is comparatively sparse."

I guessed that Dean Weigle was often called on to defend admitting black students to Yale and he needed answers that made sense. He needed to find a way to say, with conviction, that the tests did not predict our capacity to learn, but simply reflected the opportunities we had been allowed.

"Thank you, Mr. Proctor," he said. "You're doing fine work here at Yale." That was all, but I sensed that he felt relieved, too.

The day our first child was born, we received tragic news. Our baby had a severely damaged heart, a hole in the wall between the ventricles—interventricular septal defect. Through the malformed opening spent blood entered his heart and mixed freely with freshly oxygenated blood from the lungs, depriving the baby of adequate oxygen. Our doctor told us that we could not expect our child to live beyond his first year, or possibly two. He was what was called a "blue baby."

I desperately needed to find a way to finish my degree closer to Providence, so I could be home every night with Bessie and our baby. Boston University, where the curriculum was also dedicated largely to Christian social ethics, was ready to give me credit for my Yale work, plus a tuition scholarship. Most important, I could manage the commute between Providence and

Boston without spending a night away from home. I stretched my energies, and Bessie's patience, by crowding my days and nights to complete my doctoral courses and examinations within two years. By May of 1949, I was finished except for the dissertation. And I had learned as much about God by coping with the needs of my family as I learned in the library at Boston University.

The next step was to get a better-paying job. We hated to leave the warm and beautiful people at the Pond Street Baptist Church, but an offer from Dr. John M. Ellison, my mentor and the president of Virginia Union University, brought us back to the campus where we had met.

Once settled in, we tracked down the cardiologist that everyone was talking about, Dr. Paul Camp, a legend around Richmond and heir to a large paper manufacturing fortune, Camp Paper Mills. The word was that Camp did not treat black patients. But I was always willing to offer anyone a chance to live above his or her worst reports, so we went to see him, Bessie carrying our little Herbie in her arms. He was now four years old.

Ordinarily, we would have been looking for resentment on the faces of the receptionist and nurses, watching for any sign of reluctance to see us, glancing at other patients to see how they reacted. But Bessie and I learned to put Herbie's recovery above everything else. There we stood with all of this anxiety, but with a clear focus on our son.

Dr. Camp, his brow furrowed, held out his arms for our child and laid him gently on the examining table. Then he bent close and listened to his tiny heart. He couldn't have been more tender if he had been touching his own child. In a flash he got on the phone and made an appointment for us at Johns Hopkins in Baltimore, at that time the only hospital in the country doing "blue baby" surgery.

Herbie was so weak that he got pneumonia in the hospital before the surgery and nearly died. We had to bring him home until he recovered. It was a six-week delay, and we learned to live without time consciousness. Days and hours are not counted in this kind of situation—it is all one extended *moment*. All desire and meaning is squeezed into one flash of eternity, and all of life is defined by one event.

At last, we were able to take him back to the hospital for a "shunt" operation, in which an arm vessel was sent around the heart defect to increase the supply of oxygenated blood. Herbie survived. That was in 1950. The attention and professional savvy that Dr. Camp directed toward our son was convincing evidence that the solid wall that excluded blacks from the main flow of life in America was wavering.

The shunt operation that Herbie received gave him a lease on life, but only marginally so. He could not run, do stairs normally, or play active games with his friends. He had to limit his output to match his heart capacity. It was all a matter of waiting until he was big enough to undergo open-heart surgery.

So, while other young mothers rolled their children up and down the aisles of the supermarket, watched them romp in the grass, and splash in warm ocean waters, Bessie had to find things for Herbie to do in his tiny world that matched his strength and also supplied him with self-affirmation. My function was to manage my work at the college, while carrying a constant shadow that my own efforts would be adequate to fuel the needs of my wife and son.

Meanwhile, we were fortunate to have another child, Timothy, who seemed to have been born grown-up. He took over the care and companionship of his older brother like a life's assignment and geared his program to suit his brother's pace. It was beautiful to see the tender, gracious behavior they displayed together. We were all able to cope with our family's challenge because we had so much fun together.

An event such as we experienced involves many people. My brothers and my sister responded as though Herbie were their child. Our parents were ever so close. My wife's mother practically gave up her life in a focus on Herbie, and her eyes and the muscles in her face spoke her feelings when words were few. Our neighbors and colleagues on the faculty defined their relationship to us with Herbie as the fixed item.

All of this happened during my first year of college teaching at Virginia Union where I was assigned six courses in philosophy, ethics, sociology, and biblical literature, each requiring new and separate preparations. Four classes met on Monday, Wednesday, and Friday, and two met on Tuesday and Thursday. Fortunately, having just come from six solid years of graduate study, I was brimming with ideas and data. My ambition also helped keep the adrenaline pumping, and it seemed like fun.

Students inspired me with their serious and open class discussion, and their obvious appreciation of my efforts. I spent hours painstakingly correcting and adding salient comments to every paper submitted by every student. In between, I struggled to finish my dissertation in time for graduation in May of 1950. My students were as ecstatic as I was when I received my doctor of theology degree from Boston University and put on my scarlet gown with three black velvet bars on each arm and marched in Virginia Union's 1950 commencement procession.

I COULD FEEL CHANGE IN THE AIR. BLACK GIs WHO HAD returned home after the war left thousands of their buddies buried under small white crosses on the hillsides of Burma, in grassy plots near the Anzio beach landings in Italy, and the sun-baked military cemeteries of Tunis. They were impatient for change, and their government promised that the time had come to guarantee their full rights.

It took ten years, but the government did fulfill at least part of its promise. By 1954, the armed forces had been integrated and the NAACP had won significant cases that eliminated all legal standing for segregation. This was tantamount to a new emancipation, an inclusion that we had never before experienced.

Every time a new decision in our favor came down from the Supreme Court, we gathered around our radios to listen to the announcements. And every time we heard another one in our favor, it seemed like the Kingdom was getting closer. Churches held services of thanksgiving, affirming that the hand of God was writing in history. This direct connection between God and politics made religion a totally relevant experience for me and many others.

I was fighting on two fronts. I wanted to encourage white and black Christians to lift up and examine the issue of race in the light of their Christian commitments, and also in the light America's message of equality and freedom. I also wanted to see black people acquire the intellectual, economic, and political clout to improve their condition. The classroom and the pulpit were my obsessions, and I wanted to get better at both jobs.

I found myself being invited to speak at venues outside of of my small Baptist college. Before I knew it, I was speaking at Penn State, Bucknell, the University of New Hampshire, Duke University, and Riverside Church. Now the American Baptists had me lecturing every year at their annual Green Lake assembly. Indeed it did seem like a new emancipation was in the making.

At the same time, the move for decolonization around the world began. New winds were blowing everywhere and it had become less feasible for white Americans to be running schools, hospitals, colleges, and seminaries nine thousand miles away from home. It was time to let go. I took a bounding leap into the larger human struggle in 1953 when I was asked by the American Baptist Foreign Mission Board to join a team of clergy traveling into India and Burma to execute the transfer of institutions from American to indigenous ownership.

Our job was to consult with the American staff of the Burmese and Indian missions, and help them put in place procedures for the transition. You can imagine the sensation I created when I climbed down from the little crop-duster airplane, on a remote landing strip in India, along with three white executives. The local Baptist pastors, school heads, and health care providers were speechless. White missionaries who had been living abroad for years were unaware of the changes taking place in the United States. They were warmly hospitable, but hardly knew how to receive me.

Sometimes the visiting team all traveled together, but occasionally, in the interest of efficiency, we separated and visited some missions alone. In one isolated station in northern India, in the province of Assam, my plane landed on a narrow, grassy airstrip where a small family of missionaries waited to greet me. As I deplaned and started walking briskly toward my host, who was standing with his wife and two young children, I lifted my fist in greeting and shouted, "Don Crider, Altoona, Pennsylvania."

He beamed at me. "Wow," he said, "it's sure good to see a white face again!" I acted like I didn't hear it.

Later that night, as we chatted about ballgames and politics, Crider's little girl said, "Daddy, when Dr. Proctor got off the plane, why did you say you were glad to see a white face? Dr. Proctor's face is brown."

"I didn't say any such thing."

"But you did, didn't he, Dr. Proctor?"

Don Crider was embarrassed. "I guess it was hearing you belt out my name and hometown," he said. "You were like a friendly voice from home. All my American signals turned on."

I never looked any farther than that for an explanation. To him, living out in that wilderness station, my dark brown face represented America. To me, the incident signified that on a deep emotional level, like it or not, we blacks, even with our marginal status, were inextricably attached to this country. We were Americans. Looking at it from that point of view, the only question is whether our attachment can become realigned to reflect greater justice and fairness.

Everywhere I went in India and Burma, I was constantly required to redefine myself for local people who had never seen a black person in such a significant role. Our Baptist missionaries, themselves so far removed from modern American life, were supposed to reflect the American democratic ideal, and their behavior toward the Indian and Burmese people was supposed to display America's greatest strengths. And when I showed up, suddenly discussions turned to the black presence in America, and suddenly they were required to face up to the flaws in our society. My participation on the study team, the candid discussions that my presence evoked among Indians and Burmese people in the presence of white missionaries, were all clear omens that something new was going on in the world.

When I returned home after ten weeks in Asia, I found myself once again on the road to Green Lake, Wisconsin, to report to the Baptist Foreign Mission Board on our visits. This time I was driving with my wife. On the highway to Racine, just above Chicago, we stopped at a restaurant whose manager refused to serve us because we were not "members." We could not "join," he said, because the membership had just closed. That was in December of 1953, fully six years after my encounter with the hotel porter in Detroit on my first trip to Green Lake.

It seemed that trying to get to equality was hopeless. But these two events were only part of the story. On the one hand I confronted raw racism, face to face, on my two trips to Wisconsin. On the other, the Baptists were transferring American mission hospitals and colleges to indigenous ownership and control, and two white pastors refused to stay in a white YMCA if I could not. It was this kind of reckoning that enabled us to keep faith alive. Before giving in to cynicism and letting ourselves be overwhelmed by negative experiences, we always factored in any positive element we could lay our hands on.

If the restaurant manager had known that I was on my way to speak of world events to an audience with much greater influence than his few customers would ever have, he would have known that his world was dying. My world was coming alive, and what a squalling, noisy birth it was.

ON THE DOMESTIC FRONT, EVERY SIX MONTHS ANOTHER NAACP victory was won before the Supreme Court. The 1954 school desegregation case was the climax. On a large scale, segregating black students automatically imposed inferior status, which supported racial hatred. Further, black schools did not have the facilities, books, or any other educational tools that white schools had.

From a more intimate perspective, however, these segregated schools were ours. Black teachers, principals, choir directors, and coaches made their schools a refuge from an ugly world that constantly looked down on their pupils. They monitored behavior and supervised manners. So while everyone knew that education would answer our aspirations, not every black person was optimistic about instantly dissolving black schools, reassigning black principals into subordinate positions such as "directors of federal programs," and shifting black children into newly integrated schools.

But it was heresy to speak against desegregation, no matter what the consequences. Sadly, the consequences proved to be disastrous. Some school districts dismantled all black schools, so that whites would not have to attend a "black" school. In such cases all black students were shifted into white schools, where they were largely unwanted and unprovided for. Then, rather than attend schools with blacks, whites fled.

It's ironic that at the time that school integration began, its enemies had no idea we would end up the victims of our major achievement: Today, forty years later, all big-city school systems are largely black and failing; whites and middle class blacks have fled to the suburbs or private schools. Indeed, effective school integration today is a myth. Instead of attending warm and dynamic schools where they are sponsored and affirmed, black students today are educationally crippled, too often abandoned in urban, drug-infested, violent crime-ridden holding pens and dealt with like cattle. Clearly, something radically new must occur to generate a fresh start in educating masses of urban black youth.

Surprisingly, school integration's greatest success came in moderate-sized southern towns where the black population was in the minority, and thus less threatening to whites; or in towns with a solid black middle class which had high expectations for black student performance. In Prince Edward County, however, near where Virginia Union was located, the local white leadership was vehemently opposed to "race mixing." Rather than integrate, the county closed all of its public schools. Our college faculty helped to set up an alternate school for black pupils in the First Baptist Church in the small town of Farmville. One morning I looked out into our front yard and saw the ashes of a cross lying in the grass. During the night some fanatic had been sneaking around. We ignored it and went right on doing what we had been doing.

By this time I had been made president of my alma mater. Since, in the black community of the South, the pastors and college presidents are regarded as pilots and representatives of the people to the larger public, whatever I did or said was conspicuous in the community. Bessie and our two sons had become accustomed to the loss of privacy. The boys knew that I marched at the head of the line, my picture was in the papers, and that civil rights leaders visited our home and campus. They knew that because the spotlight was always on us, they bore an extra load, and that threats came with the territory. If I made a speech supporting school integration, it was echoed throughout the area. Finding a cross burning on the front lawn was no big surprise, but it was frightening. We knew the Klan was dangerous and that its activities frequently, and without warning, went far beyond burning symbols. But Bessie and I tried to minimize the fear to our boys, who were seven and ten years old. The police chief came out, offered his help, stood around chatting and generally showed concern and sympathy. Then he took me aside and said, "Brother Proctor, you know we can't protect you around the clock, so you had better take this." He handed me a heavy box and I knew what was in it before I even opened it. Inside was what looked like a brand-new .22 caliber pistol and a package of shells.

IN THE MIDST OF THE LIGHTNING AND THUNDER THAT accompanied the storm of school desegregation in our area came occasional moments of calm. Richmond, Virginia, had a strong and solid Jewish community. Generally, blacks and Jews fared well together, and blacks knew that many Jews worked for social progress and black liberation. But when racial lines were drawn, it was expected that Jews would sacrifice their black friendships and stand with the whites. In purely economic terms, it seemed too expensive to do otherwise.

One organization of Jewish women used to hold its weekly luncheon meetings in the dining room of Richmond's Byrd Hotel, where they discussed current events and planned various community services. In the fall of 1955, they invited me to deliver a series of six lectures on different world religions, including the black church. I prepared extensively and the meetings went well. The women always invited me to eat lunch with them in the hotel dining room where blacks worked, but could not dine. The black waiters beamed with delight when they saw me walk into the dining room. Those stylish, intelligent, and charming women always made me feel comfortable.

For the next five years I was their annual lecturer. Then one morning I received a casual phone call from one of the club women saying that their next meeting would be at the YWCA, rather than the Byrd Hotel. I complied and paid it no mind.

Thirty years later, on the anniversary of my first lecture, the women's club invited me to come back to Richmond from New Jersey for a celebration. Now they held their weekly meetings in the commodious, well-equipped Jewish Community Center. They were as warm and welcoming as ever. One of the original group, a woman now in her midsixties, introduced me to the audience of about forty-five people, explaining that when we were together earlier in the 1950s, they had to move their meeting from the Byrd Hotel to the YWCA because the hotel manager refused to let me continue to eat lunch with them. In all those thirty intervening years, I had never known that. These had been crucial years in the civil rights struggle when even small acts of integrity took courage and made a large impact.

As she spoke her voice trembled and her eyes flooded. She was so embarrassed to recall that once I had been barred from eating with them, and overjoyed that now we were together under a new set of rules and free to talk about it.

Today, the struggle is far from complete, but it's important to acknowledge where we've been and how encouragement came from many sources.

BACK IN 1950, I WAS INVITED TO RETURN TO CROZER Seminary to make a chapel address. One of my old professors told me about a new student, a bright, promising alumnus of Morehouse College. After lunch that day, I went over and talked with the young man in his dorm. He was Martin Luther King, Jr., the grandson of Dr. A. D. Williams, a veteran Baptist leader in Atlanta, and the son of Alberta Williams King, a Spelman alumna, and Martin Luther King, Sr., a Morehouse graduate.

Martin talked slowly, delivering every sentence with Delphian assurance and oracular finality. He encapsulated the Morehouse mission—to lead, to be up front, and to be right and effective. It was immediately clear to me that I was talking to a prodigious candidate for leadership.

He asked me which books had influenced me the most. I told him that Reinhold Niebuhr's *Moral Man and Immoral Society* and Harry E. Fosdick's *The Modern Use of the Bible* were first, and the work of Walter Rauschenbusch followed closely. He nodded approvingly, though he was eight years younger than I. He then paid closer attention, eyes to eyes, and asked me to characterize famous black church leaders as he called the roll: Joseph Jackson, president of the National Baptist Convention; Benjamin Mays, president of Morehouse College; Mordecai Johnson, president of Howard University; Vernon Johns, pastor of Dexter Avenue Baptist Church in Montgomery; John Ellison, president of Virginia Union, my predecessor; Richard McKinney, philosophy professor at Morgan State College; and Adam Powell, Jr. and Sr., pastor pastor emeritus and of the Abyssinian Baptist Church. He seemed to be measuring where he would fit into this panoply, staking out his own turf for later. That afternoon, in the middle of the day and the middle of the week, he wore a collar, tie, and three-button suit. He was a small-framed person, who walked and talked slowly with a kind of Napoleonic assurance. He looked like a major event about to happen.

Over the next few years Martin stayed in close touch and we met several times at the annual meetings of the National Baptist Convention. Whenever I visited Boston, where he was working toward his Ph.D., we would meet at the School of Theology and continue our conversations. Occasionally he would meet my train and drive me to my hotel, talking all the way. He loved to debate theology and philosophy with me. Martin was very career oriented and fixed on the future. His goal at that time was to succeed Dr. Benjamin E. Mays as Morehouse College's president.

It was no surprise to me when he was called to preach in the front-line, silk-stocking, Dexter Avenue Baptist Church in Montgomery, succeeding the inimitable Vernon Johns. Johns, a brilliant, radical graduate of the Oberlin School of Theology, had a well-earned reputation for throwing caution to the winds in the cause of freedom and justice. In a certain sense, he had prepared the congregation at Dexter Avenue for Martin. They were solid citizens with a preference for orderly change, but after spending a few years with Dr. Johns they were capable of taking on more dramatic action. They were primed to speed up behind leaders with integrity.

By then I was vice president and dean at Virginia Union, and I often invited Martin to speak to our student body. Like an old man, he was deliberate in everything. But when he spoke, his rhythmic cadences, his flow of language, and his sagacious finality about big problems captivated the students. Martin disarmed his listeners with his simple idealism and his unapologetic allegiance to the most sublime ideals that have echoed through the long corridors of the centuries. He had answers, and everything he said was true.

Martin gave no quarter to compromise, to the accommodation of evil, to caprice or calumny. I often think of him now when I read newspaper columns written by prominent black conservatives, like Dr. Walter Williams and Dr. Thomas Sowell, who are partners with those who consistently try to keep black people from pursuing simple fairness. With their scholarly cant they cloud the issues and drum on themes that draw applause from their cynical sponsors. I wonder if they are ever frightened when they look around and notice who is applauding them.

Shortly after Martin settled in at his new church, a black citizen of Montgomery was asked to give up her seat on a bus to a white man and move to the rear. In effect, Rosa Parks' heroic refusal began the legend of Martin Luther King, Jr. Martin led a bus boycott that effectively eliminated segregated seating in public transportation. Many other black pastors also had talent and courage, but they didn't have Rosa Parks! She was the right person, at the right place, at the right time.

Rosa Parks was a soft-spoken Christian woman active in her church, well prepared and well versed in the policies of nonviolent social change. She wore her hair combed back in a soft bun, and used no lipstick, rouge, or eye shadow. She never used profanity, drank alcohol, or chewed gum. She wore modest clothes and low-heeled shoes. She looked like a temperance advocate.

Martin, on the other hand, had the charisma of an old-fashioned Baptist preacher, with a catalogue of ideas rooted in the radical social message of the eighth century BC prophets of Judaism who spoke of justice rolling down as waters and righteousness of a mighty stream. Most of all, he believed that love—without thought of reciprocity—had inherent power and intrinsic authenticity.

Together, Rosa Parks and Martin Luther King, Jr., became the defining moment for real social change in America. Their witness was the zenith of the long struggle for full emancipation. Some secular critics said King was naive to believe that a reservoir of white good will existed out there somewhere. They could not conceive of change without bloodshed and wholesale killing. But Martin recognized that our very existence in a free society, with its accent on equality, derived from the ultimate victory of the One who died on a Roman cross with a crown of weeds and thistles on his brow.

Martin was right. He believed that in order to achieve a moral end, our movement had to be morally correct. This attitude has always been more typical of black striving than violent acts.

Martin invited me twice to speak at Dexter Avenue for his Annual Spring Lecture Series. Other black churches had revivals, but Martin's congregation, largely comprising faculty and staff from Alabama State College, preferred more sedate activities. He often told me, bragging of course, that he had thirty-nine Ph.D.s in his congregation. And I would always reply, "And how many Christians?"

One day during the Spring Lecture Series in 1956 he had to go to Tuskegee, about thirty miles away, to arrange to buy gasoline for cars that were transporting blacks boycotting the bus line. In Montgomery, any gas station owner who sold to blacks was denied his supplies. To keep Martin company, because you never knew what might happen to a radical black man on the highway in those days, I rode along with him. An Alabama state trooper followed us every inch of the way, about a yard behind Martin's old Pontiac station wagon. We were both frightened, perspiring profusely, and silent. When we reached the edge of Tuskegee, the trooper pulled over and stopped.

We spent an hour or so in town, while Martin conferred with black gasoline station owners. Then we started back. The same trooper picked up our tail as we left town, and trailed us all the way back to Montgomery. The cop's childish game of intimidation barely registered on our Richter scale. He probably would be furious to know how small an impact his harassment made on the larger purpose.

Incidentally, not long ago I was caught in a terrible rain storm while driving from Mobile to Atlanta. Driving frantically, hunched over the wheel, I found myself traveling on that same road between Tuskegee and Montgomery, now widened and renamed Martin L. King Jr. Highway.

Back in the mid-1950s, the table was set, but I wondered, when do we eat? We were naive in believing that legal victories alone would mean social change. Institutions like the Boy Scouts, YMCA, churches, labor unions, lodges, and fraternities—all operating under lofty creeds to serve humankind and promote good will—sought loopholes that allowed them to remain segregated and immune from court orders. Those "born again" Christians would not do it.

RICHMOND WAS A GOOD PLACE TO BE DURING THE GREAT transition because it had a large, educated black population with a polite connection with the white establishment. Life was tolerable, not stifling, even though resistance to change was firm. We did not experience the fear and violence that we learned about in the deep South.

We had married during the war years when so much was unsettled, and Bessie had some college credits to complete for her degree. Consequently, our home was tightly organized around her writing papers, the boys demanding attention, and my six courses which kept me buried in books. Preoccupied with Herbie's health, Bessie's final courses, and my workload, we hardly had time to reflect on larger issues.

Our lives were full of college sports events, church programs, college concerts, children's activities, and family visits. We were frequently visiting my wife's home in Fredericksburg and my own family in Norfolk, and it seems that I was always speaking in some church, conference, or school. Bessie was always busy packing and dressing the boys to get us ready to pile in our station wagon and hit the road. We knew every filling station, hamburger stand, and ice cream store in Virginia where blacks could be served without insult.

By 1955, I had become president of Virginia Union. That same year I had the privilege of awarding the bachelor of arts degree to a Mr. D. B. Jaycox, the oldest student on our campus— or any campus, perhaps. Mr. Jaycox had been the principal of my elementary school. When I was a boy, I always thought he had second sight. I'll never forget the day when little Vanetta Morgan was leaning over the drinking fountain, with her long braids hanging all the way down her back. The sight of those braids was too tempting and, after being certain that no one was looking, I grabbed both of them and yanked hard. Before I knew it, Mr. Jaycox appeared out of the mist and whacked me across the fanny with his hickory cane.

Like many black teachers in those days, Mr. Jaycox had earned a teaching certificate, but had never graduated from college. After he retired, he came to Virginia Union at age seventy-five to earn what he considered the ultimate prize, his baccalaureate degree. When he stepped up to the platform, he didn't look nearly as fierce as I had remembered him, so as I handed him his diploma I brazenly reminded him of Vanetta Morgan's braids. He grinned at me. "That's why you're where you are today," he said. "I kept you straight."

He did indeed. And placing a college diploma in his hands was one of the most rewarding moments of my life.

As DESEGREGATION TOOK HOLD, SOME HARDENED ATTITUDES also began to change. Under the threat of court orders, a handful of black students had been enrolled at Duke University, and Dr. Howard Wilkerson, the chaplain of Duke University, asked me to speak in their chapel. Duke's president, however, told Dr. Wilkerson that no black would preach in that Gothic church unless it was over his dead body.

Two years later, the president unexpectedly died. Dr. Wilkerson invited me again, and while I was seated in the chapel getting ready to deliver my sermon, I leaned across and asked him where the former president was buried. "Directly under the pulpit," he whispered. Surely enough, I was literally preaching over his dead body!

In 1957, at the height of the heat and ferment about school integration, the president of Lenoir-Rhyne College in rural piedmont North Carolina invited me to give their commencement address. That took nerve on his part, and I accepted. I spoke on Victor Hugo's phrase, "The Power of an Idea Whose Time Has Come," presenting the view that the time had come to abandon a segregated society, and for moral, intelligent, patriotic whites to take the leadership from the racists and the opportunistic politicians and stand up for a new beginning in race matters.

To my surprise, the all-white audience of students, faculty, alumni, and families stood up and applauded; I had to bow several times before they would sit down again. Afterward, as I was wending my way through the crowd milling around the campus near the auditorium, I heard a voice calling, "Dr. Proctor! Dr. Proctor!" Walking toward me was an elderly couple, wearing the marks of many winters in their wrinkled faces. They were out of breath trying to catch me. The old woman reached into a bag and took out a boxed Cross pen and pencil set and held it out to me. "We brought it to give to our grandson who is graduating today," she said, "but we'd like to give it to you instead. We can buy another one for him." I still use that pen and pencil. And I treasure that moment, granting it as much credibility as any court decision, act of Congress, or publication of any major treatise on social change. In terms of informing my heart about the future, I put as much trust in that moment as I would in a volume of speeches.

Also in 1957, Bessie and I participated in the Institute for College Administration at the Harvard Graduate School of Business. In this special program we met the best minds in the country on the subject of school management. In 1958, we joined in a retreat in Nova Scotia to study the Great Books curriculum of Saint John's College of Annapolis, Maryland, guided by its president, Dr. Weigle (the son of my dean at Yale).

I brought everything I gained at Harvard and Nova Scotia back with me and dumped it on the faculty and staff of Virginia Union. The idea was to elevate the intellectual tone of campus life and encourage challenging and stimulating discussions among the faculty. We had a great time fashioning our administration and curriculum to meet the needs of the young people coming to us.

Other movements were also spinning the political wheels of the nation, and in one way or another overlapped onto the black struggle. In 1958, at the height of the Red scare, anyone could grab headlines by becoming a virulent anticommunist. The Baptist World Alliance got the idea of sending three observers to the Soviet Union and Eastern bloc countries to look behind the Iron Curtain and see how small Baptist groups were faring under severe religious restrictions.

Anxious to show Eastern Europeans how some aspects of American life had changed, the Baptists chose me for the team. It was an honest, though less than significant, gesture and I was eager to go. In every circle we visited, questions about the status of blacks came up, even in countries like Belgium, Germany, and Switzerland where no blacks were visible and where they were not welcomed.

In Eastern Europe—in Warsaw, Riga, and Krakow—blacks were even less known, and I was proud to tell them how we had stood up and advanced in the face of rigid racial discrimination. All the Eastern Europeans knew how we had been treated, but they did not know how we had responded. I took pride in telling them that our spirits were never fully broken and that we always were able to muster the strength to protest, to march, to pray, to sing, and to go to jail to keep our movement for full freedom alive. It is a story I never tired of telling.

Under the communists, all churches and religions in Eastern Europe had been driven underground, except for one large Baptist church in Moscow. I preached there one Sunday morning with about two thousand people attending and another two thousand waiting outside. Those inside would periodically leave their seats and send in people from the outside to take their place. The sermon lasted more than three hours because every sentence had to be translated into four languages. I had to wait so long for the translations that from time to time I forgot where I was in my discourse. When I finally finished, I was exhausted. But before I could sit down, someone in the crowd stood up and asked that "the black brother from America should give another sermon."

After that, the police warned me to stop telling the Soviets that faith had enabled black people to outlive oppression. They advised me to stick to the Bible. That was curious, since the Bible— from Moses versus Pharaoh, to Elijah versus Ahab, John the Baptist versus Herod, and Jesus versus Caesar—is all about liberation.

> The Spirit of the Lord is upon Me, for He has anointed
> Me to preach the Gospel to the poor; . . . to announce
> release to the captives . . . ; to set free the [oppressed].
> Luke 4:18–20 (Berkeley Version)

We suspected that the Soviets permitted our visit in order to deflect reports that religion was stifled in Russia. But it was obvious to us that religion *was* being suppressed. We were moved to see old people coming to the service carrying huge Bibles, with lavishly designed covers, the pages inside ragged and thin with use. New Bibles had not been printed in Russia for thirty years. But the Baptists proudly took us to cemeteries and showed us new graves which bore tiny wooden crosses. In death, it seemed, people were free to declare their religious beliefs.

When I was departing from the Moscow airport, I found several wrinkled, handwritten notes that had been surreptitiously stuffed into the pockets of my trench coat. These scraps of paper were greetings to kinfolk in the United States. Where addresses were given, I gladly mailed them.

AS A COLLEGE TEACHER I WAS ALWAYS ON THE LOOKOUT for promising students. We never knew who might be sitting out there, and we always cherished the notion that if we kept pushing, someone in the group would break free and pioneer into new realms of opportunity and service. For example, in one of my classes in ethics at Virginia Union I recognized a bright young man named Douglas Wilder, although I never guessed he would become the first black governor in America, no less in Thomas Jefferson's and George Washington's Virginia.

One way to promote students' interests and expose them to larger fields of endeavor was to carry them to conferences. Anytime I was invited to speak somewhere, I would load my car and take off with five or six students. At a conference in Greenwich, Connecticut, a woman came up to me and begged me to take her son off the streets. She was terrified he was going to wind up in jail.

I persuaded him to enroll in our college. John Merchant went down with me, played basketball, waited table in the hotels, took campus jobs, and made an outstanding record. He had a kind of Yankee audacity about him and a never-give-up tenacity that made him an excellent candidate to break down barriers. After graduation John was ready to go back North, but we begged him to take on a hazardous mission. He agreed to try. John Merchant became the first black student to enter the University of Virginia Law School, the state's most sacred cow. He is now attorney for the state of Connecticut department of consumer affairs.

Today, John's mother, blind and frail, lives in a Connecticut nursing home. I recently stopped by to see her and we recalled her son's formidable journey thirty years earlier. I had the great joy of telling her that John had just delivered the commencement address at his old law school—because his daughter, her granddaughter, was in the graduating class. She wept with thanks to God. These are the secrets that faith will yield and that hardly ever get known.

At another conference in Cornwall, Connecticut, I needed a haircut. I left my students and sneaked off the grounds alone to find a quiet, authentic black barbershop, but I got lost driving around the Litchfield hills. At last, I spotted a young black hitchhiker standing at the side of the road.

"Where ya' goin', fella?" I asked.

"To caddy at the golf course," he replied.

"If you can tell me where I can get a haircut, I'll drive you to the golf course."

"You'll have to go into Waterbury to Mr. Reid's barbershop," he said. "I'm going out of your way."

I traded him a ride to the golf course for directions to Mr. Reid's barbershop. In the next ten minutes, I really went after him. I told him he needed to get out of Connecticut and join the flow of young black men and women who refused to accept the limitations others placed on them, and who planned to scale the heights. He listened as if he had never heard anything like that before.

For the next two years we exchanged letters. He kept me abreast of his school progress and, eventually, he enrolled in our college. He went on to finish law school in New York and then moved to California. Today, my caddy, William Ormsby, is a judge in the Los Angeles County Court.

Believing that change is possible causes one to act in harmony with such faith. As you live it out, the unseen evidence begins to appear. Because you *believe,* the very believing makes it so. This is the substance of things hoped for. And when faith is operational, strange things happen.

When I was a young student at Virginia Union in 1940 to 1942, an anonymous philanthropist in New Hampshire had paid my hundred-dollar tuition. I suppose the school thought if I knew my benefactor's name, I would write to him to express my thanks and respectfully ask for more! And no doubt I would have.

Sixteen years later, I was sitting in my office as president of the same school, facing a distraught premed honor student in the senior class. He was a married veteran with two children, and the bottom had dropped out of his life. He was telling me that he was stone broke, his rent was overdue, his children had been sick, and he had to give up. He already had been accepted at medical school, but he said there was no way he could go on. As we pondered the problem, the door opened and Mrs. Lytle, my ever-present assistant, came in. "Sorry to interrupt," she said, "but I think you want to take this call."

"I'm terribly busy," I said. "Can I call back?"

"I think you should take it now!"

A cracked, warbly voice came on the line. "Are you the same Samuel Proctor who went to school at Virginia Union back in 1940?"

"I am the same," I said.

"I'm the one who paid your tuition. I called to tell you that I'm satisfied that I made a wise investment. I'm pleased with your progress."

I was dazed, and I thanked him profusely. Then, God forbid, he said, "Can you find me another student that I could help? I don't have much time left and I would like to do again what I did in your case."

"Sir," I said, with an involuntary tremor in my voice, "he's sitting in front of me as we speak."

This was as close to a miracle as I have ever seen. With the infinite probability that no human could ever align random events with such precision, there must be a God somewhere! I handed the phone to my student and left the room. I have no idea what they talked about, but when he came out of my office several minutes later I was crying, Mrs. Lytle was in tears, and the student, now the fabulous Dr. Charles Cummings, a prominent Richmond specialist in internal medicine, was smiling through his tears.

This anonymous New Hampshire donor was no social theorist, no great reformer, no political activist. He was a simple Christian with a little money who looked around to canvass his options; back in 1940, he reached into the South and helped a young black student to equip himself. Now, as he faced life's sunset, he looked about again. Without anyone asking him, his heart moved, as though guided by the mysterious lodestone in a compass, and directed him, nearly twenty years later, to help another black student transcend the limitations imposed by history. This is the kind of evidence that black people always suspected existed, though ever so dormant, to justify their timeless and enduring faith.

BY 1959, THE COUNTRY HAD MADE SEVERAL JERKY BOLTS toward real racial change. The executive orders of Roosevelt and Truman, the Civil Rights Bill of Eisenhower, along with the string of Supreme Court victories won by the NAACP, had been positive indicators; now there was a kind of expectancy, a messianic hope, that someone would emerge who would dramatize change and celebrate America's true promise. Almost mystically, the rich, handsome, charismatic John Kennedy appeared.

In March of 1959, I sat next to him on the stage in a large auditorium in Indianapolis. I was there, with the forty United Negro College Fund presidents, to open our fund-raising campaign. Kennedy was there to promote his candidacy for the Democratic presidential nomination.

On my wall at home is a picture that recently surfaced of the speaker's platform that night. I am up at the podium doing my thing for the UNCF, and Kennedy, his head tipped, index finger supporting his cheekbone, is gazing hard at me.

Later that same night, Belford Lawson, a prominent Washington attorney, called my hotel room and asked if I would meet with the senator. "For what?" I asked.

"He wonders if you would take a leave from Virginia Union's presidency and work with his campaign."

I hastened to say, "Brother Lawson, let's face it. He is so young that the old folks will reject him; so rich that poor folks will deny him; and so Catholic that the Protestants will put him down.

Now, if Stuart Symington is looking for me, tell him where I am."

Lawson chuckled, and that was the beginning of my relationship with John Kennedy. While the potential for a new racial arrangement was present in Kennedy's nomination, it was by no means automatic or inevitable. It would take real people doing real jobs to make it happen, and I discovered myself inescapably among them.

THE CURTAIN CAME UP ON A DECADE OF HOT REBELLION and frenetic campaigns for change. In 1960, black college presidents found themselves in the eye of the hurricane. Our students had grown up observing the slow, begrudging changes of the Roosevelt-Truman-Eisenhower eras; they were aware of the perennial appeasement of southern politicians and their constituents. All of their lives, they had seen promised, long-overdue change proceeding at a snail's pace. They resented the stagnant political and social climate, they resented the way older blacks seemed to accept the slow rate of change. They were right. Moral goodness was on their side. No one could justify the treatment that blacks had to accept—sitting in theater balconies, getting served only at the "carry out" end of lunch counters, and being offered only menial jobs at the lowest pay.

On the second Saturday of February, 1960, the black college presidents of the Central Intercollegiate Athletic Association were holding their annual meeting on the old colonial campus of Maryland State College on the quiet, isolated Delmarva peninsula. Squirrels and chipmunks darted between silent oak sentinels; thickly carpeted lawns were bordered by immaculate sidewalks and driveways. We were dining in the trustee boardroom, with its heavy draperies framing tall colonial windows, the table set with exquisite dinnerware, and well-groomed waiters standing by. We had just begun to dig into juicy filet mignons, when one of those handsome waiters pushed open the leather-padded door and said, "There's an urgent call for President Warmoth T. Gibbs."

Gibbs, president of North Carolina A & T, tiptoes out of the room like a mortician at a funeral. A few minutes later he was back, looking tense and drawn. Two hundred and fifty of his students were in jail! Within minutes, every president there had a similar call. The sit-in movement had begun.

Our students and their advisers had held clandestine meetings and had drawn up a scheme to strike a blow against Woolworth's Greensboro lunch counters while we were away in rural Maryland, eating steak and drinking Chablis, figuring out how to accommodate visiting football teams.

The students were doing what they could do best. Their parents, who had mortgages, car payments, and tuition bills to pay, were not in the best position to stage a confrontation with authorities.

With the student sit-ins, the new emancipation suddenly accelerated. Blacks never questioned the choice to pursue change by moral, nonviolent means. It was simply their way. There is no record anywhere—Have mercy!—of black nannies poisoning white babies or putting arsenic in the family's pot of greens. Blacks never talked about putrefying the town reservoir or burning down the sheriff's home while he and his family were asleep. When some frenzied groups decided to bomb buildings and burn cities, they were rejected by the larger black community. The majority of blacks intended to fulfill their liberation and, as a concomitant, to participate in America's fulfillment as well. This was the substance of their hope

IN THIS PERIOD IN HISTORY, I SAW THE PAST BEGINNING TO fade away and a new world on the horizon. My grandmother, Hattie Ann, lived to see it, too. At the age of ninety-six, Grandma fell seriously ill for the first time in her life and we spent many hours together talking about the past. I remember her squeezing my hand one afternoon and telling me how proud she was of my achievements. "I remember when your university was founded," she said. "It was called Richmond Theological Seminary." "My university" was founded less than one mile from the Fisher plantation where she had been enslaved.

That little slave girl has over one hundred descendants who are college-trained, many of them holding professional degrees. In less than one century, they had turned their simple belief that unrequited suffering would somehow be redeemed into a new political and social theory. Beginning with their mission, the black sojourn in America has demonstrated itself to be without precedent, still calling for a new society.

CHAPTER FIVE

The Horizon of Hope

1960–1964

TWO BIG EVENTS MADE 1960 A DEFINING YEAR FOR ME. First, our son Herbert returned to Johns Hopkins Hospital in Baltimore where a miracle was performed: his surgeons, the widely known team of doctors Taussig and Blalock, built a new wall between his ventricles, virtually giving him a rebirth.

During Herbie's first twelve years of life we had organized our lives around him, and through him we learned how special opportunities for growth were strewn along life's pathway. We made thirty-nine round trips between Richmond and Baltimore, accepting the hospitality of dear friends, the Reverend and Mrs. Thomas Davis, who served a church in Baltimore. These trips were like holiday picnics. We were so glad that Herbie's operation was a success; color came back to his fingernails, his lips and cheeks. He breathed with ease, walked steadily, and smiled incessantly.

His brother, Timothy, only ten years old, made every trip with us, grabbing every brief, sneaky minute with Herb that he could. Also on every trip was Bessie's mother, who gave up all of her other interests to share our needs. She was a fixture in our home and in our travels.

Sharing our son's early life, when his damaged heart prevented him from playing baseball, swimming, and dancing or going to birthday parties, taught us lessons no doctor's degree ever could. Everyone knew how risky his life was, but *him*. Everyone knew how much he was missing, but *him*. He sang and laughed through it all, and his brave, cheerful spirit made us thankful to be alive.

Timothy shared our special family secret: Herb's needs came first. The child with the unmerited, undeserved, unearned *deficit* laid a claim on all of us who enjoyed benefits from our birth that we did not earn or deserve. For the next forty years all of my teaching and preaching has had the same hidden agenda, namely: to show that those who enjoy a fast start, fond parents, strong bodies, quick minds, and the aroma of hope following their steps owe it to those who begin life with a physical limitation, poor education, and poverty coming in the window along with the flies, the noise, and the profanity to help them get over. Herbie got over, with an awful lot of support and love and constant prayer from the rest of us. Today, after finishing college and a master's degree in social work, he is a father of three and a veteran urban school social worker in New Jersey.

Here's a footnote to his childhood. One Sunday morning I was the guest preacher at the church in Petersburg where many of the faculty of Virginia State University worshiped. I mentioned that my son's big surgery was coming up, but he needed forty-eight pints of blood. The Red Cross in Richmond, where I had many friends, would not accept blood from black donors. However, the Red Cross mobile trailer in Petersburg would. Well, I didn't know forty-eight people in Petersburg. Even worse, I was president of Virginia Union, the arch enemy in football of Virginia State.

As the congregation stood mingling outside after church, no one mentioned donating blood. But on Monday afternoon, a whole busload of Virginia State football players showed up at the Red Cross trailer; technicians stayed late into the night drawing blood from quarterbacks, linebackers, tight ends, running backs, guards, and wide receivers—for our little Herbie, who knew it would happen for him, although none of us knew how. The prime movers were their coach, Sally Hall, and a huge bruising fullback named "Toby" Tobias, who had survived a rough upbringing in a Baltimore slum. With forty-eight pints of blood from young black ballplayers who had been recruited from the ghettos of Philadelphia, Newark, Baltimore, Washington, D.C., and Richmond, the genius surgeons at Johns Hopkins built a new heart for Herbie.

The other big event of 1960 was the election of John Kennedy to the nation's presidency. To us on the sidelines it seemed that if a handsome, Harvard-trained Roman Catholic could be elected, anything might happen. His election was accompanied by a growing impatience with the pace of change, and there were demonstrations everywhere. A vanguard of courageous people threw themselves in the face of insanely angry white mobs all over the South for desegregation and voting rights. They were beaten with tire irons, chains, bats, and fence posts, had dogs and fire hoses turned on them, and many died to turn this society around. They integrated schools, opened hotels and restaurants, registered new voters, and fought for fair employment. We owe an immeasurable debt to them. Most of them have never heard their names honored in public and have never seen them written anywhere.

For so long, the Senate had been captive to senior, southern politicians, and we had seen significant legislation and big ideas lying fallow. The Kennedy rhetoric was different. He was young and idealistic, and surrounded himself with people who created an air of expectancy. Kennedy had been a friendly senator and, surely enough, when his presidency began, we felt movement. The whole national conversation changed.

As Democratic chairman of the House Committee on Education and Labor, Adam Clayton Powell, Jr., was able to pilot one key piece of legislation after another through the Congress. I served on the board of directors of the National Urban League and saw firsthand how the government could increase opportunities for minorities in business and industry, if it had the will.

For example, the Kennedy innovators created a new program in the White House which they called Plans for Progress. Certain companies—among them IBM, Xerox, Mobil, Exxon, Chase Bank, AT&T, Bell Labs, Johnson & Johnson, Ford, Chrysler, General Motors, Citibank, and American Express—felt the pressure for change gaining momentum, and were convinced to start recruiting women and minorities, and allow the feds to monitor the results. Other companies followed their example. As a result of this push, corporate America began to enhance opportunity for blacks. For the first time we saw blacks moving up through the ranks and receiving serious appointments. Many of these early jobs were in personnel and human resources, but it was a start. Before Plans for Progress swung into action, any blacks you might have seen moving around at rush hour on Park Avenue wore doormen uniforms or carried messenger pouches. But by the time our son Timothy finished his law and M.B.A. degrees at Chicago in 1975, he had already spent a summer internship at Chase Bank; he then passed the New York bar and went to work, without missing a beat, as an attorney for Union Carbide on Park Avenue. The fruits of these '60s efforts were real.

I often spoke at Plans for Progress meetings where white corporate midlevel managers would gaze at me like cows looking at a new fence. They thought I was a mutation. They had never met educated, assertive blacks in a nonthreatening setting where they could ask naive questions and get straight answers.

All of my speeches followed the same pattern: I first presented the anti-thesis: Here is the kind of America we are creating—a huge underclass, an embarrassing jail population, illiteracy at 15 percent and poverty at 35 percent. Minorities are locked into low-paying jobs and minority students have low expectations. What kind of leadership is this?

Then I presented the thesis: We can change this. We can start recruiting and training bright young women and minorities. We can encourage colleges to recruit them and offer scholarships. We can get placement officers to prime them for job success.

Today, as I reflect on those awkward events, I am puzzled that I could speak so confidently about change before such uncommitted, reluctant groups. But I was convinced that I was right, and the companies bought into it.

I had spent so much time with the great social prophets of Israel and Judah and Jesus of Galilee, I really had no fear.

By the fall of 1960, I had left the presidency of Virginia Union, and moved to North Carolina A & T State University, a larger school whose students a few months earlier had spearheaded the sit-in movement. As a college president I was on call fourteen hours a day. The biggest part of my job was trying to develop a faculty and an academic program strong enough to propel black students into a demanding future. Our students usually came from disciplined, church-going families, reared by both parents, and backed up by at least two grandparents. Now, I began hawking foundations and federal offices for money to recruit a new contingent of black students coming from stagnating poverty and cultural isolation.

Even though I felt the work of the colleges was indispensable to black progress, there was so much happening in the civil rights movement that I wanted to do whatever I could to feel part of it, too. We could not leave our campuses and follow the movement, but we took any opportunity to participate. Whenever King asked me address one of his gatherings, I would go. The campus itself was a center for student protest planning and activity. Whenever the Freedom Ride bus came rumbling through Greensboro in the middle of the night, our food service manager would haul out of bed to get meals ready and students would share their beds. We tried to be ready any time, and were prepared to go anywhere to speak and organize.

While earthshaking events raged around us, I tried not to lose sight of the personal needs of individual boys and girls. Like my mother I had a habit of poking into the lives of the young people, a kind of pastoral spillover into my academic role. Because of my position, I had many opportunities to use contacts and influence to generate some new hope in individual lives. One day our public relations officer and I attended a 4-H Club conference in a poverty-stricken county in east Carolina. The boy who introduced me was dressed in a clean, starched, and neatly ironed 4-H Club uniform, and he spoke with unusual clarity. But as he turned toward me and bowed slightly, I noticed that his eyes were severely crossed. After the ceremony I learned that his family were poor people who practiced a typical rural philosophy: love the Lord and do your best; God will do the rest.

Back at my desk at A & T, I sat gazing out of the window. There had to be an ophthalmologist somewhere in Durham who would straighten out that little fellow's eyes. I called Dr. Waldo Beach, a respected scholar in Christian ethics at Duke's Divinity School, and asked him if he knew anyone who could help. He told me that among his church's congregation were a father and two sons, all three outstanding ophthalmologists. Only one more phone call, and these prominent white specialists agreed to correct the eyes of a poor black 4-H Club child—at no charge at all.

My only task was to convince his frightened and skeptical mother that the same God whose natural order failed and let her boy be born with severely astigmatized eyes was the same God who allowed medical science to perfect the art of ophthalmology. She agreed, and the boy's eyes were operated on. He finished high school and college, completed an M.B.A. at the University of Wisconsin, worked for Quaker Oats, Gulf Oil, Johnson & Johnson, and now heads his own marketing consulting firm in Chicago. His eyes have been busy, and Bob Hughes has done well.

I had many similar encounters in the 1960s, and many trials, too. Down the road apiece from my Greensboro school was an expensive private Southern Baptist school called Wake Forest University. At that time, Wake Forest was trying to ease away from religious control in order to attract scholars unwilling to teach under the rubric of religious fundamentalism. Someone got the idea of asking me to come to Wake Forest and speak to their middle class, white student body on the issue of race relations and the rising claims of blacks on the society. For the most part, these students liked things as they were. My job that day was to show them how racial discrimination hurt everyone.

As I stood at the podium pouring out my soul, the crowd suddenly hooted. I turned just in time to see a completely naked male student race across the stage behind me. I paused, and then asked the audience if there were any other volunteers. They roared with laughter.

It might have been a fraternity prank or a racist gesture. I was immune to either insults or interruptions. I continued speaking, marshaling the strongest arguments I could find to pry open the minds of those potential leaders of the new era. When I finished, they stood applauding. But none of this was easy.

I spoke to many different audiences during these years, and the questions I heard were always the same. It's hard to imagine the measure of self-control needed to face one hostile white au-

95

dience after another, looking in the faces of assorted antagonists, and pitifully ignorant, fearful hypocrites, whose agenda was to cling to their advantages and perpetuate the subordinate status of blacks. I answered their questions then as I answer them now:

"Do you believe in reverse discrimination, giving blacks preferences over others for jobs?"

Answer: Because of the long years of discrimination against blacks, and because tenure and seniority have been given to those who have enjoyed preferential treatment for generations, it's fair for qualified blacks to receive preference to correct such past abuses. How long it will take or how many cases are matters of legal judgement, but it should not be a permanent practice and we never asked for that.

"Do you believe that blacks should be granted admission to graduate and professional schools on any basis different from other students?"

Answer: Since the Emancipation, blacks have been deliberately deprived of equal educational opportunity. In many states it was illegal for blacks to be educated at all. All of my education through college was in segregated schools where the facilities and equipment were inadequate or not available. Most blacks, therefore, ended their early schooling with huge gaps in their preparation. Our scores on admissions tests often reflect this unfair disadvantage. When grade-point average, class standing, personal references, or in-depth interviews show that a black student is capable of successful performance, such evidence should take precedence over entrance exams—for the time being—as a fair corrective for the decades of unfair isolation and denial of opportunity.

"Why should this generation of whites be asked to pay for the discrimination perpetrated against blacks a long time ago?"

Answer: Just as blacks have inherited disabilities and stigmas and accrued financial, educational, and social *deficits,* so have whites accrued financial, educational, and power *benefits* while blacks were in physical bondage for eight generations and legally segregated for three more. It is fair for this generation that enjoys those unfair advantages to compensate blacks for such unfairly imposed deficits.

"What does the future hold for black people in America?"

Answer: As opportunities in education and employment improve, the quality of life among blacks will be further enhanced, as it was for the Jews, Germans, Irish, Italians, and Greeks. Our journey is harder because, unlike them, we bear the stigma that has been stamped on our color, and our previous condition as slaves. Our struggle is more tedious.

"What do blacks like you plan to do about so many blacks in prison and so many black teenage mothers on welfare?"

Answer: Blacks in prison read at the fourth-grade level and were reared without fathers. Whites in prison are the same. Whatever caused whites to end up in jail caused blacks also, and whatever corrective works for whites will work for blacks. It is a national problem, like air pollution and alcoholism, not a black or white one.

There are more young, white mothers on welfare than black. They also read at the fourth-grade level and most of them were reared in single-parent families of mothers who were also children of unwed parents. We need to work on the poor education and the family dysfunction that produces both black and white teenage mothers.

The causes of all these problems relate to ignorance and poverty, not skin color. Sadly, the questions I hear from audiences today are virtually the same. Prejudice is deep, strong, and intractable.

ALL BLACK LEADERS AND EDUCATORS IN THE 1960S WERE well aware that the causes of crime and social dependence were endemic among blacks, and caused our data always to be embarrassingly negative. But we also knew the causes behind the data, causes so deep and impenetrable that they would require serious national attention. We did what we could, and from where I was, I felt proud of the results that we generated.

The goal of black progress was clear: we wanted *in*, to become full participants and not marginalized mendicants. Ironically, two new black groups rose up to challenge the premise that blacks could eventually find a place in the mainstream of the society. First came the African culture advocates. They thought that equal participation was misconstrued to mean the "whitening" of black Americans: the abandonment of black heritage and identity, a sense of shame among blacks for being black. Consequently, they rejected the adjective "black" in favor of Afro-American. They put down black leaders who worked with white leaders, and all black organizations that cooperated with whites.

African cultural advocates believed that we should insulate ourselves from all white influences in the same way that the Amish and the Hasidic Jews had isolated themselves. They believed that we should run our own schools and ask for full political control of our communities, like an urban reservation.

Black separatists had a somewhat different agenda. They too believed that whites would forever look upon blacks as inferior, world without end, Amen. They advocated federal reparations to finance blacks wishing to relocate to a newly acquired African state, or even in a newly set-aside settlement in America, out West somewhere. It was more a mood, a feeling, than a well-thought-out strategy.

Of course, there was also a third, even smaller, group of blacks who wanted peace and tranquility at any cost. They blamed blacks for their plight, and thought we should stop "whining and bitching," as Judge Clarence Thomas puts it today. These men acted as though their own good fortunes rolled in softly on a gentle tide. Yet they enjoyed an education and job placement that would never have occurred without the steady protest and advocacy of black agitators.

Although these splinter groups attracted a great deal of attention from the media, most blacks continued to stay in touch with the larger society and maintain contact with people of good will.

A lot of black special interest groups at the time were trying to recruit our students for various campaigns and purposes. We taught them to ask relevant questions, look for the facts rather than propaganda, and opt for the position that was not self-contradictory. We honored our heritage, taught black history and black pride, and worked for a national community of diversity, compassion, and justice.

One particular student was always hanging around my office, darting in to snatch a few words with me between appointments, clinging to me like a vine. He was Jesse Jackson, bright, bold, and destined to be *somebody* in this country. Jesse had come to us as a transfer student from Illinois. He came to my attention when he turned up on our campus one day, seeking admission and financial aid. My public affairs officer came into my office, puffing and blowing, begging me to intercede with our registrar on this young man's behalf. "Dr. Proctor, please, don't let them turn that fellow away. We need him here!" I never knew exactly what Jesse had said to impress him, but it was immediate and indelible.

Jesse had spent a year at Illinois as a football recruit. That was a long way from home for a Greenville, South Carolina, boy, raised by his mother and grandmother in a modest public housing project. But he was adventurous enough to try anything. He gave up after a year and opted to come to us, with no money and ineligible for an athletic scholarship, pleading to be admitted. Even in his interviews he was so impressive that we made some very special arrangements to have him admitted. We never regretted it.

PRIOR TO THE KENNEDY YEARS HARDLY ANY BLACK PERSON ever received a telephone call from the White House. We hardly mattered at all. So one afternoon in January 1962, when my secretary buzzed me to pick up for a call from the White House operator I was stunned. There was Sargent Shriver, President Kennedy's brother-in-law, talking fast and spraying me with facts faster than I could absorb them. He was feverishly trying to get me to accept an appointment to direct the first full Peace Corps unit abroad, in Nigeria. Then President Kennedy came on, adding his persuasive charm and earnestness to the request.

The president said Nigeria was his showcase to help establish a more positive relationship with the new African states. He said it was urgent that the Peace Corps succeed there. (I did not discover until some weeks later just how urgent.) President Kennedy concluded by saying, in typical Kennedy fashion, "Dr. Proctor, your country needs you desperately."

Minutes later, the governor of North Carolina called. Kennedy had been burning up his phone lines, too. "Go, Sam. I guarantee your job when you return."

I hesitated. I knew little about Nigeria and even less about the Peace Corps. I did know that their volunteers were young, altruistic alumni of America's best colleges, and practically all of them were white. I also enjoyed my job, and felt I was on firm ground where I was, doing the work I was meant to do.

My reluctance was overcome by guilt feelings. During World War II, I had been a deferred seminary student, and dozens of my boyhood friends never returned from Anzio beach and the Pacific islands. I owed them something. More to the point, as a college administrator throughout the civil rights protests, I had done good work, but not on the front lines. I had never been shot at, beaten, thrown in a dirty jail, or chased by police dogs. I called Shriver back and told him I would go.

That night, I presented the situation to Bessie. Ordinarily, family problems and obligations would interfere with such a commitment, but Bessie knew I always weighed and debated every move endlessly. I told her I felt three powerful pistons moving me. One was the sense that America was on the threshold of something new and I thought that black people, including us, should be a living, active part of it. The president had in mind 15,000 to 20,000 young Americans helping students, many of them black Africans, in developing countries to obtain secondary educations. I had never done anything really sacrificial in my life, and this looked like it.

Next, I felt ashamed that black Americans had failed to help Africans. We made the faintest token gestures, but we had not developed a real commitment to Africa. Here was a chance.

Then, the world was changing. Two and a half billion people were about to start moving to close the gap with the rest of the world. I wanted us to be a part of that.

She listened to me and her response was immediate: "Let's do it!" she said. Bessie grasped clearly what it would take to move the whole family to Nigeria. Of course, neither of us really knew what life would be like or what the job would entail. But we were ready for the risk. After two or three hours of discussion with the boys, she had them on board. We were all excited and ready to go. For the next two weeks we had an African fit, being briefed by the state department and reading everything we could get our hands on about the Peace Corps and Nigeria.

The Peace Corps was a fully independent agency, free of the state department, AID, or the CIA. Its objectives were simple: to supply personnel in areas of critical shortages to newly developing nations, to enable Americans to learn firsthand about other cultures and ethnicities, and to allow the people of those countries to learn about Americans.

I knew that a pilot group of volunteers had already arrived in Nigeria with a temporary director, and I knew that one teacher had been sent home because of some kind of a misunderstanding. Before I could learn more, we were on our way. When President Kennedy said it was urgent, he wasn't kidding.

Once in Africa, the real facts surfaced. A young female Peace Corps teacher attending a training session at the University of Ibadan had written a postcard to her mother back in Ohio. Her message described the filthy, crowded streets of Ibadan, with pregnant women carrying babies in their arms, and holding toddlers by the hand, the odor of urine rising from drainage ditches, and beggars clogging every crowded intersection. Before mailing the postcard, she inadvertently dropped it on the campus grounds, where it was later picked up by a Nigerian student. As fate had it, he belonged to a "nonaligned" political wing, a euphemism for leftist bias. He turned the card over to the press and it was published in every newspaper in the country as evidence that the pro-western Nigerian government had made a mistake in inviting seven hundred "capitalist" teachers into Nigeria; the Peace Corps teachers, they alleged, were part of a U.S. scheme to subvert their national autonomy and to begin a recolonization movement.

To avert a national crisis, the Nigerian government demanded that the United States immediately send a black educator to direct the huge cadre of white volunteers. If not, the Peace Corps would be evicted from the country. Bill Moyers had recommended me to Sargent Shriver, by way of a referral he had received from the president of Stetson University in Florida. I had been checked out from head to toe; I was clean, but green, for the job.

In Lagos, the degrading remnants of colonialism were everywhere. Segregation was the absolute rule. Many Americans serving in foreign posts automatically sent their children to schools in Europe. We wanted our two teenage boys to live with us in Nigeria, but when we tried to place them in the local schools, we saw that they were terribly crowded, poorly equipped, and followed a limited curriculum.

When we learned that an excellent American school had been

established in Oshogbo for the children of white missionaries, we prepared for battle. Surprisingly, we met virtually no resistance at all. Through some white friends and colleagues in the States, I contacted the Foreign Mission Board of the Southern Baptist Convention. Within hours, our boys were invited to integrate the school. As a result, indigenous Africans were also invited to enroll.

Soon it became clear to me that the black struggle in America was a vanguard to rebuilding the tremendous damage colonialism had wrought in Africa. As desegregation was taking hold in the U.S., my sons were integrating a Nigerian school. The work of the Peace Corps in Africa seemed to be an extension of the faith package that we had inherited.

I had seven hundred freshly graduated white volunteers ready to learn a new language, eat a new diet, live in a strange culture, and do without supermarkets, television, libraries, buses, hot water, and, for some, electricity and indoor plumbing. Volunteers were paid fifty dollars a month, plus their living costs. Most taught in Nigeria's high schools, and a few taught in teacher training colleges. I never ceased to marvel at how these young people accepted their assignments, coped with the political skirmishes, negotiated their acceptance in the face of some bitter opposition, and maintained poise and confidence in the merit of their mission. We had so much opportunity to fail, but did not.

My family stayed in a state of curiosity and inquiry. We wanted this experience to yield a world of sophistication about Nigeria and Africa. We were less interested in African antiquity than we were in the people. Every household of a government employee came with a staff of seven servants attached to the house, whether they were needed or not. There was no question that we would keep them and pay them above the prevailing wage. Bessie is extremely gregarious and starts out trusting everyone. Her trust always begets trust, and within hours of taking up residence she had the house helpers feeling that they had known her for years.

Our sons are a copy of her. From their relationships with the household staff we had a constant source of facts on Nigerian life as lived at the grass roots. The time flew by. The house ran so smoothly and with such warmth and joy that we practically forgot that we were three thousand miles from home. Our comfort level radiated outward, and we were able to give extra assurance to the volunteers who needed it. Most did not.

These volunteers were working on the front lines of world need and they loved it. Given the political climate, a big part of my job was to make sure that the Nigerians loved them back. I had a private pipeline to the Nigerians through which I could learn of their real reactions to our efforts. Many of the leaders of the independence movement in Africa had been educated by white missionary organizations in Africa and gone to black colleges in America. Fifty-five Nigerian officials were alumni of Virginia Union. One of them, a tribal chief in Oshogbo, had finished his degree at my alma mater in 1911! My own great-uncle had been his schoolmate.

Through the day-to-day living, I had the opportunity to look closely at Nigeria. I saw sick children all day long, crippled beggars, and masses of young, pregnant women with other infants on their backs. Young men had two or three wives, all of whom were bearing children constantly. Life was cheap. It was impossible for education and the economy to catch up with needs that were leaping ahead of progress.

How could Africans with the least resources be expected to reverse such a tide of woe which had been created by centuries of abuse by European colonists? When I was a schoolboy, we had to draw maps of the world. Our teachers would ask us to paint all of the French colonies blue, the Spanish yellow, the German black, the Belgian purple, the Dutch green, the Italian pink, the Portuguese orange; we left the British the color of the paper to save paint. No one ever asked why these people were so far from home, ruling someone else.

Today we are still seeing the consequences of colonialism in a sea of humanity, largely illiterate, living in poverty in countries like Somalia, Rwanda, and Uganda. Blacks cannot redress these wrongs by themselves. This was a global sin and it calls for a global cure. (Much as the depressing situation in the former Yugoslavia is the result of earlier Austro-Hungarian colonialism that today cries out for a global response.) When we look at African states that are doing well, it is obvious that they had better access to education and literacy. While we have to approach the more technical issues of infrastructure, communication, and fiscal management on a longer-term basis, the nations of the West—the former colonists—can multiply manyfold their paltry efforts at education now. This is the basic resource on which all other progress must depend.

American blacks are caught in a moral dilemma. No other people on earth can match the experience of black Americans or compare themselves to us. No one can identify completely the metamorphosis through which we have gone. But now most of us enjoy a standard of living that is higher than 95 percent of the rest of the world's population. And we should be the chief advocates and participants for a change in the quality of life in Africa. Although we are so different from each other in so many ways, we are called together by our common social history, and our common quest for justice. It is our obligation to help Africans where we can.

MY EXPERIENCE IN NIGERIA FORCED ME TO REACH DEEP inside and probe my sense of being. Who was I, really? It is a question that every educated, upwardly mobile black person has to ask every day, but it had extra poignancy for me at this time. While I dealt with budgets, transport, housing, Nigerian politicians, and their leftist detractors, unfamiliar feelings overwhelmed me. I seemed to be hearing voices, like vibrations, and seeing visions, like mirages.

One afternoon, at Port Harcourt in Eastern Nigeria, I stood with my face to the sea and thought I could see a young African youth standing before me. The boy I envisioned had been snatched from his village and family by his own people, roped together with strangers, and marched through quiet trails at night to a waiting ship, where he was sold to slave dealers in exchange for wine, beads, and tobacco. From the very spot on which I stood, the slave traffic had flourished for centuries.

In the weeks that followed, my mind kept returning to that African youth. Every day I walked the streets of Lagos around Tinebu Square, and imagined him being chained into rows of other men and stacked like salted fish in the depths of the ship. Some captives hit their heads against nails until they died; others refused to eat and starved themselves to death, but the young man I envisioned shut down all of his human instincts and swallowed whatever was put in his mouth. After months at sea, the reeking ship finally reached shore and he was still alive. He was dragged out of the hold and sold to the highest bidder. I could see him sick and starving, unable to understand or speak to anyone, toiling in the murderously hot fields and disease-infested swamps of the Southeast. At night he dreamed of being free.

In my imagination, the African youth lived to be an old man, and despite his dreams, he never regained his freedom. But he never stopped believing that, somehow, his life had a special purpose. He might have been my own ancestor. Because of his will to survive and his faith in things unseen, I was a free person, appointed by the President of the United States to represent America in this African nation, making a small effort to indemnify the moral atrocity committed against her.

But I knew that despite my title and privileges, back in America I was not a first-class citizen. I was barred from entering some hotels, barred from eating in some restaurants, barred from using some bathrooms. When white people looked at me in

America, they didn't see a doctor's degree or a director's title. They saw a black man who was, by virtue of his color, inferior.

Every now and then an ordinary exchange magnified my dilemma. One day one of our domestic helpers turned up with a fresh haircut. "Jacob," I said, "you have a neat haircut. Where did you get it?"

"My friend who comes by on the bicycle cut it."

I thought his friend was a "bookie" who came to collect bets on the soccer matches. I knew he came by to eat, because our steward was operating a clandestine family-style restaurant in his small quarters on the compound, using our food as his supply! But now I learned that the man on the bicycle was a barber, too.

"Jacob, how much does he charge you?"

"Only two shillings."

"Well, will he cut my hair, too? I have to pay six shillings downtown."

"Oh, yes," Jacob replied. "But he will charge you six shillings, too."

"Why?"

"Because you are a white man."

There were only two kinds of people in Jacob's world: his own tribal people and everyone else. I lived in a well-equipped house with a staff; a driver carried me from place to place, and I took hot baths, wore socks, and ate a varied diet. That separated me by great lengths from his people. If I were not one of them, I had to be a white man, regardless of my pigmentation.

His remark stayed with me. I didn't seem to have a place to put my foot. As a black man I lived a marginalized life in America, and in Nigeria I was a stranger. Was I in Nigeria as an American visitor, or as a child come home?

One day an associate and I were visiting one of our volunteers in Ogbomosho. She carried us out into a small rural village where we met a distinguished-looking chief with a broad smile, a twinkle in his eyes, and three deep Yoruba tribal marks in his round cheeks. This was Chief Oyrinde, my great-uncle's classmate. For more than fifty years he had been living in that small village, running a school, managing a dispensary, and serving as the local pastor. From that village he had sent a steady stream of young Yorubas to colleges and universities all over the world. When I was president of Virginia Union, we had dozens of Nigerian students coming from the same stream. They stayed away from home and family for four years, hid their loneliness and estrangement, never displayed any negative attitude toward their black American cousins, whose lifestyle was so different and whose opportunities so infinitely greater.

Chief Oyrinde greeted me like a prodigal who had come home. And I felt like a shadow before him. I was African in ancestry; but all the while I was growing into an amalgam of European metaphors and analogies, mixed in with an American worldview, he had been living here in unbroken continuity with his African heritage.

As I stood there I felt naked; my ignorance of his life story was embarrassing. All of my schooling had overlooked a close, fair examination of Africa. We saw only the National Geographic portrayals of African people, and no one like Chief Oyrinde was ever introduced to me. I ought to have had longer, deeper, closer connections to my own people. Nevertheless, with all of this ambiguity about our identity, our context here was clear and we had to live out our lives where we were.

And as precarious as my existence was in the United States, I again confirmed, as my experience in India had shown, that I was thoroughly an American. Like other black Americans, I survived on the belief that one day our society would become fair and equal. Black Americans always have been in the process of creating their own identity. We could never stop and wait until all the ambiguities of our existence cleared up. With only shaky ground to stand on, we kept moving forward.

BACK HOME, THE CIVIL RIGHTS MOVEMENT WAS REACHING its denouement. When George Wallace, the governor of Alabama, personally barred the enrollment of two black students in the University of Alabama, President Kennedy didn't mince any words:

> This nation was founded on the principle that all men [and women] are created equal, and that the rights of every man are diminished when the rights of one . . . are threatened.
>
> . . . It ought to be possible . . . for American students of any color to attend any public institution they select without having to be backed by troops. It ought to be possible for American consumers of any color to receive equal service in places of public accommodation, such as hotels and restaurants, and theaters and retail stores without being forced to resort to demonstrations in the street.
>
> And it ought to be possible for American citizens of any color to register and to vote in a full election without interference or fear of reprisal.
>
> It ought to be possible, in short, for every American to enjoy the privileges of being an American without regard to his race or his color.

Earlier that year Sargent Shriver asked me to leave Lagos and come back to Washington to be one of his three associate Peace Corps directors. One associate director worked with the Congress and the media; one worked with host countries on feasible programs and logistics; and one recruited volunteers, selected them for their assignments, and supervised their job performance, living conditions, and personal decorum. This last was my job, watching over sixteen thousand volunteers in thirty-eight countries.

We often asked celebrities to help sell the Peace Corps to potential recruits. On the day of the March on Washington—August 28, 1963—I was in my office, trying to get Boston Celtics' star Bill Russell to help us recruit black college seniors for the Peace Corps. While black students talked about their African roots and consciousness, 98 percent of our volunteers in Africa were white. As Bill and I talked, I looked at my watch and realized it was time for King's speech. We walked over to the Lincoln Memorial and as we approached the basin we were speechless at the sight of a virtual sea of Americans come together in one great moment of celebration and commitment. It looked like something apocalyptic. They were old, young, bearded, bald, formally dressed and barely covered, serious and somber, casual and carefree. They were white, Hispanic, black, and Native American. All of us were there. And there was order and electric control from within. When Martin began to speak, he was artful in capturing the mood and the passion of that assembly, and he articulated in sonorous, rhythmic phrases exactly what they felt. For a fleeting instant, time stood still and eternity bent low over Washington, and *the word* became flesh again.

A few days later, my leave of absence was over, and I left Washington to return to A & T. I felt as if I had a secret: the country was on tiptoe, leaning into the future. A new horizon of hope was palpable.

I had kept abreast of the news from A & T and knew that the new president of the student body and quarterback of the football team was none other than Jesse Louis Jackson. For my first five days back, my wise and efficient secretary, Doris Durham, helped me plan a tight schedule: every day from 8 to 10 A.M., Doris and I would work on the piles of mail; 10 to 12 noon, I would see staff and faculty to catch up; 1 to 3 P.M., I met with deans and vice presidents for the forward look; and then, between 3 and 5 each afternoon I would see anyone who wanted to see me. Jesse made an appointment for 3 P.M. on Wednesday.

But when I got to the office at 7:30 Monday morning, there he was in a blue suit, white shirt, and a striped tie. He smiled, gripped my hand like I was a prodigal returned home, and said, "I realize that I am due on Wednesday at three o'clock, but as one president to another, I thought we should talk first before anyone else." That was pure Jesse!

From the beginning, Jesse had all of the marks of an aggressive, take-charge agent of change. Not every member of A & T's board of trustees had approved of my going to Africa in the first place. Thus, I planned to make my return from Nigeria as inconspicuous as possible. Jesse didn't see it that way. He planned a major convocation, demanded that I speak, and presented me with a handsome Omega watch that I still wear thirty years later. He was aggressive and bodacious, but he matched it with intelligence and purpose. Whatever he said, or did, he was usually right and reasonable.

Later that fall I was attending a serious policy meeting of North Carolina state college presidents, hosted by Dr. William Friday, president of the University of North Carolina at Chapel Hill. While we were trading jokes and trivia during lunch, a stocky black waiter suddenly pushed open the door, waving a large white napkin. "Somebody just killed the president!" he shouted.

We looked around at each other and whispered, "Which president? Bill Friday is right here at the table."

By then, someone had gone out to the front desk and returned, saying, "It looks like President Kennedy was murdered a few minutes ago in Dallas."

We were sealed in stony silence. Each of us canvassed his mind instantly on the long- and short-term consequences of this earth-shaking trauma. The future was bent badly, but by how many degrees no one rightly knew.

My instinct told me to capture immediately any redeeming aspect of the tragic event, before anyone put another face on it for my students. I did not want a young student leader to take charge in my absence and lead the campus into a reaction that we could not live with. I rushed to a telephone and called my unfailingly trustworthy secretary and asked her to have the choir and the band excused from class. Both air force and army ROTC cadets in dress uniform were to be in full formation on the front lawn at sunset. She was to notify the local media that we would be holding the first memorial service for President Kennedy on the steps of Dudley Hall.

At dusk, the front lawn of our campus was covered with young black students, encircled by all the people of Greensboro. I spoke a few words of tribute to mourn the passing of our president. As president of the student body, Jesse spoke next, calling on the students to renew their determination to bring about the change that Kennedy had begun. Everyone was silent in the deepening night as the college choir sang the Brahms *Requiem Mass*.

Only a few months earlier Kennedy had presented his Civil Rights Bill to Congress. Was this the price he paid for coming forth in our behalf? A week later, when all of the dust settled, and the echo of the last bugle had died in the wind, when the flowers had shriveled and the rhetoric had collapsed into one loud "Amen," no matter how you took it all in, John Kennedy seemed to have laid down his life that we might live.

MUCH CHANGE HAD BEEN ACHIEVED WITHOUT VIOLENCE, but now a noisy contingent of young blacks demanded action. Curiously, it was not black violence, but white violence that precipitated change. When a sleezy coward bombed a black church in Birmingham, killing four young girls, the Civil Rights Act of 1964 was passed; then, after the abuse at Selma, the Voting Rights Act of 1965 was passed.

By this time, with the country awash in controversy over civil rights and Vietnam, the issue of poverty lit up the national agenda. The talk among blacks was how Lyndon Johnson, scion of southern democratic political domination, had come around 180 degrees to carry the banner for black liberation.

Before I knew it, early in 1964, Bill Moyers and the governor of North Carolina were back on the telephone. Moyers had moved over to the White House with President Johnson, and the president wanted me to return to Washington as associate director to Sargent Shriver again. The first time I had joined the Peace Corps, I had been granted a leave of absence. I had been back on the job less than a year and was just settling in again. If I wanted to go back to Washington now, I would be forced to resign from my college presidency. That was the choice I made. As always, the whole family got into it. Our moving around never seemed to make our sons feel insecure. The whole society was already in flux. The news was flooded with images of Vietnam War protests, mobs confronting police, and Civil Rights demonstrations. By contrast, home and family, wherever we were, seemed like a fortress of stability. The two older boys always felt closer to us than to any fast peer friends, and they liked the adventure of living in new locations.

Bessie's mother was almost always with us, and her home in quiet, undisturbed, colonial Fredericksburg, Virginia, continued to be our haven for holidays and family celebrations. Moreover, our family considered going to Washington to serve the government personally prestigious, and also an omen that a more promising future was ahead for black people. The Washington appointment was clearly an approved move.

All over the country, things were really popping. I sometimes felt guilty as I worked in Washington in a safe, air-conditioned office with four secretaries and two deputies. Yet I knew the struggle was about blacks gaining more positions just like the many who had received recent presidential appointments. We seemed to have reaped the harvest before others could get in line, and we felt guilty about it. But we knew we were pioneers in a process that had to take place. Some people called us "tokens"; in fact, we were more like wedges, pushing doors open and then trying to hold them open.

I spent some time down in Mississippi with Medgar Evers, who was head of the state conference of the NAACP. Medgar lived with danger night and day, eschewing notoriety and working in quiet devotion for freedom and justice.

As we talked late into the night at a friend's home, I offered him a two-year appointment as a Peace Corps deputy in Ghana. I laid out all the benefits he could gain from the job: he could get acquainted firsthand with Africa, earn a good salary for a while to pay some bills and get ahead a little, and get a respite from white terrorism for himself and his family. When I suggested that he would return to the fight rested, refreshed, and reinvigorated, his eyes widened and he smiled. I gave him a week to think it over.

A few days later Medgar called me in Washington. He would like to go later, he said, but not right now. Things were at a boiling point in his state. The 1964 Democratic convention had failed to seat the Mississippi Freedom Democratic Party, which comprised black and white liberal Democrats who had been ostracized by the southern Democratic Party. When the chips were down, white liberals failed to support their cause and blacks felt betrayed. It was also a bad year for violence. Five black churches had been bombed in Alabama and Mississippi, and in twenty different instances white mobs had attacked blacks demonstrating for their rights. Medgar said he couldn't leave his country at that moment. But would I ask him again, maybe in a year or so?

Two years later, as he was getting out of his car one night in his own driveway, a gunman shot him to death. It was another cowardly, hateful act, but Medgar's tragic death added momentum to the movement.

Another great soul was given to us by Mississippi. Fannie Lou

Hamer was a sharecropper and a grassroots political organizer. I met her for the first time when I was working as Sargent Shriver's special assistant in the Office of Economic Opportunity. OEO was authorized by Congress, but had no appropriation for a while. Shriver ran it out of his Peace Corps office with the help of his Peace Corps staff.

We all worked twelve-hour days and had working sessions at Shriver's home in Silver Springs on weekends. One of the rewards of this era for me was to witness the dedication of some of the nation's brightest and most privileged people as they tried to change circumstances for poor Americans, whether they were Appalachian whites, or urban and rural blacks. Head Start and the Job Corps did not make the splash that some street battles created, but the long-term effects of such solid institutional efforts were the difference between a thunderstorm and a full season of steady intermittent, generous rainfall.

At one early OEO meeting, Fannie Lou Hamer was sitting at one end of the long conference table and Sargent Shriver at the other. I sat next to Shriver and took notes about proposed projects. In the midst of a heated discussion, Fannie Lou suddenly bellowed at him, "And another thing, what do you know about poverty? You're a millionaire sitting here planning for the poor. You're like the fox in the henhouse!"

Shriver turned red as a beet, and banged on the table: "I don't have any money! My wife has the money. I bet Sam Proctor has more money than I."

I choked. I hardly had enough in my wallet to get my car out of the parking lot. Shriver jumped up and stormed out of the room. The rest of us sat frozen at the table, but Fannie Lou didn't turn a hair.

A few minutes later, I found Shriver in the men's room, splashing cold water on his face. He raged on, "Here I am fighting these right-wing congressmen and southern senators to get enough money to change the direction of this country and I have to keep defending myself because I'm married to a rich woman who cares as much about this as I do!"

Sargent Shriver is a decent, sensitive, and good-hearted person. He really didn't have a lot of money of his own. I knew that his family lost everything in the Depression and that he went to Yale on scholarships. We joked about how staff people on the road with him often had to buy his lunch; and once in Chicago I even had to lend him a clean shirt.

As he spoke, I realized that he and Fannie Lou were speaking at each other through a solid wall. She spoke the white-hot rhetoric of those who had been waiting for so long, living cheek-to-cheek with intractable white racists. Shriver was a Yale-trained social engineer who had only an academic acquaintance with chronic and desperate poverty. I was trying to translate Fannie Lou Hamer to him, and him to her.

"Did I insult her, Sam?" he asked.

"I don't think so," I said. "This was an open debate, and things need to get said. She did you a favor by bringing an important issue to the surface. If we expect to make any headway with this program, people need to know that you're not a rich man's son dabbling around with poor folks' miseries."

The simple fact was that we did have people like Fannie Lou Hamer who were vigilant to assure that the plain truth was spoken. Fannie Lou Hamer always looked white people straight in the eye, told the truth, and *never* blinked. There were many black men and women just like her.

CHAPTER SIX

Great Expectations

1964–1968

WHILE I WAS IN WASHINGTON IN 1964, RUMBLING complaints poured in from black leaders around the country. Nothing Lyndon Johnson did was enough. It seemed that our hopes, demands, and new agendas were running way ahead of what liberal Democrats could deliver, both domestically and around the world.

President Johnson raised our expectations to a peak when he pushed through the Civil Rights Bill that year. Automobile horns were blowing all over Washington that day as liberals, white and black, passed each other on the streets and highways, flashing peace signs as recognition. It wasn't enough. Super-right-wing groups started dropping from trees and crawling out from under rocks. Even Barry Goldwater could not control the extreme far right. Whenever blacks progressed an inch, right-wing extremists reacted as though it were a mile. When Howard Hughes died, a note was found among his memorabilia saying that enough had been done for blacks to last them for a hundred years.

I suppose I, too, became a little cynical about my role in Washington. I felt like I was in the wrong place, walking the hallways of a federal office building, tied to an administration that had no popular mandate. I longed to be back at the ground level, where hearts and minds could be influenced.

By now I was weary of short-term assignments and high-pressure jobs. I longed to settle into a normal position with a challenge that was close to my training and experience. Blacks who had academic credentials, experience, and a record of satisfactory job performance were in demand. Sensitive people in high places wanted blacks to receive more opportunities, and I was contacted by several. A major aircraft corporation with huge defense contracts found itself under pressure to change its hiring policies; as a result, they offered me—of all people—an attractive position. I also had several job offers from universities, foundations, and church agencies.

I chose an invitation from the National Council of Churches, a fragile assembly of mainline Protestant churches, with no authority but with a tacit commitment to promote Christian ethics in national affairs. My job as associate general secretary was to explain the goals of the council to the country and keep the churches and their congregations behind us.

Our chairman was Edwin Espy, a saintly layman who had lived a lifetime on the side of the angels. He was surrounded by serious and committed church leaders, but they failed to recognize the huge gap between themselves and the people in the pews. When white Protestants realized what their liberal clergy were up to, the money simply evaporated. The better I explained the goals of our mission—to inaugurate a just, fair, and free society with equal opportunity and a higher quality of life for all, just as Jesus talked about—the worse our fortunes became.

Our daily mail showed just how unpopular Jesus was among those Christians. They loved little Jesus in the manger and hanging on the cross, Jesus in the hymnbooks and on bumper stickers. But on Wall Street, in the Congress, in city hall, and in the boardrooms, not many really loved Jesus.

Even so, in the 1964 election, the right wing wasn't yet powerful enough to muster the popular vote, and Lyndon Johnson was elected by a landslide. Bill Moyers called *again,* and I was headed back to Shriver for the fourth time, after less than a year with the National Council of Churches. As Shriver's Northeast Regional Director, I was now working in both the Office of Economic Opportunity and the Peace Corps.

This time it was different. President Johnson won so impressively that I thought the residual of good will in the country was broader and deeper than I had perceived. Also, it appeared that the attitude that seemed to dominate the churches was not really representative of the country's majority. There was more good will in secular circles than could be found in evangelical Protestantism, which had made a tacit alliance with segregationists in the South and ethnic pockets in the North. It was culture-bound, not prophetic; more loyal to the status quo than to the teachings and example of Jesus.

By now it was apparent that the changes we yearned for had a better chance if they were the outcome of a broad political consensus. It seemed that the church had so completely accommodated itself to the white middle class that it had little to say. Even the black churches stepped back from the vanguard and clung to their traditional role of providing nurturing and inspiration to their flocks. They resumed their identities as stabilizing institutions, and from them would emerge, here and there, a flaming prophet of change.

Meanwhile, increasing numbers of young blacks were losing hope. The line between blacks who still believed in the substance of things hoped for and those who had given up grew clearer, wider, and deeper.

New talk surfaced of a separate Afrocentric culture, resulting from our rejection as full citizens and our lack of a cultural reference. Young blacks who had courageously entered college under enforced court orders were tired of begging for their rights. Ostracized by other students, they changed their hairstyles and eating habits to reflect boldly the African culture that had been stolen from their people in the seventeenth century. They even changed their names. Black students grew zealous in their demands for separate dining halls, libraries, recreation centers, and curricula. Some also changed their manners and attitudes toward non-Africans and certain blacks whom they called "Negroes" or assimilationists.

One night during the mid-1960s, I attended a Sigma Pi Phi dinner at the Commodore Hotel in New York. This is a sort of superfraternity, founded in Philadelphia in the early 1900s to give black intellectuals a place to go for mutual support and stimulation. The group was composed largely of black attorneys, businessmen, judges, physicians, college professors, and clergy.

As I leaped up the steps headed for the meeting room, I looked back and saw a gathering of black men dressed in African attire filling up the hotel lobby.

I heard a voice call out, "Sam, where the hell are you going in that tuxedo?" It was an old friend of mine, wearing a richly patterned green, red, and black dashiki, open sandals, a huge gold bracelet, a beaded neckpiece, and a full, expansive Afro hairstyle.

I came back down the stairs to meet him and told him where I was headed. He screamed to his buddies, "Hey, y'all. Sam is headed upstairs to one of those 'Oreo' meetings with a bunch of big shots. Let's go with him and check it out." As it happened, they were at the hotel for a convention of the National Association of Black Educators.

This group was challenging the curricula and teaching style of schools serving black children. They wanted more Afrocentric materials and less of a Eurocentric focus. They wanted blacks to control the governance and policy making in black schools. The details of how this program would be accountable to the statutory schoolboards were not clear, but the agitation stage had begun.

They stormed our meeting—about forty of us and about twelve of them—demanding that we justify our existence. The late Julius Thomas of the National Urban League was there. So were Kenneth Clark of City College, Justice Delaney of the New York Supreme Court, and Stephen J. Wright, then the head of the United Negro College Fund. We represented the signs of success and change, a new image, new movement toward inclusiveness and fairness. But there we were, apologizing because our advancements seemed to be a trade-off for the denial of other blacks.

In that room in the Commodore Hotel the sharply defined paradox of black life in the 1960s was clear: one group believed that America could change; the other believed she would not.

To the National Association of Black Educators, accepting status as quasi-citizens and subscribing to the culture of America was tantamount to agreeing to inferior status unworthy of any person. But by resisting the signs of change, they were, in effect, rejecting the goals established in the 1950s.

The members of the Sigma Pi Phi fraternity, whose origin dated back to the turn of the century, had already debated the issue of identity and survival. Around 1915, they concluded that blacks had only one destiny—and it did not lie on the African continent, nor on an island in the Caribbean, nor on a bleak, arid reservation in the deserts of New Mexico, Arizona, or Nevada. Their destiny was to dig in and fight for justice and respect right at the center of America. Their destiny was to engage in creating a new culture of their own, a blending of African residuals, survival strategies learned in slavery, and consciousness of their dual personalities—U.S. citizens tacitly aware that they were participating in a unique transition that would lead America to become something entirely new.

The tuxedoed gentlemen seated at the banquet tables were not childish mimics of an artificial status. They were intentional about creating their own culture. Each one of them was involved in some cause devoted to black amelioration, and many were in the foreground of change. They regarded the Afrocentrists as cop-outs who had recognized how long and how hard the real struggle would be and chose something quicker and closer.

The Afrocentrists thought the fraternity brothers had bought into the dominant culture too deeply, had sacrificed their African identity, and had moved too far—too high—from grass-roots blacks.

I felt frustrated, feeling that both sides had legitimate platforms yet, at least that night, at the Commodore, with one group dressed in tuxedos and the other in African garb, both appeared excessive. We did need agitation to make schools alert to the needs of black students for affirmation and identity. And the fraternity members were the big link between black problems and the resources needed to solve them. They were in touch with the power structure and they were sincere in their advocacy.

At some other point in history it might have been possible to bring the two sides into alignment, but not in that decade. The debate was hot and angry on both sides. Each person believed passionately in his agenda. The argument descended to the black teachers calling the fraternity members Uncle Toms and the fraternity members calling the teachers hustlers and phonies.

SHRIVER ASSIGNED ME TO NEW YORK TO RUN THE NORTHEAST regional Office of Economic Opportunity. This was the hottest spot in the country. In fact, the protests were so frequent that I often had to leave my office and hold meetings in that same Commodore, which was one block away. On any given day I would have mothers visiting who had been evicted from their apartments, tenants bringing boxes of rats to show their living conditions, students coming to protest tuition increases, artists demanding money to put on exhibits and performances, and drug addicts and alcoholics coming to demand housing.

To maintain family stability in this chaotic situation, Bessie and I had chosen to settle in a quiet community in Teaneck, New Jersey. Our two older boys were in high school, and we now had a new baby, Samuel, who had been born after our return from Africa. We had all but forgotten what it was like having a baby in the house. He demanded more attention than any of us anticipated. I always brought my problems and paperwork home and always talked over everything that was going on with Bessie and our sons. It was not our style to separate my job from the ebb and flow of family life. It was all one. So between giggles, toddler feedings, teenage dilemmas, and dramatic reports about the latest protest at the OEO, we made it one day at a time.

Our daily travails were nothing compared to the hardships endured by those being bombed, beaten, jailed, and chased by police dogs across the South. I was willing to endure any challenge in New York to do whatever I could to bring change through the OEO. At the same time, I resented the cynicism of the protestors who came to harrass me because I was an executive of the government, and to them the government was the enemy. I thought they should have known that the White House and the courts had given us the only hope we had. Corporations had to be forced to hire us and universities had to be sued to admit us. When we were admitted to schools, we went on federal programs and grants and loans. In return, federal agents who were black were being treated like the enemy. No one was prepared for the ambiguities America was passing through. There was no limit to the name calling, the labels, the slogans, and the blame placing, and it continues today.

The whole spring and summer of 1965, I was spread out over New York, New Jersey, New England, Puerto Rico, and the Virgin Islands keeping track of how OEO dollars were being spent. Reactions to OEO initiatives ranged from cynics who thought the whole program was a hoax designed to deflect attention from a class war, to those who saw it as a political pork barrel to buy the votes of the poor or a Communist scheme to redistribute the wealth of the country. Of course there were those who saw it for what it was: an excellent approach to the needs of the poor that needed to be continued and expanded. The biggest problem was trying to involve the poor, who were inexperienced with institutional accountability, budgets, and audits, in planning and managing their own programs. Their greed and cleverness were no more sinister than the greed and cleverness at every other level of government and commerce.

By September, problems were mushrooming all over the country. I had to return to Washington as Shriver's special assistant—my fifth title with the same boss. I hardly gave it a thought. It was a continuum of the New York task, only now I had to connect with the directors of every region doing the same kind of problem solving.

So, halfway through Johnson's term I returned to Washington, and became the troubleshooter responsible for trying to remove barriers to OEO operations around the country. In one large Connecticut city, for instance, we decided to fund a tenants group that wanted to monitor housing abuses. It turned out that the chief violator they turned up was a slum landlord who contributed large sums to the Democratic Party. But we were called on by certain important senators to "unfund" that particular project. We couldn't call off the tenants group if we wanted to, and we did not try.

One day Bill Moyers called from the White House and asked

me to leave fast, go to the airport, and fly to Charlotte, North Carolina, with Billy Graham. We were helping a lot of poor, mountain people near where he lived, and we wanted to get his support.

All through the flight down we talked church, religion, and social change. When we reached his mountaintop home, we had a delicious lunch and more conversation. It all settled down to a stalemate: Dr. Graham felt that his business was to preach the gospel and change the hearts of individuals. Changed persons would then change society.

I countered with the teachings of Jesus in chapter 25 of Matthew's gospel, in which he admonished that at the day of judgement we would all be separated into sheep and goats. One got to be a sheep by feeding the hungry, giving water to the thirsty and clothing to the naked, visiting those in prison, and taking in the stranger. The sheep entered into the Master's joy. Goats did not do such things and were consigned to a burning hell.

Reverend Graham smiled and said that I was making Jesus a "liberal." It was odd, though, that while he officially avoided political involvement, he often boasted of advising several presidents. The visit was pleasant, but he did not change his position, and neither did I.

One night Shriver and I, along with his wife, Eunice, and a couple of other staff people, went to Philadelphia to attend a rally in support of a national job training program funded by the Department of Labor and the OEO. We went up to announce a $1 million grant. On our way back to the airport a black motorcycle policeman was doing some fancy stunt riding as he escorted our car through downtown traffic. His bike hit an oil slick and he went up about ten feet into the air and landed on his back, unconscious. An ambulance came and carried him to the hospital.

We followed, and Shriver and his wife stayed by the policeman's bedside. Throughout the still hours of the night they kept a vigil until the next morning, when the injured man finally regained consciousness. I was always impressed by the simple, uncomplicated commitment to people that was reflected in Shriver's choice that night. It was the same approach he had to all of his tasks. Little wonder that he moved on to head the Special Olympics.

UNDER PRESIDENT KENNEDY, THE WHITE HOUSE AND THE departments had become flooded with Harvard and MIT types, and they had many black friends in education. They were pragmatists, reaching for whatever would work. The ultimate goal was to move black youth out of poverty in a way that would be permanent and replicable, not with benign, temporary remedies. They wanted healing, not placebos.

As we kept meeting around Washington, trading ideas, it struck us that if black colleges were strengthened, with their strategic location in southern cities and their known commitment, they could become catalysts. More strong black teachers, Ph.D.s, accountants, engineers, microbiologists, dentists, physicians, nurses, agronomists, and space explorers would enter the stream and filter into the American workforce everywhere. The idea sold easily, and the Institute for Services to Education came alive. Its goal was to strengthen the faculties and programs of 105 black colleges.

Its board of directors asked me to move over from the OEO and serve the Institute. This meant leaving our Teaneck home and relocating in the Washington area. Because this was a new, independent agency, it looked permanent, worth a real investment and a long outlook. Along with our move, a fourth baby, Steven, arrived, and a new voice was added to the household. It was exciting watching a new life connect with our close unit and fight for space and attention.

I loved the new job. Working with a team of eight faculty from each school, we developed a curriculum for thirteen colleges. For once, money was no problem. We had excellent funding from various foundations and federal agencies, with seed money coming from the Carnegie Foundation. I remember walking around Washington in March of 1966, a check for $500,000 in my pocket, looking for a bank that would give us the best deal on a start-up account.

At the same time, this period brought sadness to the family. My younger brother Charles died suddenly of a heart attack. Three months later, Bessie's mother, who had been our constant companion and the real cushion in our home for all of the shocks and bounces, passed after a long bout with cancer. A year later, my mother passed, never having gotten over Charles's untimely death.

The shock of three funerals, writing obituaries, and standing silently by gravesites forced me to reluctantly accept the intrusion and the finality of death. In the midst of the frenetic excitement of Washington and the challenge of social crises, I was suddenly called into a new kind of sobriety. Death demands a longer view of things. It seemed that death was an alarm, calling us to stand up straight and stiffen the chin for life's imponderable pressures and surprises. We made a Spartan response that seemed to be the mark of maturity. The tears were mostly inside, an empty feeling of being abandoned when our parents died. Our home was so tightly knit and family was so close that we were not left alone long enough to be overwhelmed with pain.

Even as I took stock of myself, I tooled up to get ISE going. Every educator we called on for help responded by serving on committees and granting leaves of absence to their stellar teachers so they could join us in developing new curricula. We contracted for office space with the American Council on Education, through their president, Dr. Logan Wilson, a big-minded, big-hearted Texan, who saved us thousands of dollars. He managed all of our fiscal operations from his DuPont Circle building and charged us less than one half of a secretary's salary!

It was fun watching black college teachers huddled day after day with the most renowned educators in the country, searching for creative ways of inducting young blacks into the life of the mind and the world of ideas. I recall one humanities teacher running around screaming, "I got it! I got it!"

She had run upon the idea of teaching the history of ideas by a course entitled "Jailbirds," which she had developed around people who had been jailed for their innovative thinking. The timeliness of this was great. Civil rights and liberation leaders all over the world were being thrown in jail for their ideas. And there were Socrates, Jeremiah the Prophet, Jesus, Paul the Apostle, Jan Hus, John the Baptist, John Milton, John Bunyan, John Brown—all the Johns!—Copernicus, Galileo, Nat Turner, Nkrumah, Azikewe, Mandela, and Martin L. King, Jr. The list was much longer. Jailbirds 101 and 102!

OUR FAMILY LIFE WAS ENORMOUSLY RICH AND FULFILLING. Nothing can compare with the pleasure of having seen two infant sons initiated into life by their two older brothers. They found the babies to be a happy relief from the daily tensions of coping with campus violence and the vicissitudes of large-scale social change.

Of course, Samuel and Steven never knew the ways of the old South as their older brothers did; they had landed in the midst of rapid transition.

Because I was working both as a special assistant to Sargent Shriver and as president of the Institute for Services to Education, I was denied the "daddy time" the boys needed, and Bessie had to double in brass. She kept her station wagon loaded with toys and boxes, and every floor in the house was littered with signs of life.

We both recognized the need for time away from the city, and we starting spending weekends on a small farm on the waterfront of Northumberland County in Virginia. We shared this spot with nine other families, each of which had built a modest cinder-block cottage. We added to the fun with an 18-foot boat with a 40 horsepower outboard motor. For thirteen weekends each summer we went fishing, swimming, and water-skiing with the boys, played touch football and pinochle, and told each other long drawn-out crazy stories. Then, late on Sunday nights, we went back to the serious, grinding business of making a new society.

EVEN THOUGH I WAS OUT OF GOVERNMENT BY 1967, I HAD a call from a member of Hubert Humphrey's staff, telling me that the vice president had been invited by Clark College in Atlanta to give a centennial Founders' Day address. The demonstrations, Vietnam crises, and tensions in the country required the vice president to remain on board in Washington; would I stand in for him? A White House car picked me up at the ISE office, a cap, gown, and hood in the back seat, and I wrote a speech on the flight to Atlanta. When the plane touched down, the press, police, and politicians were there waiting for Hubert Humphrey. When I climbed out of the Air Force jet, we were all surprised. "What you see is what you get," I said.

A year later President Johnson was scheduled to deliver a centennial Founders' Day speech at Johnson C. Smith University in Charlotte. At the last minute, Bill Moyers called again and I had to repeat the whole exercise.

When I returned, a White House staffer ribbed me, "So, Sam, who are you replacing next?"

"I'm going home and wait for the Pope to tell me he can't make it to Notre Dame."

When Humphrey decided on short notice to run for president

in 1968, all sorts of supporters demanded his attention and his presence. Humphrey's speech writer, Van Dyke, called to ask me to write speeches for the vice president to deliver to the National Baptist Convention, the African Methodist Episcopal Zion, and the African Methodist Episcopal general conferences. He would make the speeches over the next ninety days and each would be heard live by at least ten thousand blacks and another 5 million watching on television.

That meant writing three different speeches saying the same things: things have changed under Johnson-Humphrey, but we have a long way to go. Nixon wants to go backward. We must go forward and complete the integration of education, expand job opportunity, continue the War on Poverty, remain strong militarily, strengthen new nations in decolonializing, and build in America an example of a new human community of compassion, justice, freedom, and hope.

Humphrey enjoyed giving these speeches, which I inadvertently flavored with a little Baptist pulpit rhythm and glow. He would roll along with his Minnesota staccato, and whenever an audience detected the echo of a black preacher, they raised their hands and chanted "Amen!"

I was in the audience one night at the 1968 General Conference of the African Methodist Episcopal Church. Humphrey was rolling along pretty good when suddenly a robust voice shouted out, "Preach on, brother!" The colleague next to me, who had been chuckling quietly, now fell out of his seat laughing. Humphrey looked out at the audience and said, "Where is Sam Proctor? What did you put in this speech?"

The Methodists roared. It was one of the most transparently communicative moments I have ever witnessed. Humphrey and those black Methodists were on the same wavelength. They loved him. Humphrey had always stood up for black people, even though in 1964 he had been on shaky ground, going along with the party in denying seats to the Mississippi Freedom Party. That night he could have stood there and recited the Ten Commandments to a standing ovation.

In the same year, Humphrey had to go to Africa in order to look more like a presidential candidate. He asked me to go with him. We traveled on Air Force One (which is repainted and called Air Force Two when used by the vice president). We had a great trip, stopping at Zaire, Tunis, Liberia, Zambia, the Ivory Coast, Ethiopia, and the animal preserves of Kenya. Typical of such trips we were wined and dined and superficially briefed on American relations with the host country. The embarrassing part was to see the lavish lifestyle of the ruling class everwhere we went, and the unbroken landscape of poverty and sickness in the streets where the people struggled to survive. It was heartrending. Humphrey insisted on seeing it all. And when I saw this contrast in well-being everywhere we went, I had the feeling that Americans shared the guilt, because we were friends with those rulers.

Habib Bourguiba, head of the government in Tunis, had twelve palaces! We, meaning the U.S., gave tacit consent to his behavior, just as we gave to the Duvaliers in Haiti. When we got to Addis Ababa, the students lifted up one side of our Cadillac limousine and almost turned it over, so vehement were they in their protest of our buddyhood with the royal family of Ethiopia.

Same old story. But the world was changing fast. Throughout the trip I had a chance to discuss these observations with Supreme Court Justice Thurgood Marshall and *Jet* editor Simeon Booker, an old Latin and Greek classmate from college, who were also on the trip. All of us recognized Humphrey's motives and his unpretentious idealism, but we wondered how much change he could effect if elected. Powerful economic forces were firmly in place to stalemate any significant change.

Huge corporations were involved with mega-governmental contracts, therefore contracts had to stay in place. Hiring practices were frozen in business and government, and old-boy networks kept blacks and women in the lowest grades. Cabinet offices and corporate chairs were a revolving door, and huge Washington law firms kept deals on the table with governments, fiefdoms, and sheikdoms in every corner of the planet. Politicians were all beholden to the same money. The most salutory event of the whole trip was our arrival at the Nairobi airport in Kenya. I looked out of the window and spied among the official greeters my old friend, that big bad "Toby" Tobias, who had led his football team to the Red Cross trailer back in 1960 to donate forty-eight pints of blood for my son's heart surgery. When I stepped off the plane, he gave me a bear hug, scratching my face with his wiry, tropical whiskers.

"What are you doing in Kenya?" I asked.

"Well," he said, "you recall that you and Bill Moyers let me join the Peace Corps and sent me to Iran to help the shah develop an Olympic team. After the Olympics, Kenya asked me to work for their government developing their Olympic team. So here I am."

"It was good of you to come to meet me."

"I really came to see the sergeant," he said.

I turned to see a huge, black Air Force sergeant with all sorts of stripes crawling up his sleeve and medals splattered across his chest. He rushed up to my fullback and hugged him, and tears rolled down both of those stone countenances. It turned out that as little fellows trying to survive in the slums of Baltimore, they had both wound up in a boarding school founded for black youngsters who needed an alternative home. They had been like brothers. Now the sergeant was in charge of security on Air Force Two, and the fullback was training Kenya's Olympic team. That fabulous result from the ghetto and a school for troubled boys! When your eye is trained to look for it, there is plenty of evidence that there is a faith proposition that operates, and that get results.

MEANWHILE, THE MOVEMENT AT HOME WAS ALIVE AND well. In 1968, Whitney Young asked me to preside at the plenary sessions of the National Urban League convention in New Orleans. After opening words from politicians and local officials, I began to move the meeting forward, presenting speakers and panelists. Just then, a half-dozen young men, dressed in guerrilla warfare garb suddenly appeared on the stage and grabbed the microphone from my hand. The truth was that some of the Urban League staff, including Whitney Young, were former athletes and marines. They were not about to let a half-dozen self-appointed commandants take over the convention. In a flash, Whitney, all 6 foot 3 and 240 pounds of him, reached for their leader's collar, snatched him forward, and said, "You will not interrupt this meeting. I'll give you a chance later to make a statement."

Still threatening, they backed off, and we proceeded. As promised, Whitney did give one of them the opportunity to present a statement at the end. Cogent and sincere, it bore little relationship to the reality of that moment. It was simply rage. And it was the tenor of the times: discussion and debate signified weakness, while a show of force stood for integrity.

The Urban League felt the protestors were honest in their ideals, but they believed that violence would only leave the black end of town in ashes and elect the most extreme right-wingers to Congress and the White House. Their approach was negotiation, conciliation, and persuasion.

The problem was that neither approach could bring change fast enough. All of us saw the ingredients for riots in every urban setting. In Los Angeles, for example, every black neighborhood was infested with unemployed, uneducated gang members armed to do battle somewhere with someone. Violent behavior was their shield to cover their inadequacies. In juxtaposition to them were poor white migrants from Texas and Louisiana, with their boots, their tattoos, their guitars, and their racism. The brighter of them became policemen. Every riot was the outcome of an abrasive encounter between a racist white cop and a mean, bad "brother."

But if you stepped back to get a wider perspective, it was clear that in ten short years the black condition had changed dramatically. And beneath the surface of public debate were small private gestures that never made the news.

While I was in the thicket of our work with the colleges and the White House, I had a call from a Martin England, a white Baptist missionary recently retired from service in Burma. He was now working to enroll southern pastors in the American Baptist Health and Pension Plan. He called to find out if Martin Luther King had any health or life insurance or pension plan.

"It occurred to me," he confided in his gentle way, "that Dr. King has a young family and that he lives dangerously."

Martin England would never have expressed such a concern outloud, but into my ear he spoke of life's inexorable and changing scene.

"My hunch is that Martin has been too taken up with other matters to worry much about his financial condition," I said. "But why don't you give him a call and ask him?"

For two months he tried to reach King, but could never gain admittance to the black inner circle. Martin England was a tall, thin, pale man with a balding head and dark blotches of age on his hands. Whenever he showed up, dressed frugally and driving a worn old Plymouth, the black brotherhood surrounding King with their thunderous voices and rotund physiques frightened the retired missionary into a quick exit.

But England didn't give up. He called me again and described his futile efforts. I promised to try to get him in to see King. It worked. King signed up for the plan. The efforts of this unobtrusive South Carolinian made it possible for Coretta Scott King and her children to have health coverage and a monthly income from this one source ever since. Such small and apparently insignificant gestures bury themselves in the deep reservoir of my memory, and make me immune to the cynical notion that all human decency has died.

A FEW MONTHS LATER, ON APRIL 4, 1968, A DALLAS cabdriver picked me up at Love Field. He had long, stringy blond hair, tattoos crawling up his arms, and a wet cigarette butt dangling from his lips. A pair of cheap sunglasses hid his eyes. He was trying to tell me something, but he couldn't get the words out. He began to cry and was shaking so much that he had to stop the cab to collect himself. Finally his message spilled out between sobs: Martin Luther King, Jr., had been shot to death in Memphis. I felt my heart splinter.

I was on my way to a conference with specially selected white and black teachers to devise a strategy for preparing Dallas teachers for school integration. When the news of King's death lit up the airwaves, I had to reassess whether such small efforts were worth such an enormous price. I knew how much Martin would have loved to live and see his children grow up. But I knew also his sense of destiny and that he had calculated death as a possible price. He died, really, to give impetus and sanction to every effort at building a community of justice and compassion. In order to feel some sense of continuity with him, I had to look at this conference and find legitimacy in it. I knew that making all schools work well in illuminating the minds of all children would have been called redemptive by Martin.

I clung to that belief as in one city after another, black ghettos went up in flames, ignited by hot anger in a tinderbox of broken dreams and deferred hopes. Feeding the flames were decades of police abuse, unemployment, poor education, ragged and ill-kept housing, and feelings of being unwanted everywhere.

Two months later, Robert F. Kennedy was murdered in Los Angeles. America was stretched to her limits. Every imaginable controversy divided the country: the war in Vietnam, women's rights, black rights, gay rights, abortion, school desegregation, and affirmative action.

The setting was perfect for a full swing to the conservative right. Richard Nixon got out his tuxedo and polished up his patent-leather shoes. It was a dark moment for me when Nixon defeated Hubert Humphrey. The threat was always there, in the candidacies of Strom Thurmond, George Wallace, and Barry Goldwater, that the Kennedy-Johnson initiatives would stir up a backlash. In addition, the riots, burnings, lootings, and emergence of violent rhetoric among young black rebels had eroded much of the moral beachhead held by Martin Luther King. Now, all of our friends seemed to disappear, just as they had disappeared in the early 1900s. Our agenda had become too complicated.

CHAPTER SEVEN

America's Moral Parentheses

WITH RICHARD NIXON COMING TO THE WHITE HOUSE, I'D lost my appetite for Washington. Fred Harrington, former president of the University of Wisconsin, was one of the few stalwarts of the 1960s who retained enough idealism to maintain his enthusiasm for liberal causes. In 1968, he and his able assistant, Don McNeil, invited me to join his staff at Wisconsin and to bring my ideas for improving black colleges with me.

The University of Wisconsin would be spearheading a program that would involve all of the Big Ten universities. Their goal was to increase the numbers of minority scientists and professors by strengthening the curriculum and the performance of black colleges. My job was to recruit and graduate a new pool of black

Ph.D.s, which in turn would strengthen the faculties of one hundred black colleges scattered across the South. We planned to graduate a hundred new professors each year. We had financial commitments from government and private foundations for the program.

I accepted Dr. Harrington's offer of a new post, which carried the ambiguous title "University Dean for Special Programs." I landed at Madison in September of 1968, and hit a wall of resentment. Most of the small group of black undergraduates had been recruited from the ghettos of Chicago and Milwaukee to attend that milk-white school, where they felt unwanted—a tiny island in a sea of thirty thousand students of Scandinavian and German descent.

While this trip to college was a release from a depressing and impoverished situation, it seemed to me that no one had told these kids what to expect. A few were so bright and tough-minded that you could have dropped them in Siberia and they would have survived. But for many, their first day in a college class was a shock. They had no faint notion of what their high school diplomas were supposed to have guaranteed them in terms of preparing them for college. In truth, their diplomas from big city schools often amounted to no more than attendance certificates.

The challenge, and the chill—from impolite gestures, hostile glances, and overt questions about their presence—created an adversarial atmosphere. It took very little to convince them that the school was wrong, the teachers were irrelevant, the curriculum was too Eurocentric, and that the school needed to change to accommodate them. Mistakenly, they thought I had been chosen as their new representative, without their consent.

Increasing our discord, the black students wanted to create a black enclave within the university. They demanded distinct and separate programs for blacks only. I agreed that we needed an infusion of African and African-American topics throughout the curriculum, but not solely for black students.

In one effort to be recognized, these students had demanded and received part of the budget for public speakers. One speaker they invited was an ex-gang leader from Washington, D.C., who allegedly spoke for the "black cause."

The student welcoming committee greeted him with pot and coke. By speaking time, he thought he was John the Baptist. It was embarrassing to sit in the auditorium and listen to him talk about "where it was." I already knew where it was! I had been there. It was no mystery. He carried on for half an hour, wild-eyed and thick-tongued. By then, the student committee was calling for him to leave the lectern. They had to mount the platform and usher him, delusional, to the wings. It was absurd that on this campus we had no better interpreter of our complicated social crisis than this young man.

I tried hard to feel what those students felt, but every conversation I had with them revealed a wide chasm between us. The truth was that no group of students could move that huge university to meet their tastes. The students were the ones who would have to change, and many did. The others left in dribbles.

WHITE PEOPLE THOUGHT THAT BLACKS WANTED ONLY A chance to outlive the past and to get caught up with the American dream. They thought it was enough to provide a new opportunity for success. They failed to understand the estrangement and cynicism that accompanied those black students from Chicago's South Side to Madison. Blind to the anger that would follow their academic embarrassment, and unable to see how closely resentment followed charity, no white person appreciated how uncertain these students were about their future. With cooperation on both sides, they could have topped off their weak high school experience with a solid, creative freshman year. But such pragmatism was too much to expect of college planners. The enraged students made one demand after another, some of which were acceptable and incorporated. Others were beyond what a university could do, such as the demand to allow students to hire and fire teachers.

I knew I had a pivotal program in my grasp at Wisconsin, and even in that frenetic crisis, it never occurred to me that I could fail if I applied my best effort. But eventually I was compelled to reconcile myself to the facts. The university experiment was going seriously awry. Constant demonstrations interrupted class schedules, lectures, visiting speakers, and everything else. Every faculty meeting was stopped by someone imposing another new political agenda on us.

Within our family we constantly talked about defeats and victories, mountains and valleys of black fortunes, and we kept before us a barometer of America's moral presence in the world. But while our boys always lived close to public issues, they never lived near bloody street trauma, gunshots, or hand-to-hand combat. They hardly heard any public profanity.

In this atmosphere of social challenge that kept violence in the news and campuses on the alert for student eruptions, Bessie and I tried to make sure the effervescent social climate was interpreted and digestible for our sons.

Our second son, Timothy, was caught as an undergraduate in two massive student revolts—1966 to 1970—first at Yale, and then Wisconsin. He had done his freshman year at Yale, but the student crisis there caused us to take him to Wisconsin with us. In his first year there, between 1968 and 1969, he made almost a 4.0 average and was invited to join the math honors major. The next year the campus was in turmoil. Picket lines, protest marches, boycotts, and rallies made class attendance seem irrelevant.

The fact was that Timothy and many other better educated students were unprepared for the heavy rhetoric and violent gestures that other black students felt were necessary to turn a university around. They were not certain that violent strategies had any real relevance, and felt that the consequences would be counterproductive. They felt frustrated because the mood and tempo defied reason and logic. Many young people did not make it over this terrain. Drugs and dropping out were their only answers. Others found a bulwark at home, a harbor of hope, and families stayed close to see them through.

Timothy continued to live at home. The most conspicuous concession he made to the counterculture was to buy a motorcycle, play the guitar, and grow a large 'fro.

Timothy took advantage of an early admission program to enroll in the joint M.B.A./J.D. program at the University of Chicago, without having to complete the B.A. He scored well on the admissions tests and gave his career a big leap forward. Today he has a very challenging career in corporate law.

MANY AFRICAN-AMERICAN STUDENTS BECAME SO DISILLUSIONED during this time that they began to believe that they would be wiped out if they adapted to American culture or continued to measure success by prevailing standards. They lived in limbo, stranded between fantasies about a new black homeland on the one hand, and unending, irreversible white hostility on the other.

I never felt that way. My own life had been bombarded by the same racist environment, but I had never absorbed it into my personality. I regretted so much that many students became so polarized politically that the inroads they were making into traditionally white universities were lost. I had so many secrets to tell them.

I knew I was not what white society perceived me to be, and I enjoyed proving it. During my darkest hours, I never believed that God had vanished, or that the moral order of the universe was less reliable than the physical order. I believed that justice had its own inherent validity. I believed that change would come if we continued to work at it. Believing these things, I went to church where we celebrated social change as though it were reality.

I had gone to Wisconsin to contribute to creative and systemic change. Instead, with the aborted Democratic convention in Chicago and Nixon's election, the signal went out and the student rebellion and protest gathered force. The 1968–69 student rebellion at Wisconsin was an extension of what was going on at most campuses. The moral ambiguity and confused objectives of the war in Vietnam sickened students; racism was not taken seriously by major institutions, and blacks had to take to the streets risking life and limb to secure rights guaranteed by the Constitution. The quiet power of the rich paralyzed initiatives to redress poverty and marginality.

After a year, it was clear that either the white radicals and black students would close the university, the president would be fired, or the state would call a halt to special programs. Although I remained an unrepentant optimist, over the years I had also become a realist, at least in the sense of being able to gauge the level of public resistance to change.

I left Wisconsin feeling defeated. I was forty-eight, with half of my career behind me. Fortunately, new job offers started coming in during the early weeks of 1969. Dr. John Elder, dean of the graduate school at Harvard, invited me to be an associate dean. I could spend the first year dreaming, speaking, and scheming on how Harvard could reach out to the best and brightest black doctoral candidates. On Sundays, I could preach anywhere I was invited. The Harvard job seemed like a miracle. We had gone where we were needed, and fought battles where we found them. Now my family and I needed a period of stability.

As I was getting ready to accept the job, another offer came from Dr. Mason Gross, president of Rutgers University.

"What would it take to bring you to Rutgers?" he asked. "We want you to settle down and finish your life's work with us. Would you consider an appointment as the Martin Luther King Memorial Professor in the School of Education, with full tenure?" There was no such position, until he thought it up right then.

Heaven was smiling on me. At Rutgers I could write my own courses and teach on my own schedule; in the summers I would be free to write, study, and reflect. Rutgers was situated in the most thickly settled state in the Union, in the epicenter of Boston, Philadelphia, Washington, D.C., and New York. And the appointment was out of the pathway of administration, fund raising, public relations, and budget balancing.

One problem: the Harvard letter of acceptance was in my pocket. How on earth could anyone say no to Harvard? I talked it over with Bessie and our sons. We were all so anxious to settle down after Wisconsin that it did not matter if we went to Cambridge or New Jersey. The two younger boys only wanted to be with us anywhere; and the times of change and challenge that buffeted the lives of the older boys caused them not to worry too much about me. Literally, they trusted in some abstract process that would not let us fail. I prayed a little prayer, and then called Dean Elder and turned down the Harvard appointment, with sincere thanks and deep apologies.

In March 1969, we moved to Rutgers at New Brunswick. Over the next twenty years, that old colonial Dutch Reformed institution that had become New Jersey's state university, spreading out on both sides of the Raritan River, became my home.

I came into the university with tenure, at the top of the line, having had two careers already as president of two schools and a stint with the Kennedy-Johnson crew. I also came in at a time when Rutgers was hunting for blacks who were more than merely certified, but who could bring experience and seasoning to the campus. And, yet, no matter what I was otherwise, I was still black and that meant that I had to prove *everything*.

At Rutgers I was expected to do what I had been doing for several years: help increase the flow of black academics into the graduate school so they in turn could teach and help other black students fulfill their rich potential. Improving the life chances for my people changed the tone and thrust of the school itself. In the next twenty years, over a hundred of my black students graduated with doctoral degrees. Nine are teaching in Mississippi colleges, and three are college presidents in the Northeast.

Time flew. Rutgers was good for me and good to me. It was a privilege to come to work every day, and I could not wait to get into the classroom. It offered me a chance to wrestle with ideas and get to know people who had spent their lives in the pursuit of truth. Our two youngest sons grew up in the shadow of Rutgers. One of our sons did all of his college work there, while the other three did graduate work. I saw Rutgers grow from a small, Ivy League school into a major university with fifty thousand students and fourteen schools, and with the most multicultural faculty and student body found anywhere in the nation.

All of this activity was set against a hostile panorama. In 1971, President Nixon promised the nation that he would *diminish* federal enforcement of school desegregation orders. In 1972, he crushed George McGovern at the polls.

The passive indifference of the Nixon-Agnew days were in sharp contrast to the vigor and clarity of the Johnson years. Our communities were terrorized by waves of violence and the polarization of the races. Police were given a national mandate to allay black street violence, but there was no national mandate to deal with the causes of that violence.

To me, the most shameful behavior during this period was the posture of the white churches and the mean-spirited fundamentalism that was spreading around the country. All across the South sprang up television preachers in silk suits, jewelry dangling from every appendage, and fancy hairdos, a Bible raised in one hand and the other hand gesturing wildly about "born again" religion. The following that grew up around them became diverted into a right-wing political base that opposed "race mixing" in the schools. These preacher-organizers played on the ignorance and fears of their poorly educated parochial followers who never got a chance to hear any other points of view, and they built little power bases on the issue of integration.

Some were able to organize private schools and lure white pupils away from integrating schools. They did this in the name of "morality and Christian principles," and they called their schools "Christian academies."

The country was desperate for leadership, and the need was most heavily felt in the black community. The symbolic leadership of Martin Luther King, Jr., could not be easily reassigned. Roy Wilkins, Whitney Young, Jesse Jackson, and the Black Panthers had their followings, but the rhythm and the cadence did not click. We lost our magnetic pole and became fragmented. However, it never occurred to me that we needed a single leader to drive us forward. We had many dedicated servants devoted to our cause, faithfully at their posts, in every corner of the country.

Despite the diversity of our leadership, the media continued to crave a single spokesperson. The hungry television cameras drew charlatans, opportunists, misguided ideologues, and self-serving sensationalists. Our condition lent itself to easy exploitation, and prompted glib answers to complicated problems. Seizing this opportunity, several universities hired "house conservatives" who used obscure language to insinuate that blacks caused their own problems and deserved to suffer.

To present a so-called "balanced view" the media also paraded a string of unemployed militants who made a living on ranting and raving about separation and black nationalism. Many of these later turned into Reaganites, fundamentalist preachers, local politicians, or "consultants."

The business of manufacturing a leader is tricky. If people insist on having one, they come crawling from under rocks. I believe we should have many leaders, in every field, and in every state and region of the country. There is so much talent, wisdom, and energy out there that it needn't be packaged and delivered to us by the media.

EVERY SUNDAY WAS A PREACHING DAY FOR ME, SOMEWHERE. I had taught ministers in Virginia Union's School of Theology for eleven years; as a result I had alumni scattered all over the black churches in the East, and they called on me continually. I enjoyed having reunions with them and seeing how well they were doing. As a guest speaker I also met pastors up and down the length of the Atlantic Coast and across the country to Chicago, Seattle, San Francisco, and Los Angeles. Every August I was invited to preach at the magnificent Riverside Church and at small storefront churches in Harlem. I found myself as much at home in Brooklyn's fabulous Concord Baptist pulpit as in a white congregation's clapboard church on a hillside in rural Virginia.

Despite the social upheaval of the time, my religious ideas and social concerns remained intact. But I never spoke about current events, unless I first processed the information through my own experience. No matter where I spoke or the nature of the occasion, my authority was rooted in three principal biblical sources: the monumental eighth century Jewish prophets (Micah, Amos, and Isaiah), the life and teachings of Jesus, and in Paul's understanding of the transforming power of Christ as the object of one's faith.

I never asked my audiences to leave their minds outside when they came into church, and I never felt obliged to preach about *everything* I read in the Bible. Some of it reflects a world that is flat, with a burning hell underneath and a jeweled heaven above. Some of it reflects a primitive view of women, killing, slavery, and war that is far short of Jesus' teachings. Our world was much too complex for simple dogma.

I kept busy speaking across the country, and into Asia and Europe. I also spoke to employee groups at giant corporations and even at the CIA, the state department, and the agriculture department. In the late 1960s and early 1970s, these audiences were almost always composed of white men. I never attacked like a junkyard dog, and never wanted to leave a room filled with angry people. I always wanted to leave it filled with people resolved to do something for change, however small. I viewed these talks as teaching opportunities. Many white college graduates were immune to informed, thoughtful dialogue about controversial topics. They seemed to have been rehearsed to find the conventional views on everything and stay pat.

The invitations to speak came from people appointed by their companies to be "human resources" administrators, equal opportunity directors, or affirmative action programmers. In the wake of the riots and new federal initiatives, such men were found in every major corporation. I could never tell who was genuinely committed and who was merely a hireling going through the motions, but I always appreciated the audiences. It was our only chance at some of these bright people, so I never passed up a corporate opportunity.

With Nixon in the White House and Clarence Thomas in charge of the Equal Employment Opportunities Commission, we didn't expect much, but we kept pitching. Once, while speaking to the agriculture department's super grades, in a room filled exclusively with white men, a well-dressed black man carrying a large alligator briefcase entered, wearing a sharply pressed sharkskin suit, with conspicuously matching tie and pocket handkerchief. I asked his name. He answered, then added that he was the "equal opportunity officer" for the agency. His job purportedly was to encourage the hiring of more women, blacks, and other minorities—but he was the only visible outcome of his efforts. He had used up his whole office on himself!

That's what it was like then. The approach in Washington was to hire blacks who did not support government intervention in racial matters. Benign neglect was Nixon's policy, and it took root.

When we read about Richard Nixon's values, it's enough to make you weep. Only days after his death in May of 1994, H. R. Haldeman's White House diary was published. Haldeman revealed that Nixon resented the Jewish "domination" of the media and said that Billy Graham had told him that the Bible referred to "satanic Jews."

Nixon reserved his worst comments for blacks who, he said, were the only people who had never had a great nation and were the "whole problem." He wanted to eliminate welfare because it "forced poor whites onto the same level as blacks."

The president of the United States was a Quaker who graduated from Whittier College and Duke Law School, but he did not know any black lawyers, writers, clergy, or university professors with whom he could communicate. Howard University was only ten minutes from 1600 Pennsylvania Avenue, but Nixon ignored that rich resource of scholars who had spent a lifetime studying issues that affected the whole country, and instead relied on his "Uncle Tom" sycophants and a television evangelist for information.

ONE OF MY FAVORITE PLACES TO PREACH ON SUNDAYS WAS the Abyssinian Baptist Church of Harlem. Black Baptists had established the church in lower Manhattan in 1808, when Thomas Jefferson was president, and named it in honor of some visiting Ethiopian (Abyssinian) seamen whose ship was berthed in the port of New York.

Dr. Adam Clayton Powell, Sr., who became pastor in 1908, brought a passion for social justice and personal renewal to the church. Under his stewardship this modest-sized black church moved to Harlem in the 1920s, and became one of the largest Protestant congregations in the world, with a membership well over its current seven thousand. The church became a social service agency as well as a vital religious center.

In 1938, the pastorate passed to Dr. Powell's son, Adam Clayton Powell, Jr. By virtue of his huge personal popularity as Abyssinian's pastor, Adam was elected to the city council in 1941, at the age of thirty-two. Four years later he was elected to the United States Congress, where he served for fourteen terms. Such heavy responsibilities pulled him away from church duties, and I was often asked to fill the pulpit in Powell's absence.

Powell had reached out for me before. In 1962, when I was in Nigeria, he cabled me through the state department and asked me to head up one of the antipoverty social agencies in Harlem. His telegram sounded so urgent that everyone at the post offered regrets that I was leaving. Shriver hit the ceiling when he learned that Powell was trying to steal his staff! But that was Powell's style: he was direct and bold, and let other people do the adjusting.

Someone once said that Powell's attention span was ninety seconds, and that seemed to be the truth, because he had no patience with pedantry, literal- or closed-mindedness, perfunctory traditionalism, or superficiality. He wanted conversations to get to the point fast. He lived in a hurry and he always had an important goal in front of him.

Powell was both feared and hated by the established political machines. At the height of his congressional career in the 1950s and 1960s, he chaired the powerful Committee on Education and Labor, from which he successfully piloted sixty-seven pieces of social and economic reform legislation. Working for Sargent Shriver, I had to testify for our legislation on several occasions before Powell's committee. He and his staff were truly formidable.

Adam Powell allowed few people into his inner circle, and he required unquestioned loyalty and confidentiality. His private life stayed private. But his inability to trust and delegate to his aides limited his leadership. My own dealings with him were very sketchy. We first met when I was a college student and a chauffeur for the president of Virginia Union. I had to meet Adam when he arrived at Richmond's Main Street train station, a segregated facility. He did not walk through the "colored" waiting room, but strode boldly through the main lobby for whites only.

He was a gifted, spell-binding orator, who could get furious over matters of injustice. I'll never forget when he spoke in our college chapel in 1941, shortly after his election to the city council. "I can't stand conservative Negroes," he said. "They don't have a damn thing to conserve!" I have never forgotten how vehement he was when he said that.

His sermons were usually on issues of civil rights and racial pride. He has never been fully credited with the contributions he made, because he was not a collaborator, never a gregarious glad-hander, and always operated alone. His blunt, straightforwardness was often taken as arrogance, but it was the result of the fact that he lived in a pressure cooker.

In 1969, he lost his seat in Congress to Charles Rangel. His health declined, and he spent most of his time in Bimini, his favorite retreat, to escape public view. In 1971, the church requested that he either resign, retire, or return. When Powell failed to respond, they declared the position of pastor vacant. Adam Powell died in April of that same year.

The church officers of the Abyssinian Baptist Church asked me to deliver his eulogy. Adam's funeral filled the two-thousand-seat sanctuary and the entire block from Seventh to Lenox on 138th Street. Most people did not even know that he was no longer pastor when he died, and I conducted the funeral as though he were.

A few months later, I was asked to accept the pastorate. I I really had not anticipated beginning a new chapter in my life at age fifty-one. Our two older sons were away in school and the two younger boys were settled in their schools in New Jersey. We could not envision moving to Manhattan and starting life all over again. But it did seem important to help Abyssinian regain her posture.

I accepted the pastorate on the condition that I would continue my work at Rutgers and share church duties with other staff ministers. We continued to live in New Jersey, and I shared the pastor's salary with an extra assistant pastor.

Bessie had made such a smooth adjustment to two new sons after thirteen years, moving from America to Africa, back to Washington, to Greensboro, to Washington again, to New York, to Washington, to Wisconsin, to New Jersey—commuting to New York (thirty miles on the New Jersey Turnpike) three times a week was a snap. We sang and joked through the nagging commuting like it was recess time.

It was a constant, nagging tug on me to try to replicate Adam. He was brought to the church as an infant in 1908 and had been nowhere but there until 1971. Everyone in the church grew up with him. It would have been nonsense to imitate him. Powell was larger than life, obsessed with the concerns of the last, the lowest, and the least. His political articulation set in motion a spirit of courage and commitment that became the ignition for the entire civil rights movement.

Still, the church was warm and cooperative, and my family and I felt wanted and appreciated. Some wanted the church to remain a political center; but when I was appointed, it was clear that I would leave political offices to others and make my contribution in other ways. My training and experience were far better applied to a teaching-preaching service than to one as a New York politician who knew nothing about New York. As always, I set my priorities and my pattern of work with God's guidance.

Soon, Abyssinian was home to us. Smiling, talkative women,

friendly and supportive officers, an appreciative handclapping, singing, and responding congregation. And the excitement of Harlem was such a consuming atmosphere that it was like a new life.

All the while that I worked at the church and the university, I felt enriched by both. Religion and education are symbiotic. Each energizes the other, and I benefited greatly from two incomparable growth opportunities.

MEANWHILE, MY COURSES AT RUTGERS DREW LARGE numbers. It took personal courage for black graduate students to withstand the wintry stares of white campuses like Rutgers when they first began to enroll, and consequently students I had recruited thought of me as a big brother. I had taught many of their parents, pastors, coaches, and former teachers, and they were always baffled that no matter how remote their hometown, I could name someone they had known back home. They crowded into my tiny office as if it were a lifeboat.

Through my door came a steady flow of black students wanting to unload their problems and frustrations. Some distrusted all blacks over forty, and thought people like me were too well off to be of any use in the struggle. My brand of optimism met a cool reception in many quarters. Here we are, I thought, with much of the worst terrain already crossed, and I can't convince my African-American graduate students that the glass is half full. I would tell them how my brothers scuffled through medical and dental school, and how my son was battling his way through law school. They shrugged off these examples and called them "bourgeois." I reminded them that presently we were not loved by those in charge, and we couldn't afford to call each other names. Certainly we couldn't afford to call all educated and successful blacks "bourgeoisie," because we had to make hard work and success attractive.

One of my less committed students came to class one evening walking a large, dirty white dog on a frayed rope pieced together from fragments. The dog was happy to be in a warm room on a cold night and most students gave it a pat or a scratch on the neck, but a few moved their chairs away from the dog and its ill-kempt master.

I got that student's message: he wasn't going to take me or the course seriously. I asked the class how many had dogs. Almost every hand went up. I asked if they felt entitled to bring their dogs to class if this student could bring his. They agreed that they did. I asked if we could all concentrate if everyone who had a dog brought it to class.

They shouted, "No."

I asked the student to tie the dog outside the door or leave the class, and told him that any similar incidents in the future would earn him an absent mark; if he missed a fourth of the sessions, the course credit would automatically be denied.

He called me a czar, a tyrant, and worse. Afterward, he told me that I was following "white" standards which did not fit blacks. I said that our experiences were indeed different, but blacks and whites shared the larger areas of human concourse and that most life behavior had no racial tag. I meant it.

One of my white students entered an elevator that I was in already, and I removed my hat. "Dr. Proctor," she said, "why in hell did you take your hat off when I got on the elevator? You're living in the Victorian age." She laughed congenially.

"If you'll get off the elevator with me for a moment, I'll tell you." At my stop, we both stepped off.

"I'm not a Victorian," I said, "but some things stay in place from one generation to another, and certain manners stand for values that I hold dear. I believe that a society that ceases to respect women is on its way out. Women bear and raise our children, they are bound to them in early infancy; they need our support and security through this process. When we forget that, the keystone of family and home is lost. When we neglect and abuse women, the family falls apart and children are less well parented, and they fill up the jails and are buried in early graves. I believe that respect for women is the linchpin of the family and the society. Therefore, when you entered the elevator, I wanted you to have automatic, immediate, unqualified assurance that if the elevator caught fire, I would help you out through the top first. If a strange man boarded and began to slap you around and tear your clothes off, he would have to kill me first. If the elevator broke down and stopped between floors, I would not leave you in here. If you fainted and slumped to the floor, I would stop everything and get you to a hospital. Now, it would take a lot of time to say all of that, so when I removed my hat, I meant all of the above."

Tears sprang to her eyes. There are some values that abide. They have no racial or ethnic label. It took a lot to convince students that equality was possible, but we had first to define the optimum human condition and call *everyone* to embrace it.

Some of my students were incredibly successful. One day a book salesman from San Francisco came by my office to introduce his company's latest publications. I interrupted his singsong sales pitch to ask him a few basic questions about himself: "Where were you born? Are your parents living? Are you married? Where did you go to school? Did you play sports? How did you get this job? Is this your future? What would you rather be doing?"

His patience ran out. "If you must know," he said, "I want to be an orthopedic surgeon. What are you going to do about it?"

"I'm not sure yet. But you don't look like a salesman to me. Maybe we can get you off this book route and on your way to medical school. What were your grades like in science?"

He was stunned. "My grades were good, but I left college to play pro basketball. I didn't make it, so here I am."

I sent him over to our medical school to talk with Dr. Harold

Logan who could evaluate his chances for entering Rutgers. We had so few successful black applicants for medical school that I thought it was worth a try. Dr. Logan gave him the third degree and asked other faculty to talk with him. Then he struck a deal: if the young salesman would quit his job, enter summer school right then, make top grades in microbiology and invertebrate zoology, they would let him in on probation. In the fall, he would have to pass the regular admissions tests.

Four years later, I spoke at his commencement in the Garden State Art Center. An elderly professor from the medical school came to me after the exercises and thanked me for sending that student to them. Today, Dr. Michael Charles is one of the most popular sports orthopedic specialists in the San Francisco Bay Area. There is a catalogue of people like him whom I had the pleasure of knowing as students and who kept my faith alive that we were indeed capable of erasing the stereotype, reversing the bad data, and securing justice in America. I found recruiting and graduating a steady stream of doctoral students from Rutgers a source of pure delight.

I HAD MY OWN SPIRITUAL TRAIN GOING FROM THE CLASSROOM to the church, carrying lessons back and forth between the two. And the messages were always compatible. One Sunday morning, soon after I took over at Abyssinian, the deaconesses (wives of deacons who volunteer for special functions) said that several parents had brought their babies to be dedicated to God. While Baptists baptize only those old enough to acknowledge their faith for themselves, we also commit the church to serve and care for infants.

I went into the room where parents and infants were waiting and looked over the cards with the names of the four babies and their parents and godparents. I tried to match each baby's name with the tiny, round faces and jeweled eyes gazing at me with grave suspicion from under pretty lace bonnets. I noticed that two infants had the same last names as their mothers, but different from the fathers who were present. I asked those two fathers to step outside with me. We left the deaconesses and other parents looking puzzled and confused.

Apparently there had been a tacit agreement not to challenge these unmarried fathers who showed up to stand beside the mothers of their infants. It was another concession made to a declining order of things, and a statement to the whole community that a young man could impregnate a young woman and walk off without responsibility.

I took the two men into my study. "Brothers," I said, "are you the fathers of these children?"

"Yes."

"Do you intend to marry?"

They were not sure.

"Do you want the whole church to know that you are the father?"

They did.

"Do you want me to tell the congregation that you're not married and have no plans to marry?"

They did not.

"Do you have other children, either in our church or somewhere else?"

One did.

"Are that mother and child present today?"

"I don't know."

"If they were, how would they feel seeing you here with another unmarried mother and a new baby? What should we do if you come back six months from now and stand with another unwed mother and child?"

They both looked at the floor sheepishly. It hurt me to turn them away, but how could I stand in church and approve a practice that was destroying our families and communities? It was one

thing to present an infant and mother to God. It was another to
ask the church to celebrate casually a father who assumed no responsibility for parenting.

I told the two men that they could sit near the front of the
church with other worshipers, but the infant dedication service
would take place without them. I offered to counsel them, at
their convenience, about marriage, schoolwork, or whatever else
they wanted to talk about.

In the same way that popular culture can have a negative influence on education, it can also creep into the church and play
havoc with our basic life values. Some of us have become so
compromised that the rest of us have to be doubly certain that
our institutions protect our gains, and continue to prepare us
for a higher quality of life.

At Abyssinian we saw life in all of its extremities. We saw people whose devotion and steadiness would put the rest of us to
shame. They gave and served without thought of return. We saw
single mothers rear children and send them off to college. And
we also saw intelligent men and women throw away their values,
their goals, and their futures to drug dealers who had no con-
science at all.

One day our membership secretary, Esther McCall, noticed
an unusual-looking envelope in the mail addressed "To the
church pastors." There was no return address, so Esther set aside
the envelope. Over the next couple of weeks, several more came
in, addressed the same way. We received our share of crank mail,
and Esther simply let the envelopes accumulate. The pile grew
so large that she finally opened the envelopes before tossing
them in the trash. Inside, she found bank cashier's checks, postal
money orders, and commercial money orders made out to the
church. More and more envelopes came in until the total value
amounted to $48,000. We opened a special escrow account and
held the money in limbo. Since the source was still unknown, we
decided that eventually we would use the money for our youth

sports program.

One afternoon one of our three sextons announced that a huge black Mercedes-Benz with smoked windows had pulled up out front. A man emerged from the car wearing a black leather jacket, diamonds on both hands and in one ear, gold around his neck and wrists, and expensive alligator-skin boots.

We activated our little security system: one sexton stayed out in the lobby to be free to run for help; one stayed at the telephone in the office next to mine, with the door cracked, to listen for trouble and call the police if necessary; and the biggest one sat in front of my office door, keeping track of the conversation.

The visitor spoke softly. "I'm the one who sent the money," he said. "I got it in the streets and I want to do some good."

Then he began to tremble and, wiping tears from his eyes, beneath his dark glasses, he asked me how he could make a new start in life. He sounded like a drug dealer. He said that if he turned his back on his "associates," he would have to leave the city.

I told him that he would be better off leaving. Staying here he had no life anyway, and he was destroying other lives every day. We prayed together. He squeezed my hand with a kind of finality, and backed slowly out the door without even telling me his name.

Later, a relative of his called and asked us to write a letter to the parole board explaining what a benevolent and charitable person our mystery man was. The caller told us his name. But we couldn't write the letter he wanted. We could acknowledge only that he had made anonymous gifts to the church over a six-month period, but other than that we knew nothing about him. We asked the caller to stay in touch with us, or have the dealer call us, but we never heard from either of them again.

OTHERS FROM AMONG THE DISPOSSESSED CAME TO US. FOR many years it was my habit before Sunday service to enter the sanctuary and walk down the long side aisle against the wall to the deacons' room. The first time I took that walk I passed by a family seated on the aisle: three neatly dressed middle-aged women, a man who could have been brother or husband to one of them, and a young man with Down's syndrome. I couldn't guess his age. He was very stylishly dressed, and seated securely between them.

He looked up at me with shock. I was wearing a black gown with scarlet arm bars, and a scarlet paneled hood lined with my school colors. It was a colorful get-up. He fixed his gaze on my face. I think he was looking for Adam Powell, who had been 6 foot 4, weighed around 210 pounds, and was fair-complexioned with straight black hair. I was 5 foot 10, 190 pounds, ginger-colored, and had short, matted hair. He stared hard.

To reassure him, I gave him a wide smile and a soft pluck on the head. He beamed. The next Sunday when I came down the same aisle, he raised up in his seat and leaned his head toward me; I gave him a little tighter, stronger pluck. Every Sunday after that, I had to give him that little sacredotal, ecclesiastical, liturgical pluck! It may not have meant much to anyone else, but his world was small and uneventful, and few things happened to accentuate his presence. What seemed negligible to others was highly significant to him.

The church filled the vacuum for blacks in so many ways. What was left out of their lives all week long was supplied by the church on the Lord's day. Those who did not register as important in the secular world found that they mattered greatly in God's house.

This was especially true for women. All week long, black women were on the bottom—beneath black men, white women, and white men. On weekdays they were somebody's cook, typist, nanny, file clerk, maid, housekeeper, nurse, or office helper.

But on Sunday they were in charge. Hardly anything happens in the black church without the support and sponsorship of women. Finally, they are moving into the pulpit. Hallelujah!

Black women are enrolled in seminaries in strong numbers. When they are allowed to preach, their success is remarkable. Sadly, however, among Baptists, where most blacks are affiliated, some pastors still argue against women preaching.

Recently, I listened to a group of pastors talking about excluding women from the clergy because Jesus did not have women as disciples. Well, Jesus did not marry, either, so all pastors should be single and celebrate, and the married ones fired. His disciples didn't have college degrees, so ministers today should go directly to ordination without stopping by the Ivy Leagues. His disciples were not salaried, and had no pensions or health benefits. That calls for some changes, too. Neither did they speak English, and all were Jews. This excludes all English-speaking pastors who are Gentiles.

It would be odd indeed for God to create men and women equally, and then reveal God's truth only to males. Historically the black church has been our great liberating agent, and it is past time to liberate its women completely.

At Abyssinian a wonderful female seminary student joined our staff, and when she graduated we decided to ordain her in our church. The church called a council of sixty ministers to examine her for ordination, but only three showed up. Since the council is only advisory among Baptists, and since we had the authority to ordain whether a council met or not, the three ministers conducted the examination and Reverend Sharon Williams was ordained. She remained to serve on our staff for a brief time, and then was called to a Brooklyn parish where she still serves successfully.

The woman I remember best from Abyssinian was not a seminary student, but a worshiper who occasionally came to church a little inebriated. One Sunday morning I was rolling on in my sermon about how Jesus had a circle of friends that we wouldn't want to be seen with—harlots, poor people, the demon possessed, and those with leprosy and lame limbs. His friends were the lost, the least, the last, and the left-out. "We prefer to have friends who are the first, the finest, and the foremost," I said. "If Jesus gave a party, you all would not even want to go!"

This lady screamed from the balcony, "That's a damn lie. I would go to Jesus' party."

"I know you would," I called back. "You would go to anybody's party!"

Yet I relied on her presence—and those like her—every Sunday morning. When our fortunes were reversed, when the backlash confused our hopes, we all needed the church more than ever to keep us on track. The church held us together and warmed our hearts. The church provided sanctuary and rest for all those who were heavy laden: "Whosoever will, come!"

SEVERAL YEARS LATER, IN APRIL OF 1984, COUNT BASIE'S widow asked me to deliver the eulogy for her husband's funeral at our church. The Count was a highly regarded member of the black community, a good neighbor in St. Albans, Queens, and a family man who had lived in the same house with the same wife for forty years. Mrs. Basie could never guess what I was thinking about. In the first place, I never believed Count Basie could die, he was bigger than life to me. And second, in a way he had helped pay my way through college.

When I had been a sixteen-year-old student at Virginia State College, twelve of my classmates and I had a little jazz band. On weekends we each made seven dollars a night playing around town and at the officers' club at Fort Lee. While I stumbled through my solos with pedantic stiffness, our pianist, seventeen-year-old Billy Taylor, sparkled with precocious virtuosity at the keyboard. I spent hours trying to learn the alto saxophone riff in Basie's "One O'Clock Jump," which was our main number.

As awkward as my playing was, "One O'Clock Jump" was good enough to keep us working and we went wild with that song three or four times a night. Now, many years later, the great Count Basie was being buried out of the church where I was pastor and I felt a deep emotional stirring.

On the day of the funeral, the church was packed with twenty-five hundred people. Mrs. Basie had asked some of her husband's old buddies to say a few words of tribute, but when they got to carrying on, things got morose. Those who had been helped by the Count when they had been down on their luck wouldn't give up the microphone. They kept on groaning and crying and calling the name of the deceased in grateful remembrance. I finally got up the nerve to point to Billy Taylor, who was sitting in the front row. Yes, the same Billy Taylor who had played in our little college jazz band. Without any hesitation, one of the finest jazz pianists in the world stood up and went over to our grand piano.

The church was packed with musicians. "Please learn a little song for our dear and beloved Count Basie," I said. "It has only three verses, one line each, and you repeat it four times." Our organist, Dr. Jewel Thompson, played the tune through once and I spoke the words.

> Woke up this morning,
> With my mind stayed on Jesus. ♪♫

Halleluh, Halleluh, Hallelu-u-jah!

Well, this great audience of jazz artists took hold of this little tune. With Dr. Thompson on our five-manual, 67-rank Schantz organ, Billy Taylor on the grand piano, the world's best harmonizers, improvisers, and rhythm artists sang those words to a sassy Basie beat, rocking and clapping hands, heads tilted up, eyes closed, and tears streaming down their cheeks.

Then the tall, slender balladeer Joe Williams, wearing a blue blazer and gold slacks, signifying a happy mood for a homegoing celebration, floated down the aisle with his toothy smile, slapped Billy on the knee and said, "Duke's 'Come Sunday,' in E flat."

Billy swung into the song, and those unfamiliar with the *élan vital* of the black church didn't know what had hit them. They had one dramatic introduction to the kind of spiritual uplift and revitalization black people use as a respite from the degradation and disgust that life dumps on them every day. Since the earliest days of slavery, in an unbroken refrain, we have been singing the songs of Zion in a strange land.

CHAPTER EIGHT

Crisis!

━━

ONE MORNING IN A POUNDING RAINFALL I DROVE MY TWO younger sons to their schools. A heavy curtain of water was blinding us, and I planned to carry them right up to the school doors. But the youngest insisted that I stop the car and let him out before we reached his junior high. After we left him on the corner, I asked his older brother why he was so adamant about getting out in the rain.

"He didn't want the other kids to see that he had a daddy who would drive him to school," he said.

Among many blacks in the school, especially among his peers, it was assumed that your daddy, if you had one at all, was missing. The children had romanticized the absent father, along with the other deficits of poverty and school failure. The year was 1975, but it might have been today.

When I saw this attitude in my son's all-American school in a middle-class neighborhood, it wasn't hard to imagine what was happening to our children growing up in urban slums. Faced with empty hours and detached loyalties, they see themselves rejected by everyone, even their own families. It is hard to stand erect and pledge allegiance when you are hungry, poor, and overlooked. Like their ancestors, there seems to be no future for these kids. In these mean streets, alienated teenage fathers walk away from their children, teenage mothers continue to bear children, young men maul elderly women for their Social Security checks, and rob schools of typewriters and computers to get money for drugs. They have given up on the future.

These young people did not choose the chronic poverty, the total social rejection, begrudging educational opportunities offered them, and denial of a fair chance at employment. They are stranded—in the streets, in jail, and stretched out in mortuaries and morgues.

These sad facts are largely the legacy of Ronald Reagan, combined with leaps in technology that caused anyone who was poorly educated to lose all hope of a decent job. Then, under Bush, we drank the bitterest dregs of contempt in the appointment of Judge Clarence Thomas to the Supreme Court. This cut deeper than can easily be imagined. We knew that Bush was a conservative politician, but we never thought that he would insult black people by placing on the highest court of the land a person who had so blatantly operated for his own personal comfort at the expense of his people.

Against this backdrop of national events, life went on. During the 1980s my third son, Sammy, entered Yale University. But when he got there, he and the other black students did not feel welcome. As a result, many of them shunned school organizations that white students controlled. Sammy was a computer science and economics major, but he did not join the computer science club or the economics club. Instead, he signed up for the all-black glee club, the black chapel group, and the black social services organization.

Sammy could have gone to other colleges closer by, or to one of the black schools in the South. But he wanted what he considered the strongest academic challenge. He had heard about the cold social climate on campuses, yet he found it strange when he was largely ignored by white students and faculty. So Bessie and I tooled up again to provide the auxiliary support system that he needed to get through. We did, and he did.

Countless black families all over the country found that the euphoria of having their son or daughter admitted to Yale, Wellesley, or Mount Holyoke was soon dimmed by the reality of late-night calls and rebellion against Anglo-cultural presuppositions. Many of these young people who had been warmly affirmed at home and heralded as successes and role models in their communities found themselves numbered among the "disadvantaged," the "diverse," the "high risk" and the "equal opportunity" students. This was true even for those who had no financial aid, high SAT scores, and a strong academic average.

Their families had to function as emergency first aid counselors, helping good kids negotiate the treacherous waters of Ivy League schools during a time of transition. It was all novel and unprecedented. They were making leaps to distance themselves from the stereotype that followed blacks like a shadow from slavery into the late twentieth century.

In addition to giving support to our four sons and trying to maintain the success of black graduate students at Rutgers, I was doing my best to be the spiritual leader of Abyssinian's large urban congregation. Its huge Gothic edifice stood in stark contrast with much of its surrounding community. Housing was rundown, and the neighborhood bore the scars and bruises of a defeated people.

Once the membership of the church had come from the neighborhood, but as their fortunes improved, they moved to Westchester, the Bronx, Queens, North Jersey, and Long Island. Now every Sunday, well-dressed, well-educated blacks who had moved out of the neighborhood paraded back to their shrine, bedecked in furs and jewelry and effusing exotic fragrances. It would be easy to call them snobs, or elitists, or something worse. It wasn't so obvious that most of them had grown up doing manual, farm, or domestic labor, shining shoes, hauling freight, and cleaning hotel rooms and hospital wards. They had gone to school, taken whatever jobs were available, saved money slowly, bought homes, educated their children, and stayed firm in their belief that they could make it in America.

By contrast, the people living in the surrounding ghetto were defending what little pride they had left. Despite their destitution and isolation, they wanted to claim their own standing in the world. In a sense, they looked at the church people as enemies—those *other* people. The church continued to reach out to them, though—through any means we could.

The great choir at Abyssinian was under the gifted leadership of Dr. Leon E. Thompson, music education director of the New York Philharmonic. Dr. Jewel Taylor Thompson, one of the country's finest exponents of liturgical music, was our organist. The choir performed with both the New York Philharmonic and the Boston Pops, as well as making many other special appearances. With such a magnificent choir the congregation decided to make a huge effort to purchase a spectacular new organ. The base price was $250,000.

One afternoon the church secretary buzzed me in my study and announced that a group of young men wanted to see me. They didn't have an appointment, but I told her to send them on in. About six or seven of them shouldered their way through the door, dressed in faded dungarees, leather jackets, and T-shirts with violent slogans printed across the chest.

"Sit down, gentlemen," I said.

"We don't need to get so damn comfortable," their obvious leader said. "We're here on the peoples' business and all we want is some answers from you."

He proceeded to chastise me for buying an expensive organ for a Harlem church in a neighborhood where 250,000 hungry blacks lived.

"Let me propose a deal," I said. "Suppose we give up the organ and instead we give you the $250,000. You can give a dollar to each of those 250,000 people. McDonald's runs ninety-nine-cent specials; and each one could get one small hamburger, one small bag of French fries, and one small Coke. Four hours later, each person will be hungry again. We won't have an organ, the money will be gone, and you'll be back in here begging. Does that make sense?"

The tight-jawed youths just stared at me. I continued, "Now, the people in this church who saved the money to buy this organ started out poor, too, but they were lucky enough to have patient and caring teachers, and parents who loved them. Even so, nobody here inherited any money and they all worked hard all of their lives. They want to keep pace with the dreams of their parents and grandparents who started with even less, but who praised God in the beauty of holiness. This organ is their testimony of thanksgiving and praise. They didn't ask anyone to buy it for them.

"More important, these people are *organ listeners*. They sit here every Sunday and hear that great instrument copy every sound of nature—the rolling thunder, the wind whistling through the trees, and the thrush singing a love song. The music cleanses their spirits, drives out ugly thoughts, puts wings on their prayers and wafts them heavenward. Oh, yes! The organ *works* for them! They can go out of here and find a job, do it well, get paid, and eat on time. They are not hungry. They have an organ in their lives!"

I admit, when I have an audience, it's hard to stop me.

"Now, here you are, unemployed yourselves, representing hungry people. None of you is an organ listener. So I suggest that you get out of here; go and round up the 250,000 hungry constituents that you claim to represent. And bring them over here every Sunday morning and let us make organ listeners out of them. They won't be hungry long. They will change from within; and that change will be a prelude to change without. Eventually, personal hunger will not be their concern. They will be full enough themselves to start worrying about the hunger of children in Africa and Asia and Latin America, and the hunger of the elderly poor right here. My soul! Organ listeners have strange behavior."

The young men left my study, mumbling. They left behind an indelible portrait of a community in crisis. The time had come when one approach to the future had clashed head on with the other. Those propelled by the faith that we can make it here were making it come to pass. And those for whom racist intransigence was too rigid and endemic, poverty too burdensome, political indifference too powerful, and resources too shallow were wallowing in the muck and mire. They had run out of answers and their circle of options was narrowing.

This had been a creeping trend, but by the 1980s, it had reached a crisis level. When substantial opportunities for minorities opened up in the 1960s and '70s, and when the job market simultaneously became more demanding of literacy skills and mathematics, blacks with education seized their new opportunities and began to put a new face on America. Although large numbers were finding their way into better education, better jobs, better health, better homes, and enhanced general well-being, it turned out to be largely an individual matter, and the massive bottom failed to rise.

This social paradox has wrought havoc in the black community. Some people are now so angry that they want to turn their backs completely on the white world. While this is basically impractical, it *feels* like action and deludes many young people into giving up on any concentrated, sustained hard effort. Just a few young people in this frame of mind can wreck a classroom and poison the atmosphere of a whole school.

When people have no functional relationship to the larger society, when their options are cut off, frustration builds, and the time is then ripe for ideologues and false messiahs to emerge with fantasies about race, culture, and destiny. Meanwhile, illegal hustling, crime, drugs, suicide, and homicide become the only game in town. It seems easy to target achievement-oriented blacks as the enemy. Any black person, it follows, who is successful in any field must have sold out.

It's far from clear what would happen to us today if we assumed a cultural insularity similar to small groups like the Hasidic Jews or the Amish, for example, which—on the surface, at least—appear to maintain separate islands in a sea of Americana. However, their communities abound with compromises and contradictions.

The Hasidim benefit daily from values generated by the larger, multicultural political institutions: freedom of religion, freedom of speech, and freedom of assembly. They enjoy the Protestant legacy of separation of church and state, without which they could never exist here. So, while they appear to live in an insular community, the whole society blesses them.

The Amish keep their children out of public schools, and arbitrarily deny them a chance for university education. Yet that same community depends on ophthalmologists, veterinarians, meteorologists, physicians, dentists, engineers, pilots, judges, and the United States Army to service their needs. It's a gross contradiction to reject formal education and then count on its benefits being available every day.

The idea of 25 million blacks going it alone in America is fantasy. Moreover, what moral basis have we for trying to separate from the society in which our forebears invested so much? We cannot undo the past four hundred years and divest ourselves of all the cultural accretions we have absorbed and invented.

We African Americans do have a distinct culture of our own, comprising African residuals, strategies for surviving slavery and segregation, plus an abiding determination to live out the promise of the Declaration of Independence. Why would anyone want to erase a culture that has been so hard-won and for which such enormous sacrifices have been made? It is the honest outcome of our struggles.

To replace it, we would have to expend our meager resources to construct a new infrastructure in a separate place, new economy, and a new civics of our own. Even if we did, what guarantee do we have that we would thus escape racism?

This schism in the black community is a crisis of the first order. The Afrocentric movement causes young blacks to behave tentatively and thus lose important ground. So much attention is paid to the cosmetic aspects of living—dress, hairstyles, music, diet, art, social gestures—that the main requirements for survival—economic independence, career preparation, sound health, stable families—are often left in fragments.

I find myself searching for a metaphor exact enough to embrace all of our African roots, and at the same time accept that we are fully involved in this nation's life and destiny.

I have a Native American friend who similarly grieves over the tentative outcome of his people. They were driven from their land and forced into the mountains and deserts where no one else could survive. Without a long-term strategy, they have somehow managed to scrape by on a minimal economy and government grants. It's a haunting, dehumanizing set of facts to pass on to one's grandchildren, and the future does not promise change. What choices might they have made that would have changed the outcome? What choices do they now have?

Whatever strategy they devise to participate in America's future must also honor their past. Is it possible?

THE CRISIS IS UPON US. ON THE NIGHT OF AUGUST 30, 1994, a young black bandit broke into the home of Rosa Parks on Detroit's west side, cuffed her around, and threatened to kill her if she did not give him all of her money. He left the 80-year-old civil rights heroine badly bruised and semiconscious. He had brought to that moment the whole package of poor rearing, poor education, and poor jobs. Added to that impoverishment was a poor self-image and an inadequate response to his plight. He is part of the crisis.

The crisis comes with hopelessness. The crisis grows as frustrated blacks fall behind in school and become comfortable with failure and nihilism. Their violence and adversarial posturing are childish responses to their confusion.

Next, the crisis breeds half truths, spurious anthropology, historical hearsay, and propaganda. Finally, the crisis spirals ever upward as racists grab each opportunity to amplify all the bad news.

The news is loaded with the trial of O.J. Simpson and the collapse of leadership in the NAACP. Right-wing talk show hosts and specialists in cocktail party repartee chew on these juicy items that confirm their private hopes and expectations of black failure. The crisis is upon us.

Here is a story of the crisis. On September 7, 1994, a small-framed black child lay in a wooden casket in a black church in Chicago. His schoolfriends passed by in numb silence, looking on his corpse with awe and fear. His grandmother cried hysterically.

Little Robert "Yummy" Sandifer seemed to be doomed from the outset. His father was in prison, and his mother, the third of ten children from four different fathers, was a drug addict. She was fifteen when she had her first child. Now, at age twenty-nine, she had five children besides Yummy. And forty-one arrests for mostly prostitution.

Yummy had been arrested over and over as a child offender and had already spent time in detention centers. He cursed out adults, beat up kids bigger than he, extorted money from frightened neighbors, broke into schools to steal money, and stole cars. He died at age eleven, having already been charged with twenty-three felonies and five misdemeanors. Two weeks before his death, during a gang fight, he fired a 9 mm semiautomatic into a crowd of kids playing football and killed a fourteen-year-old girl.

The last three days of his life Yummy spent running from the police while his grandmother searched for him, vainly hoping to find him alive. He ended up at a neighbor's house, asking her to pray with him and to call his grandmother. A few hours later a member of his own gang shot him twice in the back of the head to keep him from talking to the police.

In every black community today this is what it means to be young. This boy was headed for the sixth grade; he should have been getting into space discoveries, world geography, reading good books, and playing basketball. He should have been participating in church projects to help the elderly and the blind, or rehearsing for a school play. Instead, his young life was over. He had sworn his loyalty to others who had no traction, no cleats to move them forward toward sane answers about life. He and his peers were adding to the problems of their families, the society, and the whole human enterprise.

Nothing had been done to help Yummy's mother. Nothing had been done to redirect the lives of her children. From all we can tell, all of her nine siblings and her six children are still living somewhere in the margins of our society.

We must candidly face the raw data of Yummy's brief life. We have allowed some simple values to slip from us, and we seem to accept the loss without regret. A tenet of the faith that sustained us through the bitter days of the post-Reconstruction, the Great Depression, and the humiliation of racial segregation was that oppression—no matter how severe—could never destroy our character and self-respect. Now, by constantly emphasizing the details of our past, we seem to have reversed ourselves.

Curiously, the more we focus on the horrors of slavery and the more we celebrate the significance of our African heritage, the more ground we seem to lose. The bolder we are in declaring our wish to be self-reliant, the weaker the fabric of our neighborhoods becomes. Something that ought to be going forward is instead moving in reverse. And something that ought to be reversed is gaining momentum.

One of the quietest secrets in the black community is that we expected more positive results from the infusion of black studies in our colleges and black curriculum in our schools. All the classroom walls, the bulletin boards in the offices of principals, guidance counselors, and coaches are covered with pictures of Malcolm and Mandela, DuBois and Frederick Douglass. We began this thirty years ago and we thought that it would inspire our youth to claim their dignity. But curiously, this cultural elixir has left us still waiting for results. Instead, we have many more black males in jail, many more teenage mothers, and our schools are more like detention centers.

I believe that we expected too much from consciousness elevation. Africa may be too far away in time and distance for a teenager in East Orange, New Jersey, to grasp. The excitement of the street is too close. Moreover, it may be too abstract to ask a child to live in two worlds, when everything he sees and hears, and the values that propel the society, convincingly tell him that the world he sees is the world in which he must live.

We don't have long to debate this because the Yummys are all around us. It would be wonderful if we could continue to educate our youth about the great omissions of black Americans in social studies. It would be a real contribution to acquaint them with African and African-American heroes and heroines, and simultaneously keep them in step with a knowledge of world history, Western history, and all of the disciplines that will prepare them for success right here.

But somehow, all of the details of Yummy's life needed to be reversed. We must ask ourselves what went wrong on the first day of his brief visit on planet Earth. If we cannot unravel these tangled cords and reweave a new pattern for children like Yummy, we should close down all of our institutions, give away the endowments, and admit that all of our past strivings were in vain.

There must be a better answer than exonerating everyone but the real victims. Yummy did not ask to be born. Surely he did not wish to be born into the safekeeping of a teenage mother with a drug habit. But this is a fact for thousands of new lives, even as we wring our hands and spout cheap, escapist rhetoric about bigger jails, the death penalty, and no parole ever for anyone.

USING DATA FROM FEDERAL GOVERNMENT SOURCES, Andrew Hacker gave us a frightening summary of the current crisis in *Two Nations, Black and White, Separate, Hostile and Unequal.* I did not want to believe that we were dragging such awful data behind us, but his figures are impossible to ignore.

In 1930, blacks were 22.4 percent of the prison population; in 1986, they were 45.3 percent. In 1990, blacks committed 53.9 percent of the murders in America, 63.9 percent of the robberies, and 24.3 percent of the rapes. One out of every five black men will be incarcerated for a part of his life! Considering that, for most inmates, jail is really a crime school, these are frightening statistics indeed.

Parallel to the increase in crime, another problem grows: in 1950, 16.8 percent of black births were out of wedlock, and 17.2 percent of black households were headed by women. In

1990, both of those figures had more than tripled.

Many of these young mothers will turn out to be strong, solid winners and their children will do well. Most, however, will survive feebly on public assistance, suffer abuse by aimless, part-time lovers, escape into alcohol and drugs, endure more pregnancies, and eventually lose their grip on life entirely. Their children will reach seniority by chance, loaded with trouble. Meanwhile, the class stratification among blacks widens and resentment of other blacks toward these young mothers and their children grows.

Beneath these troubled waters are powerful, hidden undertows. Whoever reads Hacker's data on crime and irresponsible parenting should also read the statistics on jobs and education. Placed side by side, the data have a clear, causal relationship.

The most stubborn barrier to progress is the insistence that negative behavior stems from race, rather than from poverty and isolation. It is a scandal in scholarship constantly to report statistics by race alone. If we eliminate race from crime statistics, and measure young criminals in the light of their reading levels, family income, education of parents, neighborhood incomes, fathers in the home, and church participation, a different picture of criminal behavior emerges. Blacks who read well, whose parents are present and employed, and who attend church regularly are not in jail. And whites who read poorly, who are unparented, who grew up poor and did not attend church are in jail. Factors that lead to crime are so readily found in ghetto communities that race is mistaken as the key. Race alone has nothing to do with crime data.

The papers are covered each day with more horror stories about street crime and drug-related offenses. When blacks are involved, race is always added as an implicit causative factor. Never mind that whites have been in the news for killing infants and women, shooting a dozen students from a Texas campus tower, killing thirty boys in Wisconsin, shooting up post offices and restaurants, and killing Brinks truck guards and putting a wife in a wood-shredding machine. These crimes are not identified by "race."

There is a crime problem, and it does involve a disproportionate number of young blacks. All sorts of political opportunists who have no programs, no vision, and no imagination are thumping and screaming about crime and aid to dependent children. This is all it takes to stir up the fears of prejudiced people, cut off debate—and, unfortunately, win elections. What will the nation do after a "sweeping" election—for which only one third of eligible voters turned out—has brought to power a conglomerate of zealots who vote against gun control, but support capital punishment, reduce benefits for welfare mothers, and support vouchers for private school tuition?

Where is a vision of schools that will educate *all* of our children, a program for rebuilding our dilapidated cities, a plan for retraining our recidivists and creating viable jobs for them, and a program for health care delivery to all of our people?

It is always difficult to embrace two apparently dichotomous aspects of one issue and see the hard truth in both. Blacks have to assume responsibility for mending and restoring our own families and institutions. No one else can do this for us. At the same time, the federal government has responsibility for monitoring justice and due process, "securing the blessings of liberty" and "forming a more perfect union." The federal government is the only agent that can take initiatives to correct past discrimination, even to correct its evil consequences where possible, and remove barriers to equal opportunity. This has nothing to do with "quotas" or promoting blacks who cannot perform over whites. It has to do with giving blacks equal opportunity to earn every social benefit, even to the extent of undoing previous, gross offenses. Some call this reverse discrimination; it is simply redressing previous discrimination.

There is an answer to the crisis. Every African-American organization in the country has some program on its agenda to try to reverse the mounting data on crime, drugs, and teenage parenting. It is possible to begin to hear more about preparing young people for success, and less about the futility of trying.

From time to time I meet with a group of early parolees from drug convictions in a downtown Methodist church in a New Jersey city. They went to jail for stealing, fraud, and fencing stolen property, mostly to get drug money. They had followed the procession of their peers into despair. They are good-looking, healthy, and intelligent young men and women, but nihilism, the belief in nothing, overtook them and dragged them under.

I tell them some of my own experiences and help them revisit their own lives and review their prospects. They sit straight up and give a hard listen. It is unreal to them that any black person could have a positive outlook on life. I always try to bring something to them that they may not get a chance to hear otherwise. I try to show them how pride and self-respect derive from the spiritual core within. I talk about the need for a strong religious faith, and a worldview that holds things together. Their own lives are vacant at the center, but they always listen.

They often ask me how I found the strength to work my way through college and graduate school, and I tell them that I had plenty of strength left over. My power never ran low. If you believe that there is a purpose and a power available to each of us, you have an inexhaustible source of evergreen inspiration.

Although we must be honest in stating the facts of the crisis, if we get lost in the "paralysis of analysis" we cannot move toward change—we've lost our cleats.

Last September, I gave an address to a beautiful audience of students at predominantly black Delaware State University at Dover. I talked to them about how academic success could change the future for both individuals and society. I told them that we had the faith and the capacity to change our situation, and change America along with us. Afterward, four young black female students came running up to me. They were wearing floppy clothes and jeweled braids and they bubbled over with enthusiasm.

"Dr. Proctor, we were just talking about you," one girl said. "Your speech helped us so much. All the kids are saying that you changed our minds on a lot of things. This year will be different for us because of what you said."

I asked, "Where are you all from?"

They were from Harlem, Passaic, East Orange, and Baltimore—four of the nation's crisis pivot points. My soul! They are on their way in spite of it. That is indeed the substance of things hoped for.

CHAPTER NINE

Racism: Black and White

WHEN I WAS A YOUNG PASTOR IN RHODE ISLAND, A prosperous mortician took me to Boston to see the Brooklyn Dodgers play against the Braves. We sat in the grandstands, the only blacks in sight—except for one. Every time Jackie Robinson came to bat, epithets sailed all around us. Thunders of "nigger," "darkie," "blackie," and worse rolled around the stadium. It was a subrational tribal cry, like something primeval being vented. We kept our cool and Jackie Robinson kept his. I don't know what it cost him to do so, but I have a pretty good idea.

When I was a boy, my brothers, sister, and I were always being reminded that "colored" people had an extra burden to bear. At home, at school, in church, at our little storefront YMCA, and in Boy Scout meetings, it was drummed into us that we had to put our best foot forward at all times to prove we were not inferior. Later, in college, we got the same constant reminders.

Some black youngsters felt a special responsibility always to be clean, polite, and respectfully quiet. As if to prove our humanity, we tried to do everything superbly well. We always had jobs and succeeded in school. If we kept chipping away at the rumor of inferiority, maybe we could push some obstacles aside.

But not all our friends and neighbors were convinced of this. They joked about us being "proper niggers." They would go downtown looking "bad." They didn't care who heard their profanity and boisterous conversations. They embarrassed us, because we wanted to be seen as having pride. It was painful to see African Americans act out what whites said about us. To us, racism was at its most destructive when it earned converts among African Americans themselves.

During the bleak days of the Depression, we kids did anything to make some change for the little extras—a movie, bakery treats, milkshakes—that our parents simply could not afford. Almost always I worked for people who thought I was inferior and expected subservience from me. Even then I could recognize the difference between the person I was at home and the person I was expected to be on these odd jobs.

When I was about twelve years old, I worked after school in a neighborhood grocery store for a man named Cohen. His son also did odd jobs in the store, but when a chicken had to be killed and plucked, that was always my job. When someone dropped a carton of eggs on the floor, I cleaned up the mess. If someone wanted fish gutted and scaled, that was my assignment. And, of course, scrubbing the floor and cleaning the toilet were late-night, closing-time chores for me. I did it all with a double consciousness. Somehow, I had to do those jobs and at the same time retain my self-respect. I tried to remember that the job didn't define who I was. I separated myself from Mr. Cohen's definition of me, and chose instead my grandma's definition of me. She had convinced me that I was God's child and inherently equal to everyone else. I can still remember the schizoid feelings of those hard days.

On school vacation days my brother and I would sometimes go to the corner of Princess Anne Road and Church Street and join up with the dozens of black women and men waiting to go out and work on the farms. It was a fun ride on a big truck. Not every foreman would allow kids to get on the truck, but many of the women carried their children with them and we simply mixed in and got on board.

In the fields we played as much as we worked. We picked just enough string beans, strawberries, tomatoes, cucumbers, or peppers to exchange for coupons to carry to the owner's commissary wagon to buy a huge bottle of RC Cola and a French apple pie for lunch and still have a dollar left over for spending money.

On these days we glimpsed life lived at the survival level, where human dignity and pride were stifled by poverty and ignorance. The farmhands lived each day from hand to mouth, following orders from poor, uneducated, white foremen. They ate minced meat sandwiches and greens from a pickle jar, and the women had to go behind bushes and trees to relieve themselves. Often three generations would be working in the fields together.

My brother and I would repeat the speech patterns of the "field dialect." To a stranger it might seem that these people, mostly women, were barely human. It was not clear to us why their language was so poor and their thoughts so dull and childlike. Only much later did we realize that the only difference between them and our family and neighbors was that someone, or some thing, had intervened in our lives and opened up the future.

Without such intervention, however, it is easy to see how some African Americans never got far from slavery. For generations, abject poverty and abuse were ground into their consciousness. Feelings of inferiority set limits on their aspirations and controlled their expectations.

In this regard things have not changed very much. Recently, in one of my classes at Duke University, where I also teach, a white student asked me if it bothered me to be a "token" black on the faculty. His tone was neither hostile nor offensive. Prejudice is deep and lingers long, even among people who deny its presence.

I asked him why he assumed that my appointment had to be token. I had earned a doctoral degree from a leading graduate theological center, and had retired from a chair in a large public university with an emeritus title. I had been awarded a total of forty-six honorary degrees. Did he believe that Duke University was insincere, or that I was poorly prepared? Were *all* black appointees "tokens"? Could any blacks ever succeed legitimately?

He looked at me blankly, then asked if I felt I was being "used." He simply could not believe that it was normal for a black person to succeed. There had to be a trick involved somewhere. Many young blacks are prejudiced in the same way. If a black person advances, they believe, it must be a fluke. Because of this doubt, they anticipate—and plan—failure. When young people put achievement out of reach for themselves and pretend to prefer ignorance, noise, drugs, and sex for entertainment, they are committing a kind of suicide. Or, in the case of a generation of young people, genocide.

IN THE 1960S AND 1970S, DURING THE PEAK OF THE CIVIL rights movement, newspapers often reported that some new evidence had been discovered proving the genetic liability of African Americans. This information was always presented statistically, even though no instruments exist that can measure how self-concept, environment, and cultural isolation affect learning;

or how the historical flow, tainted by generations of legal denial of education, reflects on intelligence tests.

Recently we have been harassed by another racist theory put forth by Charles Murray in *The Bell Curve*, in which the author uses the ten to fifteen points that African Americans score lower than whites on intelligence tests to demonstrate our immutable intellectual inferiority and the futility of making any effort to erase these disparities. It is incredible that any legitimate scholar could be so eager to leap to hateful conclusions from partial and inconclusive data. Who can measure the extent to which oppression affects cognitive ability? Who knows the extent to which racism affects one's self-concept and, thus, performance?

Charles Murray has spent endless hours in television and newspaper interviews saying that he barely mentions race in his "data," but he knows full well that dressing up racism in scientific clothing guarantees a best-seller.

It is frightening to observe how one writer can generate the broad interest that Murray has. Charles Lane uncovered a chain of interacting researchers, writers, and "scholars" who compose a kind of vanguard of opinion-molders in the area of race and intelligence. He identified a journal called *The Mankind Quarterly* as one hub of their activities. According to Lane, this publication's editorial board includes a number of scientists who support racist views. In the bibliography of *The Bell Curve*, five articles are listed from the *Quarterly*. Seventeen authorities cited in Murray's book had been contributors to the journal. Ten are former editors. The founder of the *Quarterly* was Henry E. Garrett of Columbia University who provided expert testimony for the Topeka Board of Education in the 1954 *Brown v. Board of Education* case. Lane further reveals that *The Bell Curve* cites thirteen scholars who have received over $4 million in grants from the Pioneer Fund in the past twenty years. The Pioneer Fund also funds Pearson's Institute for the Study of Man, which publishes *The Mankind Quarterly*. (The Pioneer Fund was established in 1937 with the money of Wickliffe

Draper, who advocated the repatriation of blacks to Africa.)

Thus, instead of relying on expert, impartial data as claimed, *The Bell Curve* was really a megaphone for a cacophony of racist propaganda that had circulated that year. This well-financed work that attracted so much attention is dripping with stains of racist thought and is not accountable to the world of real scholarship.

In the wake of Murray's book comes *The Tragedy of American Compassion,* written by a born-again Christian named [CK FIRST NAME] Olasky. Olasky tells us that after being influenced by Watergate alumnus-turned-preacher Charles Colson, he began to study alternatives to "liberal" programs.

Olasky bemoans the fact that homeless people who show up at shelters for food and medicine are not given Bibles to bring them to Christ, and are not asked to clean up vacant lots in exchange for their food. He imagines that passing out Bibles and rakes to homeless people, many of whom are addicted to drugs and alcohol, can solve serious social problems resulting from generations of systemic poverty, poor education, and pervasive racism. It's amazing that some people call this Christian.

His strangely titled book, which was funded by the Heritage Foundation, was originally published by a small press, but later taken up by a larger publisher when Newt Gingrich used it to validate his "contract" to cut taxes and sharply reduce benefits programs. And it's no coincidence that the introduction to Olasky's book was written by Charles Murray! Clearly, a well-funded assault has been launched to rewrite history, ignoring the ugly causes that have delivered us to this moment.

Even top scientists, trained to be coldly impartial no matter how their research turns out, have been known to corrupt their own findings, simply to get eye-catching results. Back in 1977, President Jimmy Carter established the Recombinant DNA Panel at the National Institutes of Health, which was responsible for assessing grant applications for genetic research. Microbiology and DNA research were still relatively new at this time. I was among six "humanists" appointed by the president to work with the panel.

One panelist was a Nobel prize winner affiliated with one of our finest and most highly respected medical research universities. During every meeting he let us know in no uncertain terms that he objected to our presence. He grunted, giggled, and walked around with his head tilted back and his eyes fixed on the ceiling. For an intellectual of his standing his behavior was embarassing. *Although he was not implicated in the fraud,*

It was no surprise to read later in the Washington Post, March 21, 1991, that he was involved in a prolonged investigation, having asked that a scientific paper bearing his name be retracted because of evidence that it contained fraudulent data.

Almost a year later, on February 21, 1992, the New York Times reported that he had "stubbornly dismissed repeated accusations that his collaborator had fabricated data" for the article they co-authored. He suffered extensive criticism from his peers and colleagues threatened to resign under his leadership. Eventually he resigned one of the most prestigious scientific posts in the country.

Such a revelation alerts us to the awesome possibility that errors, whether intended or not, in reporting scientific data can spin off pure propaganda passing for the truth. And critical social theories may flow from such propaganda.

Whatever *anyone* wants to prove about genetic traits and African Americans would require a bona fide, pure sample. And in America, as in the rest of the world, the mixtures are compounded many times over. Biologically speaking, most scientists agree there is no such thing as "race." For a frame of reference, they arbitrarily divide the human species into three categories according to hair texture, eye shape, and skin color. The categories refer more to geographic origin than biological origin, hence the current usage of Asian, Latino, African American to designate geographic derivations.

We are all made up of millions and millions of individual characteristics, of which skin color is only one, and there there are often more similarities between individuals of different "races" than between individuals of the same "race." Even geographic origin is virtually impossible to determine. After 250 million years of *Homo sapiens* migration, and centuries of ocean-going commerce, wars, religious pilgrimages, colonization, enslavement, and resettlements, it is impossible to isolate a particular gene pool. The varieties of people found all over the globe are evidence of a human blending that defies discreet racial or geographic labels.

In 1953, I remember meeting a Negroid Palestinian soldier who was a Moslem. His duty assignment was to guard the Church of the Nativity in Bethlehem. The soldier told me that he was descended from African Moslems who fled from the Crusaders in East Africa in the thirteenth century. He spoke fluent German, which he had learned at a Lutheran mission school. His is a typical story of *Homo sapiens* on planet Earth.

In 1975, my son Sammy and I visited New Zealand. We stopped first at the Fiji Islands which, we were surprised to discover, are populated by Negroid people. The Fijians found it hilarious when I told them they couldn't possibly be from Fiji, but must have been born in Bedford-Stuyvesant in Brooklyn.

On another leg of our interminable flight to Aukland, we traveled with a large group of distinguished-looking gentlemen who had distinctly African features. It turned out they were actually from New Guinea—at least five thousand miles from the coast of East Africa. Then we visited Melbourne, where we saw dark-skinned people with light grey-green eyes and blond hair!

We see similar mixes all over the United States. On a recent visit to Shenandoah University I was met in the Charlottesville airport by a gentle white male student. On the drive to campus he told me he was a piano student from Blakesly, Virginia. Now, my grandfather had a cousin Bessie from Blakesly. His mother and cousin Bessie's mother were twins. The sisters never spoke about their paternity, but it was said they were the offspring of a black slave woman and a white father.

I asked the student who had started him on the piano. He said his first teacher was a lady everyone called Miss Bessie. When I told him that I was a third cousin to her, he looked at me in shock. "Was she black?" he asked.

Well, there is the question. Was she?

Is there any such thing as a person who is purely black? Or purely anything else? And what purpose does it serve to try to figure it out?

Those who are eager to see every individual fulfill his or her highest potential don't waste time trying to twist spurious anthropology or bogus evidence to prove pseudoscientific prevarications about race—pro or con.

By contrast, people who have a keen interest in race theories generally have some ulterior motive driving them. They propagate theories about a particular group in order to put that group to some advantage or disadvantage. For example, those working hard to prove the genetic inferiority of African Americans may wish to preserve our status and remove us from competition; they may want to exploit us economically; or maybe they simply want to stay in office by appealing to people's worst instincts. Or all three. Today, these people often use code words—like "disadvantaged," or "inner city," or "marginalized," or "underclass," or "high risk," or "poor and underserved"—that allow them to converse freely and appear fair-minded. Every one of those terms means "black." And there seems no end to it.

Some people are loudly claiming that the lower Scholastic Aptitude Test scores of black college candidates proves that they are less intelligent and unable to perform at the college level. Thousands of African-American students are currently enrolled at Harvard, Duke, Princeton, UCLA, Stanford, Rutgers, Ohio State, and other major universities. Every black college is brimfull, and community colleges dotted around the country have large black enrollments. If blacks are intellectually inferior, who are these students? Are they qualified to be on college campuses?

A close look at the college admission tests reveals these informative data: black youngsters from families earning $10,000 to $20,000 a year scored 704 on the SAT, while those whose family incomes exceeded $70,000 scored 854. Whites from families of the same incomes scored 879 and 996 respectively; Asians scored 855 and 1066. (It's worthwhile noting that over half of the Asian youth had parents who were *college educated*.)

The fact is that the SAT scores show that blacks—like whites, Asians, and Hispanics—demonstrate greater success and achieve higher scores as their family incomes rise, and at about the same pace. Even though blacks begin at lower scores, they advance at the same rate as others as their incomes increase. Better incomes reflect opportunity, discipline, intelligence, seriousness, and moral discernment. All of these factors lead to higher school achievement.

Yet it is also true that even though scores go up as income increases, black candidates still lag 150 to 200 points behind on the SATs. Even well-educated, relatively unbiased academics have trouble understanding why SAT questions are fundamentally unfair to blacks. If you compare blacks with whites of similar incomes and similar social isolation, the mystery of the scores disappears. People compelled to live in a separate community, barred from the main flow of the dominant culture, have a total exposure different from that reflected in the test. For example, cultural isolation has the same affect on everyone. Poor African Americans have the same problem with the SATs that Kentucky and Tennessee mountaineers would have if they took the tests. (Appalachian whites with poor educations don't usually take the SATs, however. Blacks, by contrast, are so preoccupied with the quest for liberation that many who are poor take the SATs even though they have not received adequate preparation in high school.) The evidence is overwhelming that blacks are also isolated from the larger society. Andrew Hacker's data showed that in 1992 *two of every three black children, from North to South, East to West, still attended racially segregated schools.* There is even more segregation in large urban centers of the North than in the South. In fact, when it comes to segregating children by color, only four of the southern states—Mississippi, Alabama, Texas, and Louisiana—are worse than the large northern urban centers. *Forty years* after the 1954 decision! The SAT scores clearly reveal this isolation.

THE RACE ISSUE HAS DEEP REPERCUSSIONS AMONG African Americans. Some grow to hate their identity in such an obsessive way that it paralyzes constructive responses to the ordinary challenges of life. Some go to work every day, angry that they have to negotiate for space to feel comfortable. They bob and weave to fend off remarks that sound racial, whether they are or not. They must prove that they can think in the abstract, that they tell the truth, and that they don't steal. They must guard against any gesture or behavior that inadvertently might echo the stereotype. They must be detached, avoiding those who avoid them, and sometimes even avoiding those who want to impose their "love" on them in order to prove that they are not racist. It is exhausting to be so self-conscious all day.

An African American needs a healthy ego to shadowbox all day in a world not designed for her or his occupancy. Some, especially those without strong family supports, dodge the challenge and take refuge in a fortress of alternative behaviors.

That's one scenario. There are other ways in which we internalize racism. In college, I had a brilliant African-American professor of French who spent most of our class time telling jokes about uneducated blacks. Any success we had, he took to be accidental—except his own. I know several people like him who cannot accept their identity as African Americans. Their days are one long, tedious debate with everyone about nothing. They cannot accept a white person as a friend, or an African American as a peer. They are aliens everywhere.

More commonly, endemic racism causes many educated African Americans to create an upper caste of their own. They attend certain churches, belong to certain organizations, live in certain parts of town, and engage in a lifestyle that manifests a caste at the top.

You would think that after hundreds of years of trying to survive aggressive and suppressive racism, blacks would be the last people in the world to be racist themselves. In fact, some of us have proved to be as susceptible to the virus of class and color discrimination as anyone else.

No one likes poverty, falling plaster, telephones cut off, bathing in cold water, sharing a bed with two others and a bathroom with six others. But those who succeed in improving their circumstances have a tendency to turn their backs on those who cannot. This response is by no means a racial or cultural characteristic, but among African Americans it does have some unique antecedents.

For example, until very recently, blacks tended to choose fair-skinned leaders with white features, a practice which stemmed from a long history of giving special advantages to the "black" offspring of the slave masters. Even when the father was unknown, fair-skinned African Americans received special rank and status because both whites and blacks believed in the myth of white supremacy. As a result, these were among the first to receive college educations and other benefits. They formed a kind of privileged, closed circle, and favors began to aggregate around them.

This tendency became entrenched in the late nineteenth and early twentieth century. Black college students began to organize Greek letter societies in blind imitation of white undergraduates. Next, we were having exclusive debutante balls and cotillions. Certain lodges were known to favor light-complexioned members, and certain churches called only light-complexioned pastors. Some church sanctuaries had fair-skinned members seated on one side and those who were darker sat on the other.

This layering of color within the black community continued

for several decades. When I was president of Virginia Union University and North Carolina A & T State University between 1955 and 1964, most black college presidents were still fair-skinned. During the civil rights movement we began to put this particular form of self-discrimination behind us.

Fortunately, most privileged blacks today involve themselves in some way in the social and economic redemption of their people. Arguably, their social distance from other African Americans, as well as their ardent participation in the culture of materialism, often causes them to line up on the side of the status quo. They are likely to resist any fundamental changes that might curtail their own comfort level. In other words, they would like to cure suffering to their people, without any pain to themselves. This culpability is as pervasive among successful African Americans as it is among whites.

We cannot start the human race all over again, with everyone at the same scratch line. Nor does everyone have the same emotional makeup or internal fortitude to succeed despite enormous deficits. Some are able to suffer and endure longer than others. Some can stand up to insults longer than others. Some are more aware and perceptive than others. Some lie awake, gazing at the night sky and see nothing but the darkness, while others watching the same sky see the stars. If racial categories never existed, some humans would fail and some succeed.

But African American have to recognize that we all have common antecedents lying back in the foggy past, admit that we have arrived at widely different places on the road—and find a way to go on from here together.

ALTHOUGH THE BLACK COMMUNITY IS CLEARLY NOT monolithic, there is a huge tendency around the country to relegate the tastes and behavior of some to the tastes and behavior of all. For example, our religion is often stereotyped on the most elemental and unsophisticated level. That is racism, and even blacks succumb to the fallacy.

Along with religious expression, the accumulation of such art forms as music, dance, and storytelling have been packaged up along with the poverty and lack of education and sold as "black culture." "Black culture" became the stereotype for all African Americans, and what began as a response to oppression became known as a racial characteristic.

It is wrong to present vulgar rap songs and filthy jokes on "black" shows and networks, implying that they universally represent black culture. They call themselves "artists of protest." In my opinion they add to our burden by reinforcing negative stereotypes that are already almost impossible to destroy.

Many young blacks believe these comedians and rappers are expressing "how it is." Is this what we want to pass on to coming generations? Is this the best we can do to express anger, frustration, sorrow, jubilance, and love? Calling this, or any other single form of music, "black culture" is racist, regardless of who's saying it.

Racial theories are not always used *against* a particular group; sometimes the victims of discrimination use questionable theories to prove that their race is unique and in some way superior. This kind of racism is defensive and protective, rather than aggressive and oppressive. For example, Professor Leonard Jeffries of City College in New York has tried to enhance the image of African Americans by arguing that we are "sun people," as opposed to "ice people." To him, the extra melanin in our skin signals genetic advantages.

I admit that it's a relief to hear someone say something positive for a change. But we need to resist the appeal. Because similar anthropology and genetics have so often been used against us, I think most African Americans are uncomfortable with his arguments. Most of us are not willing to have untested, unproven race theories submitted in defense of our cause, even when put forth by an African-American academic.

Minister Louis Farrakhan has a notion that we will be better off if we stop trying to find equality and concord among whites, and instead seek a locus of our own, here or abroad, and do our own nation building. He is fantastically popular and influential, especially among young African Americans. His physical presence, and the power of his oratory, create a hypnotic surrender to his views. More than fifty years ago, Marcus Garvey advocated a return to the homeland of Africa, but Minister Farrakhan would now accept a designated space for a new nation here on the North American continent.

Those agreeing with a separatist position believe that racism is so endemic in America that nothing will alter the black condition. Some independent African and Caribbean states might be a haven for African Americans who wanted to join them and strengthen them. And there are many all-black nations available to any black who prefers to leave.

Of course, we all need to know about our ancestral home and its history. But creating a diaspora mentality is another matter. Before setting off on this course, we would need much more evidence that starting a new nation, or joining an existing all-black nation, would deliver the relief and liberation we crave. It's late to be aiming at going it alone, especially when all of the world is seeking alliances and partnerships. I believe that escaping into an all-black mythological kingdom stalls progress.

On the extreme flip side of Dr. Jeffries and Minister Farrakhan are Dr. Thomas Sowell of the Heritage Foundation and Justice Clarence Thomas, blacks who ingratiate themselves among white conservatives by claiming that we retard our own progress by failing to take advantage of opportunities.

All of these extreme positions are in heated currency now. And the majority of blacks reject them. We take pride in participating in America, with all her faults and failures. Ultimately, most African Americans have a heavy investment here and do

not plan to release this rich and powerful nation from its obligation to us. We have a mortgage on New Columbia. We have
every hope and expectation of being a part of a new America in
a new world.

TODAY OUR HARD-WON VICTORIES ARE BEING THREATENED
by amorphous racism on the part of whites, and cynicism and a
feeling of futility on the part of many blacks. But our faith is not
vulnerable to vapid challenges. It resists with vigor the tide of
hate rhetoric, black and white, that inflames campuses and further polarizes society.

It has not been easy for us to reject rejection. In the wake of
popular movements that offer more problems than answers, we
all need our faith to be edified. There can be no peace without
justice, but we must pursue both without adding to the problem
by engaging in inflammatory rhetoric that exacerbates an already polarized situation.

My own values require me to seek change by using Christian
strategies. Jesus asked us to risk loving our enemies. Jesus taught
us that it is never enough to reciprocate on a tit-for-tat basis. He
said:

> If you love those who love you, what reward will you
> get? . . . And if you greet only your brothers, what are
> you doing more than others?
> Matthew 5:46–47 (New International Version)

Jesus taught us to seek the good in others, and this means loving those who may not want our love, and even loving those who
do not seem to deserve to be loved. This is tough stuff, but it is
minimum Christianity.

It is tedious to have to watch for a sign of acceptance every
time you meet someone. After a lifetime of unpleasant surprises,

many of us wait until we receive a clear signal that the other person is not racist. My rehearsal for such encounters came from experiences gained in those odd jobs of my youth. Some were positive and some negative, and most mixed in both elements, meaning that even in the worst situation some bright light beamed. I eventually learned to enjoy anticipating people. I used my imagination and tried to understand where they were coming from. As a result, I never felt robbed taking the initiative to foster a new relationship.

By the time I reached Crozer Seminary at the age of twenty-one, I could give some slack to just about anyone in any encounter. On my first day there many students made it their business to introduce themselves and welcome me. Their courtesy cushioned me for the others who were too bound by custom to speak to me. These students refused to sit by me in the small dining room, which accommodated only ninety boarders. After a while, rushing into that small space three times a day, trying *not* to sit by the one black student got to be complicated. After ten days or so, they started sitting next to me in dining hall and chapel. Whenever one of them was in range, I tried out bits of conversation.

After six weeks it seemed that we were all going to make it together just fine. Occasionally, we talked openly about race in class, but in our day-by-day relations we put it aside. Some might call this accommodation or social adjustment, but to me it was a plain victory.

I wish every black person and every white person could have such an experience. Such experiences taught me to take the initiative in meeting people. No matter what the response, I am always—literally always—prepared to try to make any new communication a positive one.

It's true that blacks must be alert to injustice and to racial discrimination. We must be ready to use the courts, the ballot, and the boycott to complete the campaign for justice. But we need to employ a greater strategy to overcome individual prejudices. This is a moral struggle that will not yield to marches and court decisions. It requires education and persuasion; it requires exposure of blacks to whites, and whites to blacks, in close and steady relations—at work, as neighbors, as club or church members, as doctors and patients, merchants and customers, teachers and students, and students and students. It requires talking about subjects that are neutral—healing a disease, controlling a flood, getting a truck to run, painting a house, winning a baseball game, or training a racehorse—subjects without racial content. Over time, the total package of human characteristics comes into focus.

No matter how intransigent the color caste system seems, I believe that it has improved. I have seen the change over my own lifetime, although admittedly much of the positive changes in modern race relations have affected only educated and upwardly mobile blacks. In the South, however, something is changing at a level that bears more authenticity and reality. Here I have found African-American and white mechanics joking in a car dealership, and workers gossiping and teasing with perfect ease in the banks, post offices, clothing stores, utility offices, courthouses, and restaurants. This kind of change is crucial, because forward movement so often gets stalled and frustrated at the local level. If the temperature of tolerance is right, change in housing, jobs, police behavior, and education may follow.

If it were not for the efforts of institutions and political leaders to keep racism alive, and exploit it for their own benefit, I believe it could die a natural death. On a recent Sunday in October the Washington Redskins were playing the Philadelphia Eagles. The Eagles won by a narrow margin. After the game, two players slowly walked toward the clubhouse, their helmets swinging at their sides and their arms draped across each other's shoulders. They were Heath Shuler, the defeated white rookie quarterback, and Charlie Garner, the game-winning black star runner. These two young men had been teammates at the University of Tennessee. Their personal tie was more durable than any new team alliance. Sealed in their bond, I saw the future of this country.

A FEW WEEKS AGO I WAS LECTURING TO GEORGIA'S UNITED Methodist pastors on Sea Island. At lunch I sat with a white pastor and his wife, who was a teacher's aide in an all-black school in DeKalb County. She told me that a thirteen-year-old seventh grader looked her dead in the eye one day and said, "Mrs. Stansberry, are you sure you are not black?"

"Why do you say that?" she asked.

" 'Cause you got soul!"

That was a child's way of saying that Mrs. Stansberry was close, warm, and involved. She inspired trust and this girl was not embarrassed to tell her she felt comfortable in her presence. "Soul" is a human attribute that anyone may have. "Soul" has no color.

CHAPTER TEN

Can These Bones Live?

BLACK AMERICANS HAVE ALWAYS BEEN FASCINATED BY
biblical accounts of the Jews' exile in Babylon, which began in
the sixth century B.C. and ended seventy years later. Some of the
Bible's most dramatic stories derive from this one experience:
Daniel in the lion's den, the three Hebrew boys in the furnace,
Queen Esther and her triumph over Haman, and Ezekiel proph-
esying to the dry bones. In the Jewish exile slaves saw a tragedy
parallel to their own plight, and the Bible comforted them, reinforcing their faith.

The books of II Samuel, II Kings, II Chronicles, Isaiah, and
Ezekiel all echo with the cries of God's people.

[The Lord] will not grow tired or weary,
and his understanding no one can fathom.
He gives strength to the weary,
and increases the power of the weak.
Even youths grow tired and weary,
and young men stumble and fall;
but those who hope in the Lord
will renew their strength.
They will soar on wings like eagles;
they will run and not grow weary,
they will walk and not be faint.

Isaiah 40:28–31 (New International Version)

Last fall, I spoke at a Thanksgiving and homecoming celebration held at the former Alex Haley Farm in eastern Tennessee, sponsored by the Children's Defense Fund. I chose my text from the prophet Ezekiel, who tells of a vision in which the Lord sent him into a valley of bones that were very dry, symbolizing God's people in their despondency. "Our bones are dried up, and our hope is lost, and we are cut off." God asked Ezekiel, "Can these bones live?" Then God told the prophet to speak to the bones, saying "hear the word of the Lord," and the bones joined together. After the bones were renewed with muscles and sinew, they complained that they had no breath. The prophet beckoned to the four winds to breathe breath into their bodies, and the bones rose up like a mighty army.

We are once again living in a valley of dry bones. For these bones to live now, we must candidly face the raw facts: Every 44 minutes a black baby dies; every 7 minutes a black baby is born to a mother with late or no prenatal care; every 85 seconds a black child is born into poverty; and every 40 seconds of the school day a black child drops out. Can these bones live?

Most of us who made it into the mainstream in the 1960s and '70s viewed with contempt those blacks still mired in poverty, alcoholism, violence, and immorality. They were our embarrassment. In no way did we want to be approving of that type of behavior, and somehow we succumbed to the popular theory that they were largely to blame for their condition. Without knowing, we were really involved in a form of racism ourselves by failing to recognize fully the causes of the delinquency of so many blacks.

Today, we are not nearly as Darwinian in our thinking. We know we must reach back and find ways to help others come along, or the whole American nation may sink. This is the new tenet of our faith. But the problem is so large and so amorphous that people who want to help can't get a handle on it. They say to me, "Which way is forward, Brother Sam?"

It may seem trivial, but many young blacks are even confused about what to call themselves. Little wonder, when one hears us joking and calling each other "niggah." What *do* we want to be called? The major organization for our redemption is called the National Association for the Advancement of *Colored People;* and the organization that supports our history-making colleges is called the United *Negro* College Fund. Two new organizations are called One Hundred *Black* Men and One Hundred *Black* Women. Representatives in Congress have organized a *black* caucus; and new university departments are called African Studies, Afro-American Studies, Afri-American Studies, or African-American Studies.

While the term "African American" feels least loaded with color references these days, it, too, has its limitations. It emphasizes our past, not our future. If we succeed in creating a new American paradigm for the world, we will all call ourselves Americans.

WE ARE IN A POSITION TO MAKE A POSITIVE LEAP FORWARD — if we have the faith and vision to make the right choices. Even as I write, in cities across America black leaders are debating exactly what the best response will be.

We know that we are all part of an unbroken chain of humanity and we cannot write off another human being as worthless. To discount a child like Yummy as a zero is to make zeroes of ourselves, sacks of protoplasm without the breath of God breathed on us. We would all be dry bones together in the valley of death.

There is no single answer. But I believe there *is* an answer, and it is derived from five separate efforts that need to be blended together: individual involvement, family rejuvenation, specialized teacher training for public schools, more committed church leadership, and, finally, a national program to recapture failing and lost youth. There are ways to achieve each of these monumental tasks. Those that involve individuals are quite simple; those that involve churches and state and federal governments are equally do-able, but require persuasive leadership and persistent effort. All five can and should be started now.

As a primary and overdue concern, all children need to feel safe. We need to protect them and ensure that they won't be hurt in the schools they attend, the streets they live on, and in their individual homes. Every child deserves a quality education. And every child deserves an opportunity to succeed. These initiatives must be available to everyone, regardless of race or income. If we cannot do these things first, then any other measure we adopt, no matter how intense, or how harsh, will fail to make a profound change in our society.

THOSE OF US WHO HAVE FOUND AN ADEQUATE RESPONSE TO our own aspirations need to find at least one viable handle on this crisis—and pull. Everyone can show concern, either individually or through a group.

Every stable home should offer asylum for at least one life that needs direction. At the little cottage where we spent summer weekends by the shores of the Potomac and the Chesapeake, we were a part of a community of nine or ten families. It seemed natural always for our boys to bring their friends along. We treated their friends exactly as we treated our sons. Today, we have a network of young men and women who know that we are available to them, our really extended family.

A few days ago I telephoned a writer friend of mine, a stylish, intellectual, avant-garde sort of person who shares an apartment on Manhattan's Upper East Side with her husband, who is also a writer. I could hear the noise of children in the background. "Who is that talking?" I asked. "You don't have children. Is there a party going on?"

She explained that one afternoon each week she taught creative writing to middle-school kids. "What kids?" I asked.

"Just kids. They belong to a young people's athletic organization."

I pressed on. "What organization? Where?"

"Oh, uptown."

Who would guess that a dozen explosive, high-energy preteens from African-American and Hispanic families in East Harlem would have found a friend among New York's literati? A friend who welcomed them and their noise, curiosity and kinetic action into her living room, kitchen, bathroom, and refrigerator for a weekly invasion? A friend who had the patience and fortitude to teach them to write poems and short stories? The idea of individuals reaching out is not so esoteric after all. Once it was the only way to life, to share love and substance in order to attain one's own fulfillment.

I asked her what prompted her to start the class. "I always wanted to do it, because a few terrific people gave me extra help when I was growing up. I heard about the organization from a close friend who was already working with the kids and she helped me get my program started. It's a small thing, but it's something I know how to do. I know lots of people doing a lot more."

She was right, of course. It *is* a small thing. And small things add up. In other times, this kind of simple sharing and passing along was quite common. One afternoon I was waiting with Lionel Hampton in the president's office at Howard University, where we were later to receive honorary degrees. I slipped into the men's room for a few minutes, and when I returned I saw Lionel kneeling in front of a chair, his head resting on his folded hands. I waited. When he arose, his his eyes were wet with tears. "Are you all right?" I asked.

"I was just thanking God for sending someone to help me," he said. When Lionel was a boy growing up in St. Louis, a German blacksmith used to play his euphonium for the black kids who had recently swarmed into his old German neighborhood. When he noticed little Lionel showing more than casual interest, he taught him scales, fingering, and execution of his odd-looking instrument. Here was Lionel Hampton, seventy years later, a world-famous artist, remembering and giving thanks for the man who took the time to help him.

It's true that a lot of people are already working one-on-one with kids. But with so many children waiting for affirmation, we need many, many more, and they must come in huge numbers from the African-American community. You don't need a college degree or a million dollars. In our corner of Norfolk, Mr. Petty would let us sit in the driver's seat of his ice wagon and ride for hours while he dispensed his ice door-to-door; Big John Gale would let us ride on his trucks and wagons and help feed his pigs and horses; Mr. Foreman, the lawyer, would take us to his office on Saturday mornings and let us type, use his staple machine, run letters through the stamp machine, and answer his telephone. It is all so vivid in my mind, the many, many people who helped us feel good about ourselves. It's not hard to reach out. Call any school, any clubhouse, any church to volunteer for mentoring programs, reading, tutoring, or nursery care.

HOWEVER, THE CURE TO OUR CRISIS CANNOT BE FOUND with individual effort alone. If these dry bones have any chance of coming alive, the recovery must also be in the family structure itself.

Family is rehearsal for life. It is the place where mutual responsibility and accountability are first learned and practiced. Family is where soft punishments are imposed, without damage to self-esteem. Family is where we learn to receive blessings, and to return them. It's where we learn to accept forgiveness, and to give it. Family is an exercise in corporate survival—we don't steal from each other or violate each other's secrets and privacy.

Family is even more than that. There we can cry when we hurt, and show our grief without shame. Family also rejoices in our successes and we, in turn, celebrate the success of others. We carry one another in our prayers and live our days vicariously in each other's lives. In a good family no one suffers alone, and no one succeeds alone. Family is the chrysalis in which young, embryonic lives receive the germinative ingredients for living, while they are protected from the hazards and major challenges of life. In that way, a young life springs forth in beauty and strength.

Even families that are intact must look for creative ways to preserve the lives of their children. When our youngest boys reached the age of ten and thirteen, we deliberately set about finding new ways to sustain our family connections during the time of social unrest swirling around us. We went to Sears Roebuck and bought an 18-foot boat and trailer on credit. The boat was a pretty, fern-green color, with an Evinrude 40 hp motor attached. Before putting it overboard, my two sons and I ran all over Richmond looking for a loud horn, lifejackets, an oar, a towline, an anchor, a fire extinguisher, a waterproof lamp, and a bailing bucket. A trailer had to be hooked to the car to haul the boat. That meant buying a cast-iron hitching tongue, and welding flanges on the frame of the car; we had to find a hitch with a ball to hold the trailer to the car. Every time we moved the boat, we had to connect the trailer's signal lights to the car lights.

Our preparations went on and on. We had to buy a state boat permit, and learn the safety manual for boat operators. Finally, we had to study the Virginia waterways.

I could never estimate the hours and energy my boys and I invested in our little green boat. Later, we traded up to a 21-foot fiberglass one, and then another one. Now we run a 23-foot inboard-outboard, and all four boys with their friends still enjoy being together on the water, doing nothing much, just talking and laughing and talking some more. We never owned a really fancy boat, just enough boat to enjoy the water and enter each other's lives at a point of leisure and slowed pace, and to maintain our family fellowship.

In cold weather we bowled. Until I was fifty years old, I had never been in a bowling alley, but by the time our two younger sons finished high school we had two notebooks filled with bowling scores. We would bowl twice a week, and all of us became good bowlers with averages of 160 to 180. One son became captain of the high school team and the champion of central Jersey high schools.

On cold, weekend nights we had pinochle games. One could find pinochle scores on scraps of paper all over our house. This lasted for fifteen years, and it still goes on every summer.

When I was a child myself, we didn't have gang leaders interpreting life for us, offering an abbreviated code of survival that leads to jail or an early grave. We began to learn life's lessons at home from aunts, uncles, parents, and grandparents. We didn't earn this priceless beginning. We were just blessed to be born in our family's environment and not in Yummy's.

We spent countless hours around the piano trying to harmonize, making up songs, and copying the big band tunes. My daddy was a music man, and we learned to play instruments, too. We made footballs out of Quaker Oats boxes, filled with rocks and grass and wrapped in layers of discarded silk stockings. Daddy made swings, carts, and doll houses out of used fish boxes. Some of our best fun was listening to "Pop" Cherry tell us of his farmboy days near Ahoskie, North Carolina. Pop Cherry was my mother's mother's sister's widowed husband who somehow ended up living with us for twenty-five years. He was a source of endless entertainment and delight. Added up, such experiences filled any and every vacuum for us.

Part of the imperative to renew the family is that all parents should be held accountable for children to the fullest extent of their ability. No one should be riding around in a new car, pimping on public funds, and leaving his child for the rest of us to support. Both parents should work in some constructive activity to learn a skill, earn a livelihood, and break the cycle that continues to dump young Yummys on the public trust.

SOMEWHERE BETWEEN THE DEPRESSION AND THE CLOSE OF World War II, the American people lost their interest in the guaranteed full employment debate. A free economy and a democratic government, resting on a respository of moral values bequeathed in the Judaeo-Christian tradition, require a program of full employment. It is a scandal to tolerate 7 percent unemployment. How can we spend $300 billion on military defense and see the nation erode from within by perpetuating begging, selling drugs, stealing, prostitution, and depending on government subsistence, when we are fully able to devise a program of guaranteed full employment? We must have the political will and the national moral commitment to eliminate beggars, homeless persons, and unemployment. We can design a national budget that assures that no one should be a ward of the government unless she or he works at a real job doing something that needs to be done.

When a mother and child receive public funds to live on, the father needs to pay back the money to the government. If he has no job, he should be able to enroll in an honest jobs program, either in an industry subsidized by public funds, or in a public institution doing a needed function, or in training for the open job market.

Young mothers in living situations not fit for child-rearing should be allowed to share safe, clean cooperative housing with a dozen or so mothers and their young, where everyone either works to maintain the cooperative or takes a job and contributes to the expenses. Such residences would be only temporary, to help young mothers learn skills for real earning power so they can adequately care for their children.

The point is that infant children should not be penalized because of unfit parents. No father should be allowed to leave his responsibility on other citizens, and every young mother should be pointed toward education and training to elevate her life permanently. Such a program can be installed with compassion and without condemnation.

However, individual outreach and family rejuvenation are not enough. The principal intervention needed is thorough and efficient schooling, from kindergarten through high school. Schools *cannot* fail; we have no institution that can do what schools are assigned to do.

The most outrageous development of our time is that young blacks are losing the opportunity for real empowerment because they are rejecting education. I wish more people really knew how much blacks earnestly thirsted for education immediately following slavery. And I wish that more people knew how determined the slave states were to deny them learning. In Georgia, for example, the state supreme court enthusiastically endorsed laws against teaching slaves.

When the Virginia House of Delegates passed a bill to prohibit blacks from being educated, one delegate said: "We have as far as possible *closed every avenue by which light may enter their minds. If we could extinguish the capacity to see the light, our work would be completed. . . .* " (The italics are mine.) When he made this statement, my grandmother was living enslaved only a few hundred yards down the road. Fortunately, her capacity to see the light was never extinguished. In fact, her capacities grew and absorbed more and more light, as her faith in a meaningful future glowed.

Rundown schools, overcrowded classrooms, and burned-out teachers are the norm for many black children. They further lose their bearings when some black educators demand that black children be taught an exclusively Afrocentric curriculum, untainted by European influences. I agree that all students—not just black students—need to learn about African origins and African history, along with colonialism and slavery. Learning one's own roots should fill one with pride, as well as ignite one's curiosity to learn the importance of everyone's roots.

But Afrocentric learning that is narrow, chauvinistic, and propagandistic is negative and stifles intellectual growth. Shallow learning results in racism, bigotry, polarization, tribalism, war, and destruction. Whatever calls us in that direction should be avoided like the plague.

What we should care about is preparing all young minds to join in the great human conversation by learning the theories which support technology and science, and the broadest range of facts known about all the earth's people and its marvelous habitats. Black pupils need to learn about the whole planet, all of her people and her physical and chemical secrets. The deeper our knowledge, the more complete our understanding of our common origins, capacities, needs, and destiny.

Furthermore, the so-called Eurocentric learning is very eclectic, a blend of wisdom, knowledge, and religion that accrued from many cultures, including Asia, Egypt, Greece, Arabia, Italy, and North Africa. There is a large fund of knowledge, art, and music from the entire human family that should be the intellectual property of everyone. And black youth would be seriously deprived if they were denied access to that broad experience. Who would be so shortsighted as to want black pupils competing for jobs and graduate study after being denied a chance to embrace the same body of facts and knowledge that all other students enjoyed? With a broadly educated mind, young black students can fully pursue any area of interest they wish.

But the sad fact is that, currently, black students are not certain that they *do* want to learn what everyone else is learning. The consequence is that only a thin trickle of black students are prepared for tough intellectual assignments; the others are left to roam the streets and abandon the quest for learning. At the same time, educational statisticians are reducing black students to numbers and spinning depressing results into theories that blacks are slow learners, that they can run, dance, sing, make touchdowns, and sink baskets, but cannot think and reason. The mischief escalates as social theorists from *without* dampen efforts to educate young blacks, and social propagandists from *within* kill off black aspirations. The sad result will be a society divided racially, and divided again on educational lines.

One way to inspire young people to learn is through the quality and commitment of their teachers. We need to open the door wider to teaching by offering incentives to people who have the vocation and the time, but who need more training. Recently, a friend and colleague of mine in New York told me that she went to a meeting which took place in a schoolroom in a public junior high in Harlem. Classes were over for the day, but the corridors were still filled with kids playing basketball and attending special afterschool classes set up by a local youth organization. What impressed her was that the kids didn't have to be there. Nobody made them go. They preferred to be inside playing and working with adults who were interested in them. They hate the noise and filth of the streets and are afraid of the violence and danger. The problem is getting enough capable volunteer tutors or teacher aides who can be available at 3 o'clock in the afternoon to meet the supply of kids.

During my tenure at Rutgers I was able to spearhead certain community efforts through old contacts in Washington. One of my friends in the U.S. Office of Education had an idea that we could develop a new corps of dedicated teachers for tough, urban schools by recruiting people without college degrees from the community and giving them a chance to gain teacher certification. We were able to get a grant for what we called the Career Opportunities Program. We recruited students from antipoverty programs, churches, and social agencies. We subjected applicants to a rigorous, two-hour interview in which their language skills, ability for abstract thinking, and personal commitment were evaluated. Once accepted, recruits received small stipends to help with living expenses during the two-year program. When they completed their studies, they had earned a Master of Education degree and a teaching certificate.

The Rutgers faculty at first greeted the new idea with "ho-hum, just another federal give-away." But when they saw that this one, like other programs we were developing, was operating with integrity, they climbed on board.

Twenty applicants entered the program each semester for the next three years, for a total of a hundred twenty new teachers for New Jersey's secondary schools. Among those recruited the first year was Edith Jackson, who was working as an office manager for a local chamber of commerce and raising three young children on her own. After taking our program she became a social science teacher in Metuchen, New Jersey, where she was twice voted "teacher of the year." Another of our recruits was Charles Morerro, who came straight out of the Job Corps and went on to become a housing officer for Rutgers and, later, dean of students for the school of engineering and the school of pharmacy. Eugene Barrington went on to finish a Ph.D. in political science at Syracuse. Charles Holmes became a high school principal in Pennington, New Jersey.

When I described our teachers' program to various educational conferences, I got all sorts of challenges concerning proper training. My answer was always the same: good teachers can be produced if they love children, if they see hope even in dirty, mean, impolite children; if they believe that all children can learn; and if they have the energy and imagination to pursue the growth of a child. These gifts may be hard to measure in advance, but they are easy to recognize in action. The key is to try.

Some people say I lean too heavily on education as the agent of change, but I saw how much education did to help produce a stable black leadership class from 1900 to 1950. When I see today the sorry condition of urban ghettos, where young people are distracted by gangs, drug dealing, and sex, there's no doubt in my mind that schooling is the crucial variable in the current crisis.

It follows that we need to train teachers to work with high-risk kids. Recently a teacher named Troy Weaver was named teacher of the year in Durham, North Carolina. Weaver teaches juvenile offenders awaiting trial for murder, car theft, armed robbery, and rape in the Durham County Youth Home. Weaver's work reflects that love that is not measured and does not wait for reciprocity.

One day one of the detainees in Durham went berserk and began cursing and tossing chairs and tables across the room. Weaver approached him and ran into a storm of profanity. "You can curse me all you want," he said, "but I still love you."

The student stopped and let Weaver walk up to him and put his arms around him. The student started to cry. "My mother never told me she loved me," he said. "She loves the pipe [crack] more than she loves me."

Weaver is thirty-three years old, married, with children. One of his adopted children is a former detainee. With more Troy Weavers, these bones can live!

THE MOVE TOWARD PRIVATE SCHOOL AND THE IDEA OF vouchers is aimed at the final destruction of public schools. Public schools will become holding pens for hopeless children, while children from higher-income families and better-educated parents will be distanced from the masses in far better schools. America built public schools as a testimony to the worth and dignity of all people. How easy it is for those looking for a quick fix to social neglect to violate the democratic ideal and the most noble aspirations of the human spirit.

Schools are as much a public responsibility as clean water, safe roads, polio vaccinations, and licensing for doctors and pharmacists. Specially trained people are needed to do what Troy Weaver can do. Yet in my lifetime I have seen no national mobilization to put a new lining in our public schools, to generate exciting and productive teaching, or to reverse the downward spiral toward a permanent underclass. But we have seen enough strong students emerge from weak schools to convince us of what could happen with a greater effort.

Three thousand colleges and universities in America are training teachers. Yet there is practically no contact between these prestigious schools of education and the public schools struggling to stay alive. If the colleges would direct their efforts toward training teachers to respond to those most in *need* of learning, we would see a revolution in urban behavior.

We need a national program to upgrade teaching and the teaching profession. This means making a career in teaching pay at least as well as carrying mail or driving a garbage truck in New York City. It means luring the best minds—not the C+ survivors—into teaching. It means keeping schools open until 5:30 all year long, except for two-week recesses in August, December, and April.

A federally supported program like that would pay for itself. Can you imagine what we have spent on Yummy's mother, her six children on welfare, and her forty-one arrests, along with the drug programs she has visited? My soul! Compare those costs to the cost of training teachers who could have kept her in school and made her a productive, tax-paying citizen.

Training teachers is only part of the answer. Instilling order and discipline is the other part. In exchange for the money we now spend on education, we get chaos. Public schools today are coping with crime, guns, gangs, and drugs. They are more like forts than schools. As a result, we are wasting millions of dollars assigned to education. Intellectual thrust cannot be created in the midst of chaos. Teaching and monitoring discipline are two separate tasks, and personnel are needed in all of our schools to maintain order so that teachers can teach until a new generation of public schools evolves.

The extra cost of improving public schools would be offset by reduced payments to teenage mothers, lower detention and court costs for young recidivists, and increased tax revenue from a larger pool of earners. Everyone wins.

When children begin with a great school experience, the line between philosophy and the prophet fades, and the space between Athens and Jerusalem narrows. When that happens, those bones are about to live!

BUT IT TAKES EVEN MORE THAN GOOD SCHOOLS TO SAVE our children. Back in the 1920s and '30s, in the rural South, black schools were pitifully understaffed, and children attended only four or five months out of a year, with frequent interruptions for farm labor. Many had to work to survive and could not afford to go to school at all. Yet a progressive, hard-driving, proud black middle class emerged in America one generation after slavery.

Fifteen-year-old George Lewis fled a rural backwater of Mississippi and ended up working in the Omaha stockyards. But George Lewis was a religious person and stayed around people of faith. He worked hard and participated in worthwhile activities. He became the chairperson of the Board of Deacons of the Abyssinian Baptist Church, and was one of the most highly regarded church leaders among African Americans in New York City. In a lifetime of work, he never earned more than five dollars an hour, but he was careful always to save a little. When he died, Deacon Lewis owned a beautiful condominium and left his church $50,000 in his will.

Deacon Lewis told me that when he was a little boy, he and his schoolmates had to walk five miles to and from their raggedy school, where one teacher taught forty pupils in four grades. On the way, they walked by the neat white schools. As they walked, white students would pass them on the road, riding in a large wagon drawn by a team of horses. They rode, although the distance to their school was half the distance that blacks walked. George said he was glad when it rained because the side canvases on the wagons were lowered and the white students couldn't spit on them as they passed by.

In the wake of such experiences it required a strong faith to retain a sense of personal worth and to aspire to do well. Obviously, not everyone could summon such faith. Others from Deacon Lewis's background ended up with fifteen descendants on welfare, and half of them in and out of jail. Like Yummy, they never had a chance.

So even though it would seem that education is a large part of the answer, it is not all. The truly educated person, in my view, is never content until a satisfactory, operational answer is found to the questions of purpose and destiny. In our early years, school is largely in control of the life of the mind and the world of ideas. But eventually we must turn our focus outward and upward to look for our own larger frame of reference. Religion brings our quest for purpose and direction to closure and our soul to ease by revealing our place in the scheme of things.

To resolve the present dilemma and move forward, we need a major intervention from the black churches. Such a renaissance is already taking place all over the country. Locally, our churches are centers of progress. They are centers for day-care, even alternative elementary and high schools, credit unions, athletic teams, family life centers, travel clubs, senior citizen residences, low-income housing, Alcoholics Anonymous chapters, Bible study, drama groups—you name it.

The local churches are doing great, but at the national level African-American churches need a wake-up call. They are still burdened with stagnant leadership bogged down in "old boy" connections. They handle money like a mom-and-pop store, with inadequate reporting and auditing; frequent losses are almost never penalized. No real accountability goes on, and everyone retires rich, like so many American presidents.

Church officers meet constantly, staying in fine hotels, attending banquets. The meetings are largely preaching marathons. The result of all this spending is negligible. Several church-sponsored colleges have closed for lack of funding, even as the national bodies have grown and collected more money.

Nationally, leadership positions in the black churches have been mostly honorific and ornamental, without real meaning. This can no longer be tolerated. With our families falling apart and our communities disintegrating into violence and resignation, we cannot afford to have millions of people attending our churches without strong leadership at the top. Groups like the National Rifle Association, with its shadowy goals and purposes, are much better organized than we.

The African-American churches represent 20 million black Christians. If they could speak with one voice, we would hear a powerful shout. If they created only one great national television worship hour, presenting our finest preachers and choirs, we could offer the country something besides the heavily jeweled, poorly educated, bodacious, sleazy hustlers currently seen on television pilfering from the meager earnings of the elderly and the poor.

Nor would it take much to establish a first-rate publishing house and a world-class conference center. Black people have a lot to say to each other, and much of what needs to be said may not meet the criteria of the commercial publishing market. But if all of our major denominations had their church school literature printed by their own printing corporation, it would be a major enterprise. That is do-able. If a book or magazine agency were founded cooperatively, the churches could use it to publish public training material. One denomination on its own may find it a struggle, but together blacks could match what other major church publishers are doing.

Strong leadership could create a mortgage cooperative for church building. In every major city there is always a multimillion-dollar black church building project. Our own black-owned, highly successful North Carolina Mutual Insurance Company in Durham is a model of what could happen in creating a mortgage company.

For example, the millions of dollars black congregations donate to erect church buildings could be invested in their own cooperative bank. The interest earned could be used to support black colleges, scholarships, and even the development of a national, ecumenical conference site, such as an African-American theme park and vacation center. Enough African Americans are working in high-finance positions to make this one a piece of cake, but imaginative church leadership is needed.

All of this begins with the right ideas and the right people to take the initiative. Imagine what would happen if someone with the dynamism of Marian Wright Edelman were the executive secretary of the African-American Baptists? Look at what she has done with the Children's Defense Fund over a period of fifteen years: She has built it from a nonentity into an instrument of change for the welfare of all of America's children.

EVEN WITH FAMILY, SCHOOLS, AND CHURCHES DOING THEIR best, there is still that powerful draconian determinant called "the economy" which has operated so that the rich get richer, and the poor remain poor. Real change will not come until the basic economic condition of the poor changes. Unemployment, and underemployment, are heavy weights for a people to carry from one generation to another. Every conceivable human problem is aggravated by poverty.

In 1990, one of every seven white families lived in poverty, but one of every three black families did. This figure has been the same for the last twenty years. That same year, the median income for white families was $36,915 and for blacks $21,423. More telling, during the twenty years of the Nixon-Reagan-Bush administrations, median income of white Americans rose along with inflation. The black median hardly moved. The bottom half was weighted heavily with those earning below the poverty line.

What about the children growing up in Yummy's neighborhood? How much money do their households have for the bare necessities of life? Today one of every two black children lives in poverty (44.8 percent) compared to one of every six white children. Two of every three poor black children live in central cities.

Unfortunately, the prospect for getting on board economically is slim in today's market because of poor education and job discrimination. The old low-wage, manual labor jobs are disappearing; if you *can* find one, the pay is so miserable that you could work fourteen hours a day, seven days a week, and not earn enough to pay the rent and put food on the table.

Andrew Hacker, in *Two Nations, Black and White, Separate, Hostile and Unequal*, says that for as long as records have been kept, unemployment for African Americans has been twice that for whites. Sadly, one of the most visible objects in America is a black male standing on a downtown street corner, poorly educated, ill-kempt, unemployed, with the glaze of despair on his face.

A free and democratic government supposedly has built-in correctives to make up for the uneven beginnings in life. Victims of racial discrimination and poverty are supposed to have room enough to maneuver their way into the middle and upper class. It has not worked out. The gaps between those who have and those who have not are widening. And as a result the whole nation is suffering.

The power to change lies in the hands of the Congress, the president, and the corporate community. But unless there is a surge of decency and fairness emanating from the public will, these data threaten to follow us into the twenty-first century.

Can these bones live? If those who have overcome will share one-on-one their intellectual, moral, and cultural capital with those with deep deficits, if families can recover their values of nurturing and support, if we can renovate our schools and lead all of our children into the life of the mind, if the African-American church on a national scale can muster the leadership it deserves, and if we can build jobs and fair access into the economy—these bones will live.

AS WE MOVE THESE PROCESSES ALONG, WE HAVE TO administer a stop-gap measure right now for our present crisis.

There are 1.5 million unparented children today—male and female, black, Hispanic, white, and Native American—who are virtually without hope of ever becoming self-sufficient, responsible citizens. The opportunity for these 1.5 million young people to become healthy, intelligent, responsible, adults, prepared for wholesome family life, a fulfilling vocation, concerned citizenship, and a meaningful view of the world is the summum bonum.

The alternative is for more and bigger jails, more wasted human resources, more social disorder, and an outlay of $40,000 per head, per year, for costs of trials, incarceration, and probation. Our present crisis calls us to see beyond partisan politics and make a major national correction of past failures.

Many young people are now beyond the capacity of the public schools to help. My own idea is modeled on the Peace Corps, and would use deactivated military bases. I propose a federally funded National Youth Academy to educate youngsters who need a new home, surrogate parents, and an enriched educational program. These schools would be state-managed, but would have national goals and guidelines. The magnitude of the problem is far beyond the capacity of voluntary or small private efforts and more critical than merely warehousing kids to get them out of sight.

My years with the Peace Corps taught me that large organizational efforts readily reach their potential when *someone at the top says so.* The facilities to put a National Youth Academy in action are there now, idle and available. Sewer lines, power lines, water supply lines are in place. Even a cost of $16,000 per child would be less than half of what we spend on prisons now.

Our Peace Corps training programs taught us that teachers—and nonteachers—can be oriented toward a new kind of professional service. The military routinely retrains accountants, trumpet players, plumbers, and hotel waiters to man tanks and helicopters and win wars six thousand miles from home. In 1963, we had sixteen thousand of the brightest and best of our college graduates teaching in thirty-eight developing countries, speaking exotic languages and living on foods they could not even spell. They worked for fifty dollars a month and had to be forced to leave after two years. They found life's greatest satisfaction in serving those who needed them most.

Many well-educated, decent Americans are willing to give two or three years to the recovery and realignment of children who are otherwise destined for a crime career or an early grave. Today we have an army of underemployed teachers who would be delighted to take on this task. We also have a wave of energetic college graduates every year, eager to share their social and intellectual capital with others. We have retired military personnel who know how to create a healthy, orderly environment of high personal expectations, conducive to serious goal achievement. And we have a surplus of well-trained, but unemployed or underemployed, experts in a variety of professional specialties.

All of these individuals could come on board at the National Youth Academy, living and boarding on the campuses, sharing meals with the students, and earning modest salaries, health care benefits, and a bonus at the end of their two-year service.

What would happen at these fifty academies with an enrollment of some five thousand each? These youth academies would be neither hospitals nor prisons. Therefore, youngsters with severe physical or mental disabilities could not be cared for there; nor could those already seriously violent. But most of our youth on a collision course with failure could be served. They would be chosen on the recommendation of the courts, schools, and detention centers, with the approval of their parents or guardians.

The National Youth Academy would enlist the country's most experienced educators to design a six-year academic curriculum, beginning in the seventh grade. This format is largely an arbitrary decision, trying to keep costs within reason. However, seventh grade is when the most serious signs of asocialization begin to appear and what little parenting that exists begins to lapse. Six years is also an adequate amount of time to establish a foundation for good habits of work, study, and behavior. The enrollee will be ready for graduation at age eighteen, ready for college or for work, but mostly ready for good citizenship and responsible adulthood.

The curriculum would include six years of serious, no-nonsense mental challenges, especially mastering math, logic, writing, and coherent thinking. Beyond the academic work, everyone would learn to swim in the first thirty days. Being able to jump into a 40-foot tank without drowning is a dramatic way to feel mastery over one's environment. Students would learn to grow flowers, sing four-part harmony, do photography, paint landscapes, breed dogs, care for an aquarium, and play sports of all kinds. Each child would get very, very good at *something*. Everyone would use computers for the whole six years. The curriculum would also include a work program that would teach *every* student to do *every* task needed to run the school, from accounting and nursing to tuning tractor motors and cutting hair. They would know how to use every tool sold by Sears!

Above all, the curriculum would include a human development program to encourage community values. These include respect for the space and rights of others, care of the environment, self-reliance and civic contributions, and responsibility for one's own actions and choices.

What about drugs? In group living, no one would have the kind of privacy needed to easily access drugs. Moreover, with a love of learning and a program of rigorous physical development, the vacuum that drugs fill would be filled already in a positive way. There would be constant vigilance to assure that the dysfunctional world these children left behind would stay behind.

This is a fiscally conservative program. Each graduate will be an earner and a taxpayer for life. Within five years, each would have repaid every dollar spent on him or her by paying income tax. And each will continue to pay taxes for a lifetime. Anyone with a net income of $100,000 today pays $31,000 in federal income taxes. Most families that I know well have such a net and more. When I was in college, the government paid me fifteen dollars a month for nine months, over four years. A total of $540 for four years! If my net income were $100,000 I would be paying more than $540 *a week* in federal taxes! Every week for the rest of my life, I would be giving the government back in taxes more than it spent on me in four years. But without that help I would not have finished college.

Consider how many times over beneficiaries have repaid in taxes what was spent on them through the GI bill. (For example, two of my brothers were educated on the GI bill; one became a dentist, the other a physician.) Consider the land grant universities, which became our state colleges and universities. In an average career, graduates pay back the cost of their education in taxes twenty times! Consider the black colleges founded by the churches in the 1860s and 1870s. They created an entire black middle class of lifetime taxpayers.

If the government started out with fifty academies, with five thousand students in each, it would cost $4 billion a year. (The Pentagon budget runs over $300 billion each year.) Over six years each student would cost a total of almost $96,000. But if we do not spend that money now, these young losers could end up costing us $40,000 each for every year of their lives, and never pay any taxes. When they finish the National Youth Academy, they will be on their way to paying $20,000 or more each year for *forty years*. That's more than eight times the investment. Now, there's a deal!

Will there be problems? Yes. There are problems in the Vatican, at West Point, Johns Hopkins Hospital, the CIA, the New York Yankees, Buckingham Palace, and IBM. But if the people in charge are well chosen, they will be *problem solvers*. Some remarkable efforts in our world have succeeded. We did get to the moon. We do perform heart transplants. And we do have 260 million people, living in fifty states, who don't carry visas and don't have a national shootout at every election. We can rescue 1.5 million young lives from destruction, just as we have saved them from poliomyelitis.

Do we have the public will to do it? I remember when Social Security and Medicare were called "communism" by those who did not need them. If we have the compassion in our hearts and the intelligence in our heads, we can generate the consensus.

This is not a project for blacks only. It is a project for every child who needs it. If African Americans are disportionately represented in the NYA, it will be because the program responds to a need that is disproportionately felt among them. Over time, the numbers will change as opportunities increase.

After twenty-five years—with three or four cohorts of National Youth Academy students entering new lives and enhancing each thread in the fabric of American life—we would begin to see a new America. Many of our college students and our most skilled tax-paying workers, college students, artists and architects, teachers, candidates for public office will be coming from the National Youth Academy.

ALL OF THE INTERVENTIONS BY CHURCHES, SCHOOLS, families, individuals, economic equality, and government are needed, and none is independent of the other. Yet one solution need not wait for the other. We all must begin where we can. Social analysts can assemble facts to show that nothing works. But whatever has led us to this predicament can be undone; the spiral can be turned in a new direction.

The litany of sins against disenfranchised blacks is long and familiar. The question facing us now is, "Where do we go from here?" The current crisis demands that we make choices that are worth living and dying for, choices deserving of our best efforts, choices that have the best chance of steering us toward the optimum human condition: a genuine community. To my mind, isolating ourselves from the rest of American society, or relying only on our African heritage for a sense of identity and pride, are not choices that will ultimately bring us into a genuine community with fairness and justice for all.

Genuine community is possible only if we accept that our destiny lies right here, with a new America in the making. A new America that the NYA will be a part of. The success that the middle-class black population has achieved has a direct relationship to hard work, personal pride, deep faith in a future filled with meaning and purpose. Such success has been earned in the face of racism and contempt for black progress. And it has been earned because we believed in a future where we were full participants at the center of American life.

I will tell you a story. If you should visit the Newark campus of Rutgers University, chances are someone will tell you about the new Free Electron Laser Laboratory that lies near Smith Hall, in a crater ten feet deep and seventy feet long. This ten-ton miracle of technology is directed by Dr. Earl Shaw, professor of physics.

Dr. Shaw was born on a plantation near Clarksdale, Mississippi, where his parents were sharecroppers. When Earl was six years old, his father was shot to death. His mother followed the urban black migration along the Illinois Central railroad to Chicago, seeking a better life for her little boy.

Anyone who saw the young mother and child riding in the "colored" coach on the Illinois Central, eating chicken out of a shoe box, rocking and shaking for hours from Jackson to Chicago, would never have dreamed that the boy would ever grow up to be a success in these United States. According to all known predictors, Earl should have wound up a statistic in a criminal justice textbook, lumped in with the norms and means, a drug-dealing, car-thieving, teenage daddy terrifying the city and keeping his mother on her knees.

But somehow he and his mother mined that vein of faith that

blacks keep hidden in their breasts, and *believed* their way through. Earl's mother worked hard enough to get him enrolled in a good school, and at age twelve he was selected for a science high school that prepared him for the University of Illinois at Urbana. Later, he earned a master's degree in laser physics from Dartmouth, and a Ph.D. in physics from the University of California at Berkeley.

After nineteen years as a researcher at AT&T's Bell Laboratories, he was wooed by Rutgers to become its premier physics researcher. Bell Labs went right along and installed a $1.4-million laser laboratory for him there. Among other mysteries, Dr. Shaw is discovering how to make invisible light ranges visible.

Statistics can't explain how six-year-old Earl moved from the edge of a Mississippi plantation, trembling with fear and grief at his father's pine-box casket, to become one of the world's top physicists.

I believe if we can transpose young Earl's faith to the common struggles being ground out in black ghettos from Los Angeles to Boston, we can turn away the crisis and a new nation will emerge. The world has anticipated such a community since the African theologian Augustine envisioned the City of God and since the founding fathers of the United States declared that it was self-evident that all persons were created equal. Although their declaration has never actually come to pass here, we have envisioned it, and our most cherished documents say that it is possible.

African Americans bring to this moment a long tradition of seeing beyond the hard facts. We have never ceased to believe in a deliverance that will come partly by our own effort and partly by the power of a metaphysical design that made a world out of nothing. We know we are not struggling alone. Like David before Goliath, we have believed in a hidden ally.

Ezekiel saw dry bones coming together and taking on sinews and flesh. He also saw colorful, intricately designed wheels moving in the air without any visible power. The spirit of God was moving over a captive people. In slavery, African Americans made up a song about a small wheel turning inside of a larger wheel: *"The little wheel moved by faith, but the big wheel moved by the grace of God."*

CHAPTER ELEVEN

Beauty for Ashes

EVERY NOW AND THEN, A SPIRITUALLY DISCIPLINED SOUL lends his or her heart to God as a lyre, and vibrates with such ethereal strains that they echo ceaselessly through the long corridors of time. Chapters 60 through 62 of the book of Isaiah, attributed to the hand of Second Isaiah, are the most beautiful portrait of God that has survived the sifting sands of time. Listen to the King James Version:

> Arise, shine; for thy light is come, and the glory of the Lord is risen upon thee.
>
> For, behold, the darkness shall cover the earth, and

gross darkness the people: but the Lord shall arise upon thee, and his glory shall be seen upon thee. (60:1-2)

The Spirit of the Lord God is upon me; because the Lord hath anointed me to preach good tidings unto the meek: he hath sent me to bind up the broken-hearted, to proclaim liberty to the captives, and the opening of the prison to them that are bound ... (61:1)

To appoint unto them that mourn in Zion, to give unto them beauty for ashes, the oil of joy for mourning, the garment of praise for the spirit of heaviness ... (61:3)

As I fix my mind on the confusion and incoherence that stare at us every day, the words "beauty for ashes," written twenty-six hundred years ago, obsess me. All around us we see ashes that need to be exchanged for beauty.

No one really knows how well prepared we are in America for movement toward a new paradigm of the human family, one that respects everyone's innate worth, that seeks to cultivate human potential and self-esteem, and that affirms the principles of justice, freedom, and equality. We do know that such movement is thwarted by archaic and mean class divisions and intractable tribalism.

We know also that what we do here in America holds promise for the rest of the whole world. There are 5 billion people on the planet, 4 billion of whom are brown, yellow, and black. With the twenty-first century lying before us, there must be an alternative to chronic, worldwide ethnic strife, mass starvation, corrupt and brutal governments, and the vulgar disparity in opportunities for the flowering of human potential. These conditions are gross contradictions to the knowledge that we have gained and to the accumulated moral and spiritual values that are woven into the warp and woof of our culture.

While we may not have a foolproof definition of genuine community, everyone knows what noncommunity looks like. For example, there are those who continue to turn a blind eye to starvation and epidemics in the world, and all of the dread that goes before such painful deaths. Anyone who can walk away in ease from such indescribable anguish cannot talk about community.

White professors—and black professors, too—who abandon the truth in favor of their own prejudices and indulge in innuendo and fraudulent data to "prove" their case—these pseudoscholars are enemies of community.

Universities that fail to help students understand the root causes of the African-American position in America are also enemies of real community. This is what made it so dreadfully tragic when it was revealed that the president of Rutgers University—the 50,000-student state university of New Jersey, with fourteen schools on five campuses, straddling the main artery between Washington and Boston, in the most diverse and thickly populated state in the Union—said to a closed meeting of thirty-five tenured white professors on the Camden campus in November of 1994, that African-American students "did not have the genetic and hereditary background" to achieve high scores on the Scholastic Aptitude Test. His earlier conduct as an administrator had never reflected such a view, and his public speeches had always testified to fairness and equality of opportunity. But behind closed doors he made that clear statement, and not one person demurred.

Everyone in that room knew enough social and economic history to account for the lower scores of blacks on the SATs. In fact, it would defy all reason and history if black students scored higher than whites. But here, at the very heart of American education, the classic, pseudoscientific, anti-intellectual, disproven, and abandoned racist theory was alive and well.

The result of this and similar acts is that thousands of black students on college campuses all over the country are again targets of ridicule by the racist students and faculty who have found new license for their views. Black Ph.D.s, many highly distinguished in their fields, are bowed in shame and disbelief, and black alumni are horrified, being teased and questioned by their colleagues all over the country.

The president has profusely apologized, but for what? For saying what he believed? For believing it? Or for the furor it caused?

Only a few days prior to the public exposure of his speech, I had completed my task as chairperson of a Rutgers fundraising campaign to promote diversity, excellence, and community. We raised $5.4 million, and our spirits were high. Then we had to face the reality that not everyone believed, really, in genuine community.

Another impediment to real community is the control of our political institutions by those representing the wealthiest segment of society. The domination of party politics by the privileged holds the country captive to the old paradigm of the superiority of the rich. Apparently there is no way to rescue government and public policy at the present time. Even the majority of Supreme Court justices are millionaires and were millionaires before going to the bench. Imagine the president of the United States surrounded by government aides and officers who are as distant from real moral accountability as feudal lords. The indifference of people in high places is an enemy of real community, and it can only change with the political awakening of working people.

The pall of prejudice that hangs heavily on our society and seeps into the fabric of American life is an enemy of community. Only today, November 5, 1994, I heard a report, from the Centers for Disease Control in Atlanta, that cigarette smoking had increased alarmingly among young African-American women, but had decreased among young white women. Does anyone know what racial identity has to do with smoking? What can one learn by finding out how many black women smoke cigarettes as compared to whites? It is instructive, however, to know whether smoking is related to education; or whether it is a regional phenomenon relating to local customs or loyalty to the tobacco-growing economy; or the influence of advertising on smoking. Perhaps it has something to do with income, or the type of job someone has. Do more *poor* young women smoke? With this information we can do something to stem the increase in smoking. But what possible use is it to know the race of smokers?

Likewise, any data on crime, teenage pregnancy, disease, and illiteracy are always given by race, thus implying that race is more causal than other factors. This "data" treats the truth with contempt, and keeps prejudice alive. Statistical reporting by race is a barrier to community.

Those who pretend that blacks are either rapists, car thieves, and drug peddlers on the one hand, or Michael Jackson, Michael Jordan, and Magic Johnson on the other, are aliens to community.

The saddest resistance to a new human paradigm comes from the very place where it should be most enthusiastically supported, the Protestant church. A special brand of churches—usually smaller, quasi-churches on the fringes of major denominations—cluster around right-wing leaders who support nationalism, heavy defense expenditures, and Christian schools that deliberately subvert racial integration.

These people accept the view that women are subordinate based on the creation story in Genesis and the writings of Paul. They regard these stories as God's will, ignoring the rest of the sixty-six books of the Bible, which display God's many marvelous gifts to women in biology and history. Others cite special phrases in the Bible out of context to prove that races should live separately. This falls short of a thorough understanding of the Bible and a more complete view of God's creation. People with a narrow God concept see AIDS as punishment of a particular group, and ignore the many other wonderful people who suffer dreadful illnesses. They cannot see that some people used the freedom God gave them to exploit others, deny them opportunity, and impose suffering upon them. All such views misrepresent more comprehensive ideas of God and vitiate efforts at building community. Indeed, a prerequisite for the new community is having an adult concept of God that makes us immune to narrow and provincial views of people, even of ourselves.

Another barrier to a new human paradigm is the long-term dependency of the poor on public largesse. Community will be hard to achieve if an underclass of poor, uneducated African Americans and whites fails to recognize that self-reliance, accountability, and personal pride are the trademarks of a free and just society. Nothing will change significantly if the society has to provide sustenance for large numbers of people who have no hope of becoming self-supporting. Our purpose should be to protect any new life brought into the world and nurture it so that it becomes self-reliant and self-fulfilling. Consequently, we should be making every effort to eliminate the practice of young women giving birth outside of the family and without adequate support.

African Americans on the bottom have to struggle to make themselves immune to cynical, hate-filled orations that persuade them that they cannot win. Those of us who have already made a commitment to stand firm and work and sacrifice for the movement toward a genuine community have to share our faith with them. This is a matter of trust and long-term commitment. We received that commitment from our own antecedents, and it enured us to cynicism. We must now share it likewise, to the same end. Those without hope must believe that a new human paradigm is possible and that persistence will work. If they remain anesthetized by the ether of hate rhetoric and separatist propaganda, they will remain on the margins.

SOME OLD BARRIERS TO COMMUNITY ARE IN FACT CRUMBLING. The state of Mississipi, once the most violent hotbed of racism, has shown many signals of lasting change. It is a fact today that the dean of the law school of the University of Mississippi, for instance, is a black legal scholar reared in a public housing project in New Orleans.

Fifteen years ago, the Mississippi State NAACP Conference invited me to speak at their annual banquet, in Yazoo City. When I arrived at the Ramada Inn, there was a huge neon sign proclaiming, "Welcome, Dr. Proctor and the NAACP State Conference." This sign stood less than fifty miles away from the spot where Medgar Evers, that devoted and revered leader, was shot to death only a few years before.

On October 17, 1994, I addressed the "Parents University" in Hattiesburg, Mississippi. This is a sophisticated PTA program intended to get parents more involved in their children's education. I was addressing citizens of a state whose very name symbolized the old, die-hard, Jim Crow South. Yet the first thing I saw there were black and white teachers hugging each other, and moving like hornets to get the program rolling. Black and white parents were all over the place, serving finger-food and punch, hanging posters, passing out programs, and welcoming the workshop leaders. The workshops covered every relevant topic for school-age children. The superintendent of schools knew all the African-American leaders by name, and all of the faculty knew all of the parents, black and white. It was one smooth, impressive performance. Scores of American cities, North and South, would covet Hattiesburg's situation.

Real community is built on common needs, talents, and contributions—great and small. We need to share these as a nation. We need to aspire to a network of relationships that will affirm all of us in our rich diversity and decency. In a global, cosmic context, we must view every other human in a way that is compatible with one worldview.

We need to appraise honestly what is essential for a good life. We are all sojourners here, and we need each other to survive. This means that we are best off if we back away from perpetual rivalries and draw closer to an intelligent, fair basis for mutual support.

We need to revisit the past and look at the practices of previous generations that led to such unmanageable inequalities—and also at those that led to progress and achievement. Any new strategy for the future must also honor the past. The new human paradigm depends on first accepting hard facts, then reclaiming the positive, productive practices that have led to success.

When Franklin Roosevelt came to the nation's leadership, he proposed the Works Progress Administration and the Public Works Administration. All of us are accustomed to driving through tunnels built by the WPA and crossing bridges with letters burned in steel indicating that they were built in the late 1930s under the WPA and the PWA. He created the Civilian Conservation Corps so that any able-bodied young man who could not find employment in the open market could count on the government giving him an assignment. In the Forestry Service and in dredging harbors and cleaning up the wilderness, there was work to be done. It was far more honorable for the government to finance earnest labor for a just reward than to give people grants that would weaken their character and create a habit of dependency.

We need to stop wringing our hands and gritting our teeth now, and put our economists, labor leaders, and legislators to work in coming up with feasible ways to scrap the Band-aid, tentative, placebo welfare programs, and return to honest labor that builds respect and guarantees every person with a sound mind and an able body a minimum decent level of employment. Our schools in urban centers badly need able-bodied monitors in every hallway. Our parks and swimming pools need able-bodied guards for safe play and recreation. Our beaches need to be kept clean and safe. The infrastructures of Baltimore, New York City, Richmond, and all of our other older cities need to be rebuilt. Floods and blackouts occur everywhere because of the inadequacies of the infrastructure. Sewer lines, underground tunnels, electrical power lines, bridges, and roadways all need to be overhauled. There is work to be done.

Federal or state agencies can do the job themselves, or they can subsidize industries that are able and willing to perform these services on a competitive basis, using extra labor supplied by the government in order to assure guaranteed full employment. This will sound like socialism to people who have no compassion. But those who care deeply about other people will hail work programs and welcome them as an intelligent response to a chronic problem.

It doesn't mean getting rid of or even reducing free enterprise. On the contrary, the corollary to free enterprise and the other freedoms that we cherish is to establish a bottom beneath which our compassion will allow no one to fall. It is incredible that our leaders are saying that we are unable to do this when we have an average national per capita income of $34,000—when most human beings on the rest of the planet live on less than $3,400. Lord, have mercy!

And what about affirmative action? Ninety-seven percent of managerial jobs in the country are still in the hands of white males. Anyone who thinks affirmative action has been overdone should go to any airport early in the morning and see who are carrying briefcases and rushing to makes planes. Go to any office building or hotel in downtown Manhattan, and see who's riding up in the elevators. It's a myth that competent white males have been shoved out of the line and replaced by incompetent females, Hispanics, and blacks. Somewhere now and then, no doubt, there has been a less competent black in the line in front of a more competent white. But generally, competent blacks are not being considered at all. Affirmative action, by whatever name, must continue because otherwise seniority, tenure, and the old-boy network will continue the status quo in perpetuity.

The administration of welfare needs to continue at the federal level. The states are unequal in their economic sufficiency. Industrial states and states with vigorous economic activity are far more able to meet the needs of people in disadvantaged circumstance. The only agency that can achieve national parity is the federal government, not because it wishes to seize power, but because through federal taxation it has the capacity to equalize that states and counties do not have. Moreover, where is the record that shows that states are cleaner and more disciplined in handling public funds than the federal government? Where is the evidence that they care more about their people? Corruption at the state level matches anything that we've ever seen at the federal level.

The institution of slavery was a monumental moral failure, just as the slaughter and dispossession of Native Americans were. Both must be remembered, as the Holocaust in Europe must be remembered. These are indelible blots on the ledger of time, and the lessons learned must stay alive. But we also must move on: An emotional appeal to ethnic solidarity is important, but early Monday morning little African Americans and little Native Americans must step into the context of today's America, and claim the future for themselves. They need to acquire the equipment to make a living, fulfill their potential, participate in government, and take the fragments of a broken society and put them together. The sad history of ethnic conflict, religious hypocrisy, and moral collapse is the wilderness-wandering that precedes movement to a new human paradigm of genuine community.

Other prescriptions may make moving rhetoric, but when pursued to their logical conclusions, we will be standing again in the killing fields, like the Crusaders trekking from Gibraltar to the Syrian desert for hollow victories, and leaving a crimson trail of innocent blood. We are destined for something better. Blacks and Native Americans, like litmus tests, must prove to the world that we have options that we are only beginning to explore. We do not need to reinvent the wheel. We already know the price of ignorance and exclusion. We have seen the result of generations denied decent employment and we know what poverty breeds. We know what beauty and grace attend the lives of those who enjoy the proper uses of the mind and fruitful employment. Strategies based on fabricated data, systemic hatreds, and self-interests of the privileged will have to be forfeited.

Each of us, to one extent or another, is already committed to a network of community. At Christmas time I discover how vast my own is, and how it grows and grows from the center out. I have to make several greeting card lists. One is for kinfolk. Then my buddies from Norfolk, many friends for over sixty years.

My circle widens, and the lists grow, embracing college schoolmates and fraternity brothers I used to joke with about the slim prospects that a better day for us would come. Then come my seminary and graduate school friends, and my colleagues from later years. We've followed one another through the tensions of the Cold War, the Johnson gains and the civil rights struggles, the long night of Nixon-Reagan-Bush, the nagging ethnic skirmishes and the slow birth pangs of a new community. We are white, African American, Asian, and Hispanic; Catholic, Protestant, and Jew. This circle is wide and deep. Because I have been closer to this crowd, for a longer time, my bond with them is the strongest. What a blessing it has been. I have already lived in a community that I call a new human paradigm. Such a community becomes richer as the years go by.

I retired from the Abyssinian Baptist Church in 1989 and spent the next year recovering from a triple by-pass heart operation and writing the 1990 Lyman Beecher Lectures on preaching for Yale Divinity School. I spent another year at Vanderbilt, and the next as professor of Christian Ethics at United Theological Seminary in Dayton. These were inspiring experiences and splendid opportunities to be with people living, working, and preaching genuine community.

I was lecturing at Duke University one day in 1992 when I ran into Dean Campbell of the divinity school. He invited me to spend my remaining teaching time at his school. Then he reminded me that he had been a sophomore the day I preached in their famous Gothic chapel, the first black person allowed to do so. He said that he had sat there wide-eyed when the black preacher stood in the pulpit directly over the crypt of President Few, the man who had decreed that it would be over his dead body before a black would preach in that majestic sanctuary. That was thirty-five years ago. My eyes welled up at his memory, and I gladly accepted his offer. I am now at the end of my second year at Duke University Divinity School.

This semester, spring of 1995, I teach a class in preaching on social issues. It's a diverse class of six African-American students and eight whites, from all over the country, from age twenty-two to fifty-two, and from four different religious denominations. Twenty years ago, there would have been no class by that title, no racial mixture, and no African-American professor.

I teach another class called "Leadership in the Black Church in the Twenty-First Century." Of my forty students, twenty-two are white and eighteen are black. Any and every issue concerning blacks is discussed; whites are allowed to disagree with blacks, and both are encouraged to disagree with the teacher. Twenty years ago, no such course would have been offered. If it had been offered, the room would have been empty, for no whites would have taken it, and there were no blacks on campus. These classes

THE SUBSTANCE OF THINGS HOPED FOR

are overtures to the opera, a movement toward the consumma-
tion of the faith of blacks. They are the substance of things
hoped for.

When I get up to preach in a ghetto church in Bedford-
Stuyvesant, or at Riverside on Morningside Heights, in Abyssinian or in the Princeton or Duke chapel, in a rural black church
in East Carolina or in Harvard's Memorial Church, I try hard to
share with my listeners a moment of trust in our common existence. We are all vessels of clay, derivative, finite creatures, but
we are not here alone. And this is the faith that sustains us.
When we feel impelled to search for ultimate meaning, we are
sounding the alarm, ringing the chimes, striking the cymbal, and
calling attention to God's investment in our condition.

AMERICA HAS NO STATE RELIGION, NO SINGLE POLITICAL
party, no royal family, and no single ethnic root. That puts us in
an excellent position, at just two hundred years old, to create a
new model of community. As citizens of the United States we
carry her passport and her Social Security card, but such contracts do not create a meaningful, viable relationship among
ourselves. However, if we recognize and celebrate the majestic
principles on which this nation was founded, and in doing so discover our unity in nurturing the ideals of democracy, we can set
an example for the world. Other nations bond around their culture, religion, or royal family, but we are bonded by ideals of
equality and justice, which are the zenith of human aspiration.

We could all simply wait to see how we make out, swallowed
up by those who match greed against need. We can wait to see
where a culture that pivots on hedonism, prurient entertainment, and brutal industries leads us. We can hold on and continue to indulge in politics that are polarized by Darwinian ethics
versus human compassion and fairness. But we can do much better by deliberately embracing the new human paradigm.

243

For the first time in this century we are free to revise our national agenda without worrying about a contending military superpower. We can capture this rare moment of change through strong leadership from churches and synagogues, from universities, and voluntary associations, and from the inspired vision of our intellectual and spiritual leaders. They can point the way toward true fulfillment, the completion of the sublime intentions of the founders of this noble experiment. We needn't wait for some wild development to lead us there. By our own intentionality we can be bold in its pursuit, as when Alexander brought Occident and Orient face to face, and the thirteen colonies said "no" to George III.

The important thing is that we hold on to this rock of faith. By faith we know we can accomplish our goals with integrity. We will help America to redefine herself. This nation began with the ignominious dispossession and near obliteration of Native Americans. It compounded its shame with the disgrace of slavery. Yet this same nation is the world's last and best hope of a free and democratic society.

Where we are today demands that we make choices that are worth living and dying for, choices deserving of our best efforts, those that have the best chance of steering us toward the optimum human condition, a genuine community.

WHEN THE PROPHET ISAIAH PROMISED THE EXILES RETURNING from their captivity in Babylon that they would be given beauty for their ashes and joy for their mourning, the promise was not made in the name of some clever political maneuver or artful social theory. The prophet had been lifted out of his mundane, terrestrial existence, and dipped in a wellspring of new truth. He had been wafted as though on eagle's wings into celestial realms, where he communed with the Ancient of Days, the Eternal One.

Ashes will be turned to beauty by a power beyond our own

fragile will. Black people have a long history of standing up to the impossible, and making the possible real. Likewise, we know how to stay our course and ply heavy seas of disappointment. We know how to trust the most invincible surmise that the mind can imagine and that the heart can embrace. By our faith in the substance of things hoped for and the evidence of things not seen, a new human paradigm can be achieved.